Along the Potomac River

EXTRACTS FROM THE
MARYLAND GAZETTE

1728–1799

Edith Moore Sprouse

HERITAGE BOOKS
2011

HERITAGE BOOKS
AN IMPRINT OF HERITAGE BOOKS, INC.

Books, CDs, and more—Worldwide

For our listing of thousands of titles see our website
at
www.HeritageBooks.com

Published 2011 by
HERITAGE BOOKS, INC.
Publishing Division
100 Railroad Ave. #104
Westminster, Maryland 21157

Copyright © 2001 Edith Moore Sprouse

All rights reserved. No part of this book may be reproduced or transmitted in any form or by any means, electronic or mechanical, including photocopying, recording or by any information storage and retrieval system without written permission from the author, except for the inclusion of brief quotations in a review.

International Standard Book Numbers
Paperbound: 978-1-58549-688-4
Clothbound: 978-0-7884-8962-4

Along the Potomac River:
Extracts from the *Maryland Gazette*, 1728-1799

During the colonial period, residents of Northern Virginia were more closely connected with their neighbors across the Potomac River than they were with the people of the lower Tidewater because of the distance to the Virginia capitol in Williamsburg. It was said of Colonel William Fairfax, a member of the Governor's Council who lived in Northern Virginia and quite far from Williamsburg, that he only attended Council sessions when specifically called. Residents of Fairfax County might have read the *Virginia Gazette*, but they would find little information about their part of the colony in the pages of that newspaper. Culturally akin to their Maryland neighbors, Virginians were able to find more news of local interest in the *Maryland Gazette* which had been published since 1728 in Annapolis.

Discovery of this relation was made by the compiler while reading the Maryland newspaper during a research project that centered upon history of the courthouse at Port Tobacco, in Charles County, Maryland. While extracting items concerning Port Tobacco, it came as a pleasant surprise to find so much information about life on the Virginia side of the Potomac River. The river served as a highway in the eighteenth century—men owned land on either side of its waters, frequently visited back and forth, and often, like George Mason of *Gunston Hall*, married Maryland ladies. The Maryland capitol of Annapolis was much closer than Virginia's Williamsburg, and the *Maryland Gazette* covered in detail the news of interest to citizens and merchants of Fairfax County and the town of Alexandria.

Bound photostats of early issues of the *Maryland Gazette* were used at the Enoch Pratt Free Library in Baltimore. For the period 1745 to 1799, the compiler used microfilm of the newspaper that is available at the Alexandria Library. There were no issues between October 10, 1765, and May 22, 1766, due to the expiration of the Stamp Tax act. During the Revolutionary War, printing of the newspaper was suspended between December 25, 1777, and May 7, 1779, due to the lack of paper. In spite of these gaps, the *Maryland Gazette* provides many more details about life in the Potomac River region than its Virginia counterpart.

Although these abstracts are by no means comprehensive, they do offer a glimpse of the interests and activities which were of concern to families then living along the Maryland and the Virginia shores of the Potomac River.

My special thanks to Wesley E. Pippenger who finalized this manuscript for publication.

Edith Moore Sprouse
Alexandria, Virginia

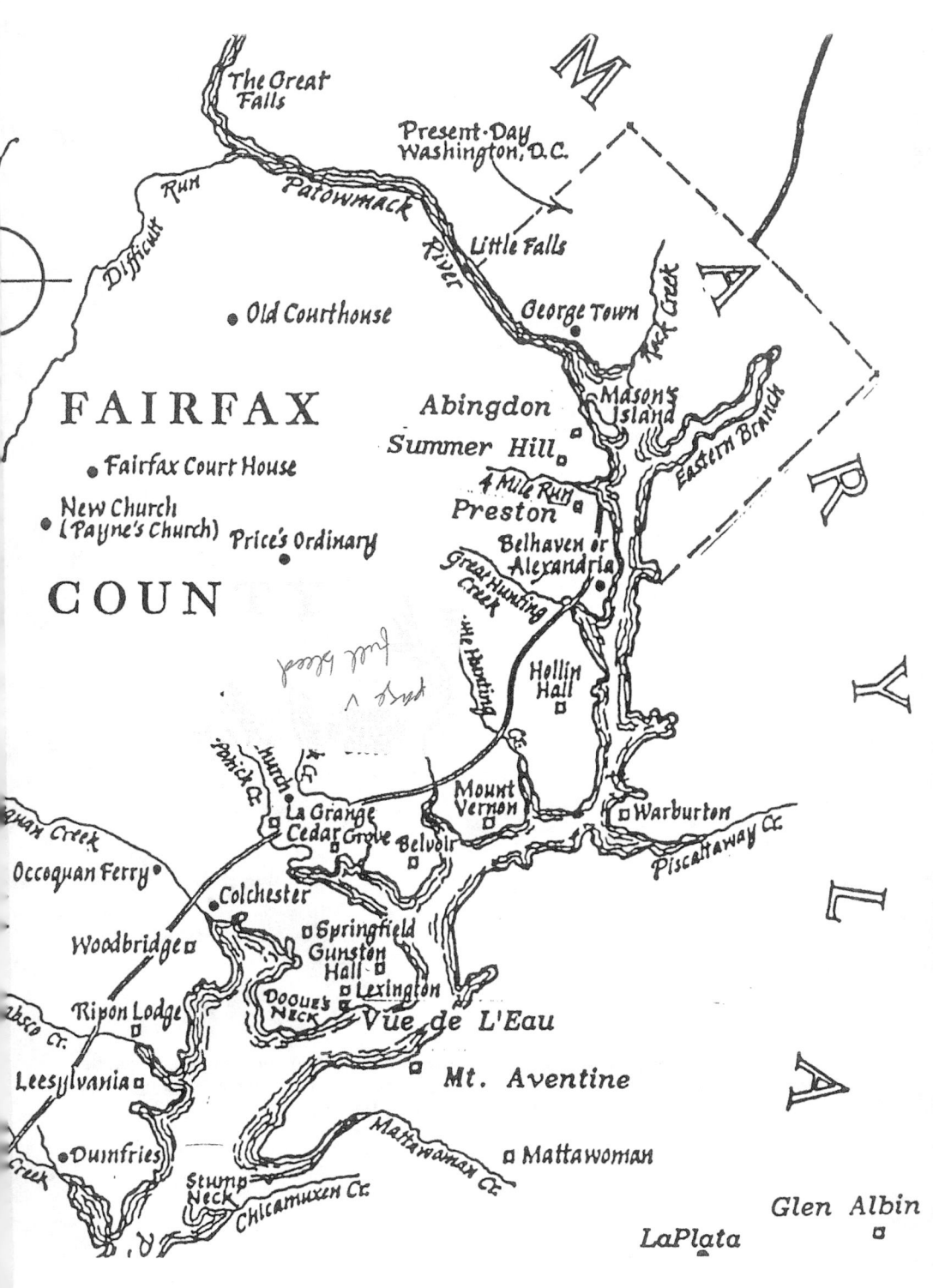

The map on the previous page is used with permission from the author, and can be found in Wesley E. Pippenger, John Alexander—A Northern Neck Proprietor, His Friends, Family and Kin (Baltimore, Md.: Gateway Press, Inc., 1990), page 290.

Along the Potomac River: **Extracts from the *Maryland Gazette*, 1728-1799**

The dwelling house of the Hon. Phillip Lee, Esq., in Prince George's County, burned. Mr. Lee lost almost all of his furniture and wearing apparel, himself and family narrowly escaping the flames. (31 DEC 1728)

Stolen from the house of Col. Thomas Lee, in Virginia, (some time before it was burned), a valuable plate [described in the text] bearing the Lee coat of arms. The Governor is offering a £50 reward. (11 MAR 1728/9)

His Excellency has been pleased to appoint George Plater, Esq., Naval Officer on the Potomac. (20 MAY 1729)

On Tuesday last, George Plater, Esq., was married to Mrs. Rebecca Bowles, relict of James Bowles, a gentleman of considerable fortune. (17 JUN 1729)

His Majesty has been pleased to constitute Sir William Thomson [uncle of Mrs. George Mason of *Gunston Hall*], one of the Barons of his Majesty's Court of Exchequer, in the room of Sir Barnard Hale, deceased. (17 MAR 1729/30)

To be sold, *A Penny Worth*, 700 acres in Stafford County, Virginia, on Great Hunting Creek, in the freshes of the Patowmack (over against Mrs. Rozer's), with a very fine landing place thereupon. Enquire of Benjamin Tasker, Esq., at Annapolis, or Mr. Phillip Key, attorney at law, in St. Mary's. (16 JUN 1730)

Last Tuesday, being the birthday of the Rt. Hon. Lady Baltimore, the same was observed here with all the demonstrations of Joy ... the Fort Guns was fired at one of the clock ... in the evening his Lordship gave the Ladies a Ball. (9 FEB 1732/3)

A tract on Rock Creek, *Knave's Disappointment*, 200 acres, and *Widow's Mite*, 47 acres, are offered for sale. (7 JUN 1745)

St. Mary's County public school wants a schoolmaster. A brick chapel of ease is to be built in the lower part of King George's Parish, Prince George's County; seek bids; £750 is available. The Vestry is meeting at Piscataway. (28 JUN 1745)

March 30th, 1745. Ran away from Thomas Lewis, living at the mouth of Dogue Creek, in Fairfax County, a servant English convict Isabel Pierce. She stole two gold rings, a silver buckle and £6. (28 JUN 1745)

Col. Benjamin Harrison, of Berkeley, and two of his youngest daughters, were killed by lightning. (16 AUG 1745)

On the 17th, a fair will be held in Prince George's County, at Mr. Murdock's Old Fields near Queen Anne town. Races will be judged by Thomas Harwood and Thomas Brooke, Jr. (13 SEP 1745)

Along the Potomac River: Extracts from the *Maryland Gazette*, 1728-1799

Advertisements and testimonials for Chinese stone, for all ailments and snakebite. Will stick fast and draw out the venom. (20 SEP 1745)

A tobacco house is to be built at Rock Creek Landing on George Gordon's land. (4 OCT 1745)

Robert Gordon is elected Mayor of Annapolis. (18 OCT 1745)

A cargo of limes is for sale. (9 NOV 1745)

An Aurora Borealis appeared for two hours. (4 MAR 1746)

Capt. John Colvill's ship was in the river 14 or 15 years ago. (15 APR 1746)

John West, Hunting Creek, Virginia, advertises for rent the place where John Pagan formerly lived and kept his store. Located at the head of the creek, it is with all houses necessary for a trading person. West lives near there. (29 APR 1746)

Lost by Patrick Doran, on the road near the Wood Yard, a silver snuffbox, gilt on the inside, the lid is wrought with several figures among which is the resemblance of a Rabbit. (13 MAY 1746)

On Saturday, May 14th, 1746, two men of Repute, fishing off Kent Island, about four in the afternoon, the weather calm and clear, saw to their great surprise, at a small distance, a man about five feet high, walking by them on the water, as if on dry ground: he crossed over from Kent Island to Talbot County, about a distance of 4 miles. (3 JUN 1746)

Henry Thompson has a ferry on Potomac River to Capt. Hooe's and Ducking Stool Point on the south side of the Potomac. (1 JUL 1746)

Charles Jones keeps a ferry from Lower Cedar Point to Virginia, by 20 miles the shortest way to Williamsburg. Edward Rumney has set up a pottery in Annapolis. (8 JUL 1746)

A ferry is established at William Clifton's plantation in Fairfax County. Good entertainment for man and horse. He also seeks a runaway servant named John Jennings. (12 AUG 1746)

A white woman was deservedly whipped and stood in the pillory here, for swearing a child to a white man, which turned out a Mulatto. (19 AUG 1746)

Humphrey Batt, at Broad Creek, Prince George's County, is selling a new 36-ton schooner, handsomely finished with a Scroll Head, fit for a Gentleman's use. Also, one only, fit for a tobacco Droguer. (30 SEP 1746)

Along the Potomac River: **Extracts from the *Maryland Gazette*,** 1728-1799

Negro Spanish pirates are near Chincoteague. (2 DEC 1746)

Hugh West, Hugh Wallace, in Fairfax County, seek runaway convict servant named Willis Duncanson who took servant Jane Williams with him. (9 DEC 1746)

Williamsburg. A grampus [young whale], 54' long, was driven ashore and killed at Jamestown. (23 DEC 1746)

The Capitol at Williamsburg lately burned down. (17 FEB 1747)

Prince George's County school advertises for a schoolmaster. G. Plater offers for sale tracts in Prince George's County, part of *Hermitage*, 873 acres; *Poplar Neck & Addison*, 400 acres; part of *Hoskinson's Folly*, 100 acres. The plantation in Prince George's County near Bell-Town, of 200 acres, is for sale for someone else. (21 APR 1747)

A fair is to be held on Rock Creek, near Mr. Kennedy Farrell's and Henry Wright Crabb's old field. Races. (12 MAY 1747)

Christopher Lowndes, of Bladensburg, merchant, married Miss Elizabeth Tasker, third daughter of Mr. Benjamin Tasker, an agreeable young lady with a good Fortune. (19 MAY 1747)

Mrs. S.C. of Patapsco, was fined 1 penny by the court for whipping R__d Mr. N__l W__r with a Hiccory Switch; it being imagined by the court that he well deserved it. (16 JUN 1747)

The Prince George's County Courthouse is now so decayed a wooden building that "shingles so much worn that in driving rain and snow the records get wet." Plans are underway to brick the walls. (16 DEC 1747)

Benedict Calvert is appointed to His Lordship's Council. (9 MAR 1748)

The court heard a breach of promise suit by a young lady. Also a case of blasphemy in which a man sentenced to being bored through his tongue and paying court costs. (13 APR 1748)

Matthew Wigfull, cutler, lives near Wood Yard, dresses lancets and razors. (20 APR 1748)

Hon. Benedict Calvert married Miss Elizabeth Calvert, only surviving daughter of the former Governor Charles Calvert. (27 APR 1748) A long "Epithalamium" on this wedding. (18 MAY 1748)

Along the Potomac River: **Extracts from the *Maryland Gazette*, 1728-1799**

Peter Wagener, of Prince William County, Virginia, seeks return of runaway servant named David Hughes, a Welshman and blacksmith. (18 MAY 1748)

April 11th, 1748. King George Parish, Prince George's County, is building a brick chapel of ease. Justices of Prince George's County to raise 54,000 lb. tobacco for repairing and finishing the courthouse in Marlborough. (15 JUN 1748)

Collin Mitchel is breaking up ordinary-keeping at Port Tobacco, and wants to rent a house and lot. He is leaving the Province. (29 JUN 1748)

Found hidden in the woods, an old prayer book. (29 JUN 1748)

Whereas Mary McLaughlin who pretends to be the wife of the subscriber, may by such pretense, contact debts... I will not pay, she not being my wife. John Carr. Whereas John Carr has published an advertisement in the *Maryland Gazette* and therein has denied me the Subscriber to be his wife: This is therefore to give notice that his assertion is false, and although I do not think he is worthy the Name of a Husband, yet he is certainly mine, as may be seen by the Registry Book of St. Anne's Parish, and can be proved by sundry living in Annapolis: Therefore those that advise him to deny me must certainly be bad advisors, and ought to consider that a Curse is denounced against such as Part Man and wife. Mary McLaughlin, as he calls me. [These notices are printed together several times.] (20 JUL 1748)

Col. Robert Hanson died last Friday at his seat in Charles County, a Gentleman who was for many years a Representative and Chief Judge of that County. (5 AUG 1748)

A large rattlesnake having 21 rattles was killed in Dorchester County. (10 AUG 1748)

Benedict Calvert offers for sale tracts in Prince George's County: *The Hermitage*, 873 acres; *Hopkins Folly*, 100 acres; *Simmons Delight*, 300 acres. (24 AUG 1748)

Lawrence Washington, seeks runaway convict servant named Robert Millby, alias Willoughby. Born in Ireland, a weaver by trade, "He has for several years been a dragoon in Lord Stair's Regiment and appears very much like a soldier ... He is much addicted to Boasting and telling of Lies, especially as to his performance in Flanders, and loves Liquor." Stole three horses, one new soldiers musket, three hunting saddles and a pair of sheets; went off in company of serving man belonging to Mr. Darrell of Fairfax County. One saddle is a large new hunting saddle with large green cloth housing, bound with scalloped leather. (31 AUG 1748)

A man stood in the pillory at Queen's Town for the crime of cutting a sealed half bushel, which he had borrowed and thereby reducing it to about a Pint below the standard. He had the word CHEAT in large letters fixed on his back, and was handsomely pelted by the Populace. (28 SEP 1748)

Along the Potomac River: **Extracts from the *Maryland Gazette*, 1728-1799**

Several persons, particularly one thus directed "to mr. jonus green prenter at anopperbas [Annapolis]", may wonder why they don't have their ads published. It did not come properly recommended. Ads are 5 shillings the first week, 1 shilling per week afterwards. (12 OCT 1748)

The Capitol in Williamsburg is to be rebuilt on the same spot. (7 DEC 1748)

A northern newspaper has published a warning of counterfeit milled dollars, dated 1741 and 1744. (22 MAR 1749)

Peace is declared in Aix-La-Chapelle. (3 MAY 1749)

For rent, a storehouse, 24 feet, near Broad Creek, Prince George's County, not more than 30 yards from a good landing and near the Inspection house and county road. N.B. There is but one store between Piscataway and the head of the Eastern Branch. Humphrey Batt. (14 JUN 1749)

May 27th, 1749. Agreeable to an Act of Assembly for erecting a town at Hunting Creek Warehouse, upon Potomack River, by the Name of Alexandria. Notice is hereby given that the Lots in said town will be exposed to Public Sale to the highest Bidders on Thursday, the 13 of July next by the Trustees. (21 JUN 1749)

A ranger of Prince George's County has two horses in custody. Peter Hoggins. (21 JUN 1749)

Races will be held at Annapolis on September 29th; also at Leedstown, Virginia, on September 17th. (12 JUL 1749)

Capt. Johnson has arrived in Potowmack River, with a number of convict servants who frequently ran away and committed burglaries. (26 JUL 1749)

William Fitzhugh, of Westmoreland, seeks the return of runaway servants. (23 AUG 1749)

Daniel Dulany, Jr., married Rebecca Tasker, on Saturday last, 2nd daughter of the Hon. Benjamin Tasker, Esq., a very agreeable young lady with a handsome fortune. (20 SEP 1749)

To be sold at the plantation lately Samuel Hyde's, in Prince George's County, 6,700 acres, *His Lordship's Kindness*, on which there is a good water mill. Several tracts totaling 2,500 acres on which are seven Negro quarters, tobacco and corn houses, a parcel of country born slaves, with cattle, hogs and horses. Benedict Calvert. (11 OCT 1749)

Arrived, 120 convicts, in the ship *Thames Frigate*. (7 DEC 1749)

Along the Potomac River: **Extracts from the *Maryland Gazette*, 1728-1799**

A tract near Rock Creek, called *Clean Drinking*, 2,000 acres, is for sale, formerly the estate of the late Mr. John Courts. John Hanson, the Younger. (14 MAR 1750)

Lent but forgot to whom the Body of Laws, belonging to the vestry of St. Anne's Parish; wrote in the beginning, "the wicked borrow and never return." Whoever has it is desired to return it to the Person who lent it, or else he will NEVER LEND IT THEM AGAIN. (4 APR 1750)

On the 3rd of last month, George Mason, Esq., of Virginia, was married to Miss Anne Eilbeck, daughter of Mr. William Eilbeck, merchant, in Charles County, of this Province; a young lady of distinguishing Merit and Beauty, and a handsome Fortune. (2 MAY 1750)

About a fortnight ago, the house of Mrs. Lucy Hatton, near Piscataway, burned. She and two sons (both young men) perished in the flames. Fire began upstairs; thought to be caused by the snuff of a candle falling into some cotton: Mrs. Hatton was once out of the house but went back to save her sons and thus perished. (29 AUG 1750)

On Friday night last the public prison in Prince George's County, in Upper Marlborough, burned; supposed to have been arson by a Negro prisoner being held for murder, who escaped. (29 AUG 1750)

A few days ago, died, Mr. John Magruder, a former commissioner of the peace for many years and Representative. (29 AUG 1750)

Dr. David Ross, of Bladensburg, married Miss Ariana Brice, eldest daughter of John Brice, Esq., of Annapolis, a young Gentlewoman endowed with every Qualification to render a man happy in the Conjugal State. (5 SEP 1750)

A libel suit against the printer is dismissed. Races to be run at Port Tobacco. (10 OCT 1750)

An Aurora Borealis has been seen in Annapolis. (24 OCT 1750)

Edward Rumney, charged with coining counterfeit double doubloons, has lately broke jail in Fairfax County, "much addicted to playing at billiards and gaming." Low Jackson, James and John Jackson, are thought to be accomplices. (7 NOV 1750)

Gerrard Alexander seeks the return of a runaway English servant named Elizabeth Bushop who "loves drink". (7 NOV 1750)

Col. George Plater's wife died on October 30th. (14 NOV 1750)

John Lammond, Musician, hereby gives notice that if any gentlemen should want Music to their Balls or merrymakings, upon application made, they shall be diligently waited on by their humble servant. The said Lammond having a good able horse will undertake journeys to any part of the province. (21 NOV 1750)

A man, as he was carrying home one of his neighbor's hogs, which he had killed with a design to make it his own, having tied the feet together and put it over his neck, he went to rest himself by laying the Hog on a dead tree, but laying it over too far, the string catch'd him by the throat and choked him, and they were found there dead: so they proved Executioners to each other. (5 DEC 1750)

The son of Hon. John Rousby, in Calvert County, died, aged 25. (7 FEB 1751)

Dr. James Somervell, of Calvert County, died February 15th. (20 FEB 1751)

Daniel Carroll died last Wednesday. (6 MAR 1751)

A storehouse is for rent at Broad Creek, Prince George's County. For terms inquire of Henry Lowe there. (6 MAR 1751)

William Digges' overseer, Donald McKenzie, was murdered. Details given. (3 APR 1751)

Upper Marlborough races are to be run at Mrs. Crawford's Old Fields. (10 APR 1751)

A lottery will be held at Belhaven in Fairfax County, for building a church and market house. 8,000 tickets, at 2 pieces of eight per ticket, with 2,000 winners. The lottery will be under the management of Col. G.W. Fairfax, Major Lawrence Washington, Col. William Fitzhugh, Mr. George Mason, Mr. William Ramsay, Mr. John Carlyle, Mr. John Dalton, Mr. John Pagan, Mr. Gerrard Alexander, Mr. Nathaniel Chapman and Maj. Augustine Washington, on the last Tuesday in May. The design, "tis the first thing of the kind in this Colony and is calculated purely for the public good, without any views of private interest." (24 APR 1751)

Ignatius Digges' horse, *Vendome*, won the race at Annapolis. (8 MAY 1751)

A one-acre lot on Great Hunting Creek, at *Cameron*, is for sale by John Pagan. It is in the center of four public roads leading up and down the county, exceedingly well suited for trade. The dwelling house is 26 feet square, brick cellar 7 feet deep, kitchen 24 x 18 feet, storehouse 24 feet square in which is a counting room 12 x 16 feet, garden 144 feet square, paled in. Also a tract ½ mile away of 575 acres. Apply to the subscriber at his house in *Cameron*. (8 MAY 1751)

John Ariss (lately from Great Britain) gives notice that buildings of all sorts and dimensions are undertaken and performed in the Neatest manner (and at the cheapest rates). At Major John Bushrod's, in Westmoreland County, Virginia, where may be seen a great variety and sundry Draughts of Buildings in miniature and also some buildings near finished. (15 MAY 1751)

Elliott Benger, Esq., sold Deputy Postmaster General of all His Majesty's Dominions in America, died in Virginia. (22 MAY 1751)

The Belhaven lottery is deferred until the third Monday in November because managers "have met with considerable Hindrance from the Surmises and base insinuations of some ill disposed Persons, so that they are apprehensive the same will not be filled by the time appointed for the drawing." If tickets are not sold, money will be refunded. They also beg leave to assure the Public, that the whole will be conducted with strict justice and impartiality, without any sinister views whatever. The lottery is to raise £690. (22 MAY 1751)

An Act is passed to treat with Anne Darnall, widow, owner of land on which the Prince George's County courthouse is built. An Act is passed to erect a town above the mouth of Rock Creek, in Frederick County, on Potomack River. (12 JUN 1751)

The Vestry of Port Tobacco Parish, in Charles County, is meeting the first Monday in August to take bids for a church in the said parish. William Hanson, Register. (26 JUN 1751)

Charles, Lord Baltimore, died at his seat Erith, in Kent, on April 23rd. His son Frederick, a minor, succeeded him. (10 JUL 1751)

Thomas Fleming and Anthony Ramsay, of Fairfax County, seek return of runaway indented servant named Robert Wisendon. With him went Sampson Darrell's servant William Hore. Darrell is living near Belhaven. (10 JUL 1751)

Land tracts are for sale three miles from Broad Creek, Prince George's County: *Saturday's Work*, 280 acres; *Speedwell*, 138 acres. Inquire of Brian Philpot, Jr. (18 JUL 1751)

The managers of the Belhaven lottery are forced to state that they will publish results immediately in the Maryland and Virginia gazettes. First price is 500 pieces of eight. (24 JUL 1751)

Rev. Jacob Henderson, of St. Barnaby's Parish in Prince George's County, died. [Ads follow for the return of borrowed books, then the sale of his library.] (28 AUG 1751)

Belhaven. The Brigantine *Fairfax*, two years old, 75 tons, to be sold at public sale on October 1; also a sloop, and 1/2-acre lot containing several buildings. The dwelling is 24 x 16 feet with a brick chimney and underpinned with stone, two rooms below and one above; the warehouse, 30 x 18 feet, smith shop, 18 feet square with brick chimney in the middle. Also a blacksmith. William Ramsay. (4 SEP 1751)

Along the Potomac River: **Extracts from the *Maryland Gazette*,** 1728-1799

A new calendar will be adopted on next September 2, but the year begins absolutely on January 1 instead of March 1. The next day after September 2 will be September 14, 1742. Feast days fall on their natural days, also birthdays, 11 days sooner than before. (25 SEP 1751)

Prince George's County seeks bids for the building of a public prison. (2 OCT 1751)

David Ross is going to England in the spring. He wants paid up the outstanding accounts for Andrew Reid of London, Reid and Stewart, Stewart & Armour, of London. (16 OCT 1751)

John Pagan again advertises for sale a lot in *Cameron*. In addition to the last ad, he is now selling a 236-acre tract that is 2-1/2 miles away, with a plantation and good dwelling house; 275 acres 5 miles away. A lot in Belhaven convenient to the landing, with a warehouse, 36 x 24 feet, with stone cellar [further details given]. All to be sold on December 10th at his house in *Cameron*. (30 OCT 1751)

Capt. John Addison is elected Representative from Prince George's County. A grey horse is stolen from *Mount Pleasant*, the plantation of Benedict Calvert. (11 DEC 1751)

A member of the new assembly has been discharged because he was an ordinary-keeper, which disqualified him. (18 DEC 1751)

An article from the *Gentlemen's Magazine*, July 1751, by a New York doctor, on "The Cure of Cancer." He used pokeweed juice externally. A medal of the Tuesday Club, Annapolis, has been lost. [Description given, with 1746 date]. Aurora Borealis has appeared. (9 JAN 1752)

William Fitzhugh, Esq., of Virginia, married Mrs. Rousby, widow of John Rousby. (16 JAN 1752)

Lots are being sold at the new town of Georgetown, adjacent to the warehouse, at the mouth of Rock Creek, the fourth Monday in March, at Joseph Belt's house. (20 FEB 1752)

Managers of the Belhaven lottery could not sell all the tickets because of "malicious insinuations." They are refunding monies. (27 FEB 1752)

Humphrey Batt, of Broad Creek, seeks return of runaway servant, a bowlegged caulker. (12 MAR 1752)

A letter on the invention of a new theodolite. (26 MAR 1752)

Died, at his house at the Wood Yard, Capt. Richard Williams, formerly a commander in the Guiney trade. (2 APR 1752)

Along the Potomac River: Extracts from the *Maryland Gazette*, 1728-1799

Wanting a place: One who can wait at a gentleman's table, take care of and curry his horse, clean knives, boots and shoes; Lay a table; shave and dress wigs; carry a Lanthorn, and talk FRENCH, is as honest as the times will admit, and as sober as can be. (2 APR 1752)

On March 17th, a tornado was in Calvert County. (9 APR 1752)

Dorothy, wife of Col. Richard Harrison, of Nanjemoy, died. She was the daughter of Col. Robert Hanson [further details given]. (9 APR 1752)

A son of Col. Blackburn, of Virginia, is drowned; also a man and wife big with child, of Quantico, and one more woman and two others. On April 4th, they had been on board a ship and got in a long boat with captain to see some seine hauling. (16 APR 1752)

William Locke Weems, of Prince George's County, is going to London. (16 APR 1752)

Benedict Calvert's house, five miles from Upper Marlborough, has burned. Mr. Calvert and Lady were about going there to pass the summer season and had just furnished it for their reception. It was difficult to save the furniture since the overseer and slaves had gone fishing. (30 APR 1752)

Mr. John Mackubin, aged 88, died. He was born in this county, and, as he died merely of old age, was a remarkable Influence of the Healthfulness of the Place. (7 MAY 1752)

Mary W__n sued Joseph W__d for breach of promise. It is the second case in a month. She got £50 damages. "A few such Verdicts, with Damages to half a man's Worth, might possibly cure some PRETTY FELLOWS of their Gallantry, and intimidate them (as nothing else will) from deluding and ruining poor innocent and credulous girls." (7 MAY 1752)

In Frederick County, a marriage was performed at night with the bride, in order to avoid carrying her debts over to her wedding, standing unclothed behind a sheet held between her and the minister. (7 MAY 1752)

An obituary states "his lamp of life went out for want of oil". (11 JUN 1752)

Business of the Assembly begins again, and is detailed. (11 JUN 1752)

A "Beggars Opera" is being performed by the Virginia Company in Annapolis. They are going next to Upper Marlborough, then Piscataway and Port Tobacco. (18 JUN 1752)

The Vestry of Truro Parish, in Fairfax County, will meet at Pohick Church the first Monday in September next, to receive proposals and agree with workmen, for buildings on the Glebe Lands, according to law; the dwelling house to be of brick, contain about 1,200 feet in the clear, one story with cellars below, and rooms and closets above, convenient as the ground will allow. Daniel McCarty, William Payne, Churchwardens. [Pencilled on the margin, "Rev. Mr. C. Green".] (9 JUL 1752)

Mr. Van Braam is teaching French. (16 JUL 1752)

Benedict Calvert's house in Annapolis was struck by lightning, taking off Part of the top of a Chimney and descending between the chimney and the wainscot (which last it split in two of the rooms) it set fire to a bed where Mr. Calvert and his lady usually lay, but they happened providentially to be out of town; and the house and furniture would undoubtedly have been consumed, had it not been timely discovered by a Servant in the family, who about nine o'clock in the evening was going up to Bed. It melted the Blade of a hangar in the same room, to which it communicated a magnetic quality, so as to take up a needle. The lightening then descended into a lower room, and split a looking glass in pieces, and the handle of a broom at the head of the cellar stairs. (16 JUL 1752)

Benedict Calvert advertises the past three weeks for the return of goods stolen from him, including two copper tea kettles, three pairs of candlesticks, and a metal mortar and pestle. (16 JUL 1752)

A description of the market house to be built in Annapolis. (30 JUL 1752)

Prince George's County school needs a schoolmaster. (20 AUG 1752)

Samuel and John Hanson seek a woman to manage a Public House in Charles County. (5 OCT 1752)

A. Pooley, Calvert County, advertises as a painter. He will do limning, altarpieces, landscapes, and views of houses and estates. (12 OCT 1752)

William Ramsay will offer for sale the Brigantine *Fairfax*, on December 1, in Belhaven. (2 NOV 1752)

John Pagan repeats his former advertisement, and offers for sale a sloop and two tobacco flats. (2 NOV 1752)

Francis Key, of St. Mary's County, married Miss Anne Arnold Ross, daughter of John Ross, of Annapolis, last Tuesday. (14 DEC 1752)

Last Monday, being Christmas, some people having got pretty merry at the house of Joseph Crouch, on the north side of Severn [river], his son very imprudently attempting to fire a gun between his father's legs, shattered the bone of one them. The father died the following week. (4 JAN 1753)

Along the Potomac River: **Extracts from the *Maryland Gazette*, 1728-1799**

Stephen West, merchant, married Miss Hannah Williams, at the Wood Yard. (4 JAN 1753)

Capt. Blackburn, is master of the ship *Prince Edward*. (13 SEP 1753)

A race will be held at Bladensburg, on October 14th. (13 SEP 1753)

Hugh West, seeks return of a runaway named Dick. (27 SEP 1753)

Anne Murdock, daughter of John Addison, and wife of William Murdock, died last Thursday. (1 NOV 1753)

Half King sends letter to the Governor of Virginia, asking that forts be built on the Ohio [river] as protection against the French. (29 NOV 1753)

Daniel Dulany has died, lived in Maryland fifty years. (6 DEC 1753)

Sold, on December 22nd, at the house of Joseph Chew, in Alexandria (alias Belhaven), the hull of the Brigantine *Success*. Carlyle & Dalton. (27 DEC 1753)

Benjamin Franklin and William Hunter are elected Postmasters-general. (24 JAN 1754)

Williamsburg. Major Washington reports on his return from the Ohio. (7 FEB 1754)

Washington's journal is published. (21 MAR 1754)

One hundred Maryland boys are at the Academy in Philadelphia. A letter suggests building one at Annapolis to keep money in the colony. (21 MAR 1754)

Joshua Fry seeks the return of deserters from the regiment. (18 APR 1754)

Col. George Dent has died in Charles County. He was a former Representative, magistrate and sheriff. In 1725, he was justice of the Provincial Court, and at his death the Chief Justice of the Province. His conduct in public office has gained him applause. (16 MAY 1754)

Captain Thomas Addison, at *Gisborough*, at the mouth of Eastern Branch of Potomack [river], has several stray cattle. Captain John Addison, at his plantation near Broad Creek, has a stray mare. (23 MAY 1754)

Hon. Benjamin Tasker, and Mr. Abraham Barnes, are appointed commissioners to the Indian conference at Albany. (30 MAY 1754)

Upwards of 300 soldiers are now at Alexandria, and more are expected every day, who are to march in a few days to join Major Washington. (27 JUN 1754)

Along the Potomac River: **Extracts from the *Maryland Gazette*,** 1728-1799

Now in the county jail in Alexandria, Fairfax County, is a servant named John Wilmington. He is supposed to belong to a Marylander. Daniel McCarty, Sheriff. (27 JUN 1754)

A Great Cricket match, for a good sum, is to be played on Saturday next near Mr. Aaron Rawlings' spring, between eleven young men of this county and the same number from Prince George's County. (25 JUL 1754)

Williamsburg, July 19th. On Wednesday last arrived in this town, Col. Washington. (25 JUL 1754)

Col. Innes reports that on June 30th the North Carolina regiment was marching from Alexandria to Winchester. (1 AUG 1754)

Thomas Harwood, Jr., of Prince George's County, challenges 15 of the county for 15 pistoles, and from that sum to 50, at the game called cricket, against that number in any county of the province. (8 AUG 1754)

A poem on what to take along when seine hauling. (22 AUG 1754)

August 11th. A letter of Adam Stephen to a gentleman in Maryland, about the surrender on the Ohio. (29 AUG 1754)

Belhaven, in Virginia. William Waite seeks return of a runaway servant Christopher Harper, bricklayer, and Ann Harper, age forty, his wife. John Edenburgh, took horse. They are thought to have taken two of Rev. Charles Green's horses, one roan, one dark bay. (29 AUG 1754)

George Washington gives notice from Alexandria that all soldiers found two miles from camp without furlough or discharge papers may be taken up for deserters. (5 SEP 1754)

George Gordon is going to move to the Wood Yard, in Prince George's County, and is offering for sale his house in Georgetown. (14 SEP 1754)

A recruiting song is printed. (14 SEP 1754)

A public sale is to be had by Daniel and Walter Dulany of their father's estate, on October 18. Furniture, osnabrigs, cotton and other goods. Also a coach, and a variety of books in English and French. (26 SEP 1754)

The races will be held in the old fields in Bladensburg, October 22nd. (16 OCT 1754)

In 1750, Matthew Steel, of Alexandria, gave a promissory note for £500 to Miss Ann Watson, of Prince George's County, only for amusement and diversion. He thought the young lady would cancel it but her father now threatens to enforce payment. (24 OCT 1754)

Last week's cricket match, played at Mr. Murdock's old field, between 11 Prince George's County and 11 South River [Anne Arundel] gentlemen, and that the Prince Georgians were beat. (21 NOV 1754)

Slaves of Daniel Dulany, deceased, are to be sold on December 3rd, also cattle, etc. (21 NOV 1754)

There is with me a young man by the name of Clajon, a Parisian born, and a Protestant, who I believe writes and speaks the French language in its utmost purity and who taught it for some time in London; he is likewise very well versed in Greek and Latin and has some knowledge of Italian and German, having travelled through these as most other countries in Europe. He wants a position as a tutor. Inquire of H. Addison, on Potowmack. (21 NOV 1754)

Captain John Addison, Mr. George Frazier and two others are elected again to the assembly from Prince George's County. (28 NOV 1754)

A donation of two guineas to the Talbot County Charity-Working School, on October 28th, was received of the Hon. Col. Fairfax. (19 DEC 1754)

One Penelope House was committed to prison here, for shoplifting. (20 FEB 1755)

To be sold on March 13th, in Alexandria, on Fairfax Court day, three tracts of land now in the possession of Mr. William Clifton: 1,800 acres on Potomac River and Little Hunting Creek; two tracts of 600 acres joining the said tract. All are well situated for trade and within five miles of Alexandria. Ignatius Digges, John Addison, or William Digges. (20 FEB 1755)

We hear from Stafford County, in Virginia, that the new church at Aquia, one of the best buildings in that County (and the old wooden one near it) were burnt down on the 17th instant, by the carelessness of some of the carpenters leaving fire too near the shavings, at night, when they left off work. This fine building was within two or three days work of being compleatly finished and delivered up by the Undertaker, and this Accident, it is said, has ruin'd him and his Securities. (27 FEB 1755)

Sir John St. Clair [Quartermaster-general] is in Alexandria. Gov. Sharpe of Maryland went there to consult with him. (6 MAR 1755)

The Governor returned March 12th. Ships from Ireland: *Fishburn*, Capt. William Tipple, and *Osgood*, Capt. Crookshanks, with 100 men and officers in each landed at Alexandria. (13 MAR 1755)

Along the Potomac River: **Extracts from the *Maryland Gazette*, 1728-1799**

William and Colmore Beans, near Upper Marlborough, carry on the business of stay-making. (20 MAR 1755)

Capt. Rawlings' ship is arrived at Alexandria. (27 MAR 1755)

Last Saturday the governor went to Alexandria, and was back yesterday. (3 APR 1755)

John Dalton, of Alexandria, seeks return of a servant who ran away on March 26th, an Englishman named James Lange. His face a little bruised and black. (3 APR 1755)

General Braddock, Governor Dinwiddie and Commodore Keppel arrived yesterday in Annapolis. (3 APR 1755)

Nathaniel Smith, going out as Sutler to the camp, is selling a one-acre lot with house suitable for a tavern, 82 feet long with a kitchen, meathouse and stable. Apply to Carlyle & Dalton. (3 APR 1755)

Messrs. Braddock, Dinwiddie, Keppel, Capt. Orme and William Shirley left for Alexandria on Monday morning. Governor Shirley, Governor Delancey and Governor Morris are arriving tomorrow. (10 APR 1755)

Last Saturday evening the mate of Capt. Montgomery, lying at Alexandria, by some accident fell overboard, by which he was much bruised and about two hours afterward, upon opening a vein, he instantly died. (10 APR 1755)

Governor Sharpe with three other governors left for Alexandria on Saturday. Most or all of the forces are marched from Alexandria west. (17 APR 1755)

Last Thursday, Governor Sharpe came back. (24 APR 1755)

A fire engine has landed from England in Annapolis. (8 MAY 1755)

Jeremiah Chase, of Charles County, is believed to have been poisoned [further details given]. (15 MAY 1755)

The Honorable George Plater died at his seat in St. Mary's County, age 66 (plus). He was a member of His Lordship's Council, a Naval Officer at Patuxent, and Secretary of the Province. (22 MAY 1755)

Spanish liquor is sold by the pound in Anna and Richard Tothill's shop. (26 JUN 1755)

Christopher Lowndes is selling at his Ropewalk, in Bladensburg, lines, rigging, etc. Lots over 5 tons will be delivered to landings on this bay. (26 JUN 1755)

Along the Potomac River: **Extracts from the *Maryland Gazette*, 1728-1799**

A land tract of 190 acres, with plantation, dwelling-house, etch and four tobacco barns is for sale at the mouth of Oxon Creek. Inquire of Herbert Wallace. (24 JUL 1755)

The death of [Gen.] Braddock is reported. (24 JUL 1755)

John Peake seeks return of runaway servant, Negro man, named Jack, "he is a very noted fellow, has crooked knees and when he walks they strike one another." Peake lived on the head of Dogue Creek. Deliver to Mr. Posey's ferry in Virginia, or to John Gibson at Alexandria ferry. (24 JUL 1755)

Humphrey Adams, Esq., a Gentleman touring through the English colonies, died in Maryland. (7 AUG 1755)

On Friday evening last, some People in Queen Anne Town, in Prince George's County, having drank too much got to making Sport, or running their Rig (as it's termed) with one of their company by tripping his heels and throwing him down on the Floor, till they gave him a Fall which killed him. Benjamin Jones had a wife and two small children. (18 SEP 1755)

Daniel Carroll has land for sale near Frederick, 300 acres called *Four and One Half Gallons of Rum*. (28 SEP 1755)

An Irish servant man named Peter Carey ran away from George Cooke near Leonardtown, and "has the Irish Brogue, and Palavers." (2 OCT 1755)

On November 18th, for sale at Alexandria, 1,400 acres, part of *Clifton's Neck*, lying on Potowmack and Little Hunting Creek on which are several plantations, with dwelling houses, outhouses, orchard and sundry other improvements. Also for sale, a tract of 600 acres formerly Henry Brent's, lying on a fork of Little Hunting Creek, within half a mile of the other tract, and on which there are likewise sundry improvements, and is very convenient to two landings, one on Potowmack and the other on Little Hunting Creek. The whole is well situated for trade and within 5 miles of Alexandria. For title apply to Ignatius Digges, John Addison, or William Digges. (23 OCT 1755)

Henry Rozer has a stray bay horse. (30 OCT 1755)

Trenches are being dug around Annapolis. (6 NOV 1755)

Heathcoat Pickett notes the report is false of French and Indians being within thirty miles of Baltimore. (13 NOV 1755)

An earthquake in Annapolis and Prince George's County was felt for one minute. No damage is reported. (27 NOV 1755)

Along the Potomac River: **Extracts from the *Maryland Gazette*,** 1728-1799

Mr. Clajon, recommended by Rev. Addison, with whom he has resided for 18 months, is now assistant in the public school in Annapolis. He proposes to teach young gentlemen French in the Evening School. (27 NOV 1755)

Last Saturday, several of the gentlemen of our neighborhood who lately went out as volunteers, to the Westward, returned home again after having seen no Indians, except one, and he was very quiet, for they found him dead. (4 DEC 1755)

The late earthquake is described. In Boston, 800 chimneys were torn down. It may be a warning to sinners. "To enumerate the Particular Vices that abound among us, would fill up more room than a Sheet would contain." (19 DEC 1755)

John Belaa, Jr., living on Ackakick, near Piscataway, is selling land. (26 FEB 1756)

George Washington was in Annapolis on Monday last, en route south to Virginia. (25 MAR 1756)

Mr. Daniel of St. Thomas Jenifer, is elected Representative from Charles County. (15 APR 1756)

To cover mares of any size, a Jackass named *Tickle Pitcher*, in Queen Anne's County. "As he came of a very plain, laborious family, there can be little said of his beauty or pedigree..." (29 APR 1756)

Capt. William Baylis commanded Fort Peircall, which is garrisoned by Prince William militia. Baylis scalped an Indian. (15 JUL 1756)

War is to be declared against the French. (16 AUG 1756)

Thomas Baker has a Pot House (pottery) at the head of St. Mary's River. Wholesale and retail. He has workmen from Liverpool and Philadelphia. (16 AUG 1756)

John Tayloe and Presley Thornton have dissolved their partnership with John Ballendine (i.e., he is no longer an agent for their Occoquan Furnace or elsewhere). (25 NOV 1756)

Philip Barton Key died a few days ago of pleurisy at Chestertown, on his way home from the northward, a young gentleman lately sheriff of St. Mary's County. (2 DEC 1756)

Alexandria. William Ramsay seeks a person who understands mining; may meet with employment in a copper mine. (27 JAN 1757)

Jonathan Tipton, born in Kingston, Jamaica, died at the age of 118 years. (27 JAN 1757)

Along the Potomac River: **Extracts from the *Maryland Gazette*,** 1728-1799

Carlyle & Dalton want a sloop or schooner, or hull on stocks. (27 JAN 1757)

Thomas Hewit, master of the ship *Alexandria*, of Alexandria, was the man mistakenly identified in the last issue. He arrived at Dartmouth in an open boat with twelve seamen on September 22nd, having found means to escape from a Prison in Morlay, France. (27 JAN 1757)

William Ramsay, Alexandria, has for sale four carriage guns, six-pounders. (24 FEB 1757)

Samuel Gaither announces that he is reconciled with his wife Ann. In the same advertisement he promotes his tavern on the dock in Annapolis. (7 APR 1757)

John Copithorn has for sale at his store in Alexandria, a long list of cloths and clothing. [Pencilled in the margin, "Carlyle"]. (30 JUN 1757)

The Vestries are to make out lists of bachelors for tax purposes. (7 JUL 1757)

George William Fairfax seeks return of runaway servant named Billy. "Has stooping in his shoulders and a shy look." Formerly belonged to Mr. John Pagan, merchant, near Alexandria. Often had travelled with his master and thought to be heading for Philadelphia. (7 JUL 1757)

John Ariss seeks return of convict servant runaway Thomas Hayward, from Mr. John Pettit's, Westmoreland County, Virginia. (21 JUL 1757)

A dancing school has opened in Annapolis, by John Ormsby. He proposes also one day a week at Baltimore, and one at Upper Marlborough. (4 AUG 1757)

Benjamin Fendall is in the business of baking ship bread at his house in Charles County, on Potomack near the Naval Office. (11 AUG 1757)

Mrs. William Digges, of Potomack, died suddenly on Sunday. (18 AUG 1757)

Stolen from the old church in Port Tobacco, on August 31st, a gold watch and case, gold dial plate, and an egg of gold to put a sponge in, also a woman's sewing case. William Waite. (8 SEP 1757)

On the 2nd, died at his seat on Potomack, greatly and justly regretted, the Hon. Col. William Fairfax, President of His Majesty's Council, etc., in whom were happily united the amiable qualities of a polite Gentleman and a solid Christian. (15 SEP 1757)

Fredericksburg. Thomas Frazier, our faithful diligent Post Rider, getting into some dispute in a tavern with an officer of the Virginia Regiment, the officer gave him a blow

Along the Potomac River: Extracts from the *Maryland Gazette*, 1728-1799

in the face, of which he died in three quarters of an hour. The officer immediately gave himself up to justice and ordered a decent burial last Thursday. (22 SEP 1757)

At an irregular election in St. Mary's County, Mr. Edmund Key had treated several of the Electors between the date (of announcing) and date of Election. Key was dismissed. (13 OCT 1757)

A poem written at *Belmont*, on Occoquan [River], on August 31st, by the author of The Little Book, entitled "The Stage Coach from Bourn, Imitated & addressed to Mr. Hogarth." It describes discomforts. The last stanza: "If one was sure in each Stage coach to meet; A company so sociable, so sweet; E'er I would trouble them again with mine; Instead of riding one mile, I'd walk nine." (13 OCT 1757)

Philip Ludwell Lee, of Stratford, seeks return of runaway, Charles Love, aged about 60 years, professes music, dancing, fencing, and plays extremely well on the violin. He took with him a bassoon... fiddle, and his own flute. (20 OCT 1757)

William Vennell, brickmaker, near Annapolis, charges 2/6 per thousand, plus provisions, and two men and three boys to help. (10 NOV 1757)

At Piscataway, the concern of Edward Trafford, Esq. & Sons, of Liverpool, desires all debtors to pay bills. George Bowdon. (10 NOV 1757)

On Sunday, November 27th, Elizabeth, wife of Daniel Jenifer, and daughter of Walter Hanson, died at the age of 25 years. (22 DEC 1757)

Shocks of an earthquake were felt. (23 MAR 1758)

To be sold at Public Vendue, at Broad Creek, in Prince George's County, materials of an old ship, about 120 tons, consisting of three anchors, seven cables, sails, masts, etc. Benjamin Dowson. [Pencilled in margin, "C. Digges"] (15 JUN 1758)

On Saturday last, a man who belonged to a ship in South River was committed to our gaol, for the unnatural and abominable crime of Beastiality. (13 JUL 1758)

Wanted: a Light Lad, about 12 or 13, to ride from Annapolis through Queen Ann[e] Town, Upper Marlborough, Piscataway, Port Tobacco, Newport and St. Mary's, and back again the same road, once a week for Eight Months of the year, and once a fortnight the other four months. Enquire of the Printer. (3 AUG 1758)

Robert Gordon, staymaker at Annapolis, is having imported a quantity of English whalebone, tabbies, and other stay-furniture. He hereby gives notice that he will supply his new customers with stays, Robe-coats and Loose Slips to take off at Pleasure. (10 AUG 1758)

Along the Potomac River: **Extracts from the *Maryland Gazette*, 1728-1799**

A detailed description is given of a lost ferryboat. (5 OCT 1758)

Robert Johnston, of Alexandria, seeks return of a runaway convict servant named John Morphy, on September 22nd. (19 OCT 1758)

Found on the road between Piscataway and Port Tobacco, tied up in a handkerchief, is a pair of tabby stays, not half worn. (23 NOV 1758)

Hilleary Lyles has a stray horse at his place in Prince George's County. (4 JAN 1759)

An act is passed to enable Charles County justices to levy tax not more than two pounds of tobacco on taxables of Port Tobacco Parish for support of an organist. (4 JAN 1759)

An act is passed for selling land where the free school stood in St. Mary's County, and for rebuilding a schoolhouse. (4 JAN 1759)

Daniel Dulany is made Commissary-General of the Province. He is also a member of His Lordship's Council. (4 JAN 1759)

At the house of Mr. John Duncastle, in Charles-Town, on Patowmack, alias Port Tobacco, will be sold riggings, sails, etc., of a ship lately lost on Smith's Point. (25 JAN 1759)

Landed at Mr. Richard Graham's, merchant in Dumfries, on Potowmack, and by him sent to my house as belonging to me, a box marked "H.M." containing six pairs of kid mittens, etc. The box was misdirected. John Mercer. (8 FEB 1759)

Piscataway. James Marshall is going to Britain, and asks to have the accounts settled for those owing to John Glassford & Co. Their store at Piscataway will be continued. William Gammell, a factor at Port Tobacco for Glassford & Co., is also going to Britain. (15 FEB 1759)

A race is to be run for on April 17th, at Walter Maddox's Old Field in Charles County. Francis Triplett. (22 MAR 1759)

Benjamin Whitcomb, Staymaker, is living in Port Tobacco. (26 APR 1759)

Richard Graham, in Dumfries, advertises for the return of two runaway Irish servants. (3 MAY 1759)

A comet appeared, and is doubtless the same as that which appeared in 1531, 1607, and 1682; which return was forcast by Sir Isaac Newton to be about 1758. (3 MAY 1759)

Along the Potomac River: **Extracts from the *Maryland Gazette,* 1728-1799**

A lottery will be held for the building of a wharf at Upper Marlborough and clearing the west branch of Patuxent River. (10 MAY 1759)

Piscataway. Whereas small-pox is rife at Bladensburg to the detriment of trade, George Bowdon announces that the store belonging to Edward Trafford & Sons, of Liverpool, and at present under the management of Mr. Richard Writtle, is now removed from Bladensburg to Mr. Magne's house at Eastern Branch ferry. (17 MAY 1759)

Allen McCrae, of Dumfries, seeks the return of Mulatto slave named Dick. He was "much addicted to liquor and stammers when drunk. He had on a good dark Bearskin frockcoat..." (24 MAY 1759)

Fairfax. William Bronaugh, Jr., Gent., one of His Majesty's Justices of the Peace for the said County, sends greetings to John Heryford, George Heryford and William Moore of the same county. Whereas William Bronaugh, Sr., did on April 14, 1759, at his plantation, take up as strays three horses and has advertised them to no avail, he does make claim to them. Therefore, you are authorized to value and appraise the said strays in current money to me. (2 AUG 1759)

Just arrived in the Potomack River, from Africa, the Ship *True Blue*, with a cargo of three hundred and fifty Gold Coast slaves, the sale of which will begin at Nanjemoy on Monday, August 20th. John Champe & Co. (16 AUG 1759)

John Carlyle seeks the return of two convict servant runaways that were bought for Col. Byrd and sent toward Winchester. (16 AUG 1759)

At a Public Sale to be held in Alexandria on October 16th, court day, will be sold a 1/2-acre lot belonging to Mr. William Sewell, Peruke-maker, with three houses 20x16 feet, bake house, and shed with bakeoven, two small houses, a well walled with stone, 35 feet deep, and a garden. Houses have brick chimneys and are well plaistered and whitewashed. (13 SEP 1759)

George William Fairfax seeks the return of a runaway Negro named Davy, 15 years old, who "speaks fluently, and is very ready in his reply." (25 OCT 1759)

Carlyle & Dalton and John Baynes, have for sale for the benefit of the insurors of the Snow *Alexandria* and her cargo, on November 13th, at Wicomico Warehouse in Westmoreland County, with 125 hogsheads of damaged tobacco. Also, on Tuesday, the 20th, in Alexandria, the snow itself will be sold and 25 hogsheads of tobacco. (1 NOV 1759)

Piscataway, October 30th. On Friday last, there was a day of public rejoicing here for the success of His Majesty's arms in the Reduction of Quebec. There was the greatest concourse of people assembled on the occasion that was ever seen at one time in this place. Upwards of fifty Gentlemen and ladies dined in an elegant manner, and many

Along the Potomac River: **Extracts from the *Maryland Gazette*, 1728-1799**

loyal and patriot toasts were drank. At night the town was illuminated, and a Ball given at Mrs. Plasay's, at which the ladies made a brilliant appearance. (8 NOV 1759)

Thomas Hanson Marshall, executor of the estate of the late Thomas Marshall, calls for settlement of accounts. (8 NOV 1759)

On December 10th, there will be a public sale at Piscataway, of a parcel of choice country-born slaves. James Marshall. (6 DEC 1759)

A comet was seen on two previous days. (10 JAN 1760)

A theatre is being built in Annapolis by permission of the Governor. (10 JAN 1760)

John Craig, administrator, calls for settlement of the estate of the late David Craig, merchant, of Alexandria. (28 FEB 1760)

Last Monday, the theatre was opened. Plays begin at 6:00 P.M. (6 MAR 1760)

6 JAN 1760. For rent, in Alexandria, the George Tavern; three fireplaces below stairs, a very good bar and six rooms above, kitchen adjoining with two rooms above and below, 24 x 18 feet dining room and room of the same dimensions above in which is a good London BILLIARD TABLE. Also, a garden, smokehouse, and stable. For terms inquire of William Ramsay (or in his absence of Mrs. Ramsay). (6 MAR 1760)

To be run at the usual race ground near Alexandria, on May 29th, a purse of £30. The track is 2-1/2 miles around, three times around the track. Enter horses on the Monday before, at the courthouse with Mr. Carlyle, Adams or Hunter. (13 MAR 1760)

Edmund Key, of St. Mary's County, has gone to live in London. (13 MAR 1760)

There has been a terrible fire on Boston; said to be the worst of any ever in all of America. (13 MAR 1760)

A lottery will be held in Alexandria for raising £250 for enlarging and repairing the public wharf, and erecting a grammar school. Managers are George William Fairfax, William Ramsay, John Carlyle, Gerard Alexander, John Dalton, George Johnston, George Mason, John Hunter, Robert Adam and John Muir, Trustees of the said town. Tickets may be obtained from the managers or from Col. John Champe, or Allen McCrae, merchant at Dumfries; Hector Ross and Benjamin Grayson, merchants at Colchester, etc. (3 APR 1760)

Benjamin Grymes, in Virginia, has built a forge. He needs a clerk who will act as manager. (3 APR 1760)

Along the Potomac River: **Extracts from the *Maryland Gazette*, 1728-1799**

The ship *Phoenix*, now in Potomack, is taking on tobacco for London. David Ross. (10 APR 1760)

Last week died here, of extreme old age (a distemper which few die of), a Negro man, who had lived here an old man of great many Years: by his own account he must have lived 125 years. He said he was a Man Boy, waiting at dinner, behind his master's chair in Barbadoes, when they received the news of King Charles being beheaded, for he remembered it by a particular circumstance, that on hearing the news, they all flung down their knives and forks, and arose from the table. (17 APR 1760)

Lost: in Alexandria, on March 18th, ten Frederick-town lottery tickets. John Muir. (17 APR 1760)

To be let, a tract belonging to Charles, Earl of Tankerville, in Loudon County. (12 JUN 1760)

To be sold at Alexandria, on July 21st, the Brigantine *Molly*. She has made only one voyage and is a prime sailer. Carlyle & Dalton. (26 JUN 1760)

Charles County, June 22nd. John Fendall seeks return of a runway convict servant man named John Winter, a very compleat house painter; covers floors as neat as any imported from Britain. The time of his going is uncertain, as he was hired to a gentleman in Virginia who can give no account of the time. The last work he did was a house for Colonel Washington near Alexandria. He must be pretty well known there, having worked at his business several months in that town. He is a very impertinent fellow, pretty tall, and very red about the neck and face... (10 JUL 1760)

Abraham Barnes, in Leonard Town, has for sale several plantations and his dwelling-house in Leonard Town. He is leaving the Province. (17 JUL 1760)

Gerard Fowke, on Nanjemoy Creek in Charles County, has a stray horse, as does Ignatius Semmes, in Port Tobacco. [The law required that all strays be advertised in the *Gazette*.] (17 JUL 1760)

One evening last week, some frolicksome Blades, more merry than wise, were at the pains to take off and destroy the cross piece of the gallows; having, it is like, forgot the old proverb, that "it is dangerous playing with edge tools." (31 JUL 1760)

To be run for, on September 4th, at the plantation of Mr. George Fraser, about one mile below Piscataway, a purse of £15. Managers of the race are Mr. Baynes and Mr. Bowden. (31 JUL 1760)

John Patterson, Alexandria, offers a £20 reward for the return of a runaway convict servant man named John Murphy, a joiner. He is about 5 feet 4 inches tall, well made, of a dark complexion, and has a large beard and large eyebrows and a pale face.

Along the Potomac River: Extracts from the *Maryland Gazette*, 1728-1799

He has been on the stage, is deemed to sing extremely well and appears to be the complete gentleman. He speaks proper English. He will, perhaps, change his occupation as he is acquainted with many branches in the mechanical way. He had on a pair of black knit breeches, fine cotton stockings, and several good wigs. (7 AUG 1760)

Last week, sailed from Patuxent for London, the ship *Wilson*, Capt. Judson Coolidge, with passengers George WilliamFairfax, Esq., his Lady and family. (28 AUG 1760)

Last Monday, the windmill on Windmill Point, in Annapolis, began to grind. (4 SEP 1760)

Printed is a letter from Piscataway, from Rev. Henry Addison, concerning the proposal to build a brick school. The school would have two masters. Forty boys may be boarded with reputable families nearby. (4 SEP 1760)

Alexandria. Carlyle & Dalton seek whereabouts of five fagots of steel, marked "C & D," imported in the ship *Baltimore*, Capt. Francis Lowndes, in 1759, and which was landed at Benedict but never reached us. (4 SEP 1760)

Thomas Contee has a store in Port Tobacco. (11 SEP 1760)

The Brigantine *Hawke*, John Craigg, master, is now lying at Alexandria, and is taking on tobacco. Apply to Carlyle & Dalton. They seek a mate for the ship. (11 SEP 1760)

Left at Robert Adam's store, in Alexandria, a box of felt hats, marked "I.S." (2 OCT 1760)

John Kinsman, lives at Port Tobacco. (2 OCT 1760)

Ran away from the mouth of St. Mary's River, on September 15th, two servants, in a schooner-rigged boat, decked to her stern, with sheets painted green, with red and yellow streaks, and on her stern, a coat of arms. She is the property of Henry Rozer, Esq., on Potowmack, and formerly belonged to Mr. Edward Neale on the Eastern Shore. The men are Daniel MacKenzie, a Scotchman, and John Wade, born about Piscataway, who wears his hair, has some defect in his walk, and understands the water well. They are carrying books, etc., to Mr. Jernegan, on St. Mary's River. William Digges. (2 OCT 1760)

Several of the managers of the Alexandria lottery, being members of the general assembly of that colony, and obliged to attend an unexpected meeting of the Assembly, and others having business at the general court... (postpone the drawing for four weeks). Those reasons ONLY occasion the postponing, the tickets being all engaged. (9 OCT 1760)

Along the Potomac River: **Extracts from the *Maryland Gazette,* 1728-1799**

William Smallwood is chosen as Representative from Charles County, in place of Capt. Lee, deceased. (23 OCT 1760)

Daniel, of St. Thomas Jenifer, seeks the return of two runaways from the ship *Jenifer*, James Chambers, Master, lying at Nanjemoy, on the 12th. James Deering took with him a silver watch, money, a piece of chintz, a piece of striped lutestring, a chintz counterpane, a black satin waistcoat, and a pair of black silk breeches. (23 OCT 1760)

Benjamin Tasker has died. He was Secretary of the Province of Maryland. (23 OCT 1760)

John Patterson, Alexandria, is an agent for the Earl of Tankerville, and is renting John Colvill's *Kittockton* tract. (23 OCT 1760)

In a hard storm in Dumfries, a new dwelling house was burned down. (30 OCT 1760)

The amount of £1,980 in paper currency has been collected from Maryland for the sufferers of the Boston fire, £1,717 from Virginia. (4 NOV 1760)

A lottery will be held in Winchester for the building of a market house. The managers are George Mercer, James Craik, William Ramsay, etc. Tickets are at Carlyle & Dalton. (17 DEC 1760)

The George Tavern, Alexandria, is for rent by William Ramsay. Includes a stable with stalls for ten horses. (1 JAN 1761)

The house at Mrs. Addison's ferry landing is now in the possession of Michael Seelig. (1 JAN 1761)

King George the Second died October 25, 1760. (1 JAN 1761)

The letter which William Digges sent to Mrs. Margaret Taylor, at St. Mary's was never received. (1 JAN 1761).

The prizes are listed from the Alexandria lottery. (8 JAN 1761)

Two cows and a yearling are at the plantation of Col. John Addison, near Broad Creek, Prince George's County. (12 FEB 1761)

On Monday, January 19th, died at her house at Oxen Hill, in her 72nd year, Mrs. Eleanor Addison, relict of the late Hon. Thomas Addison, Esq. (12 FEB 1761)

On January 22nd, died in childbirth, in the 33rd year of her age, Mrs. Sarah Carlyle, wife of Col. John Carlyle, merchant in Alexandria. She was the daughter to the late Hon. William Fairfax, Esq., President of Virginia. A lady of the most amiable character,

Along the Potomac River: **Extracts from the *Maryland Gazette*, 1728-1799**

endowed with excellent qualities, and her death is universally lamented by all who had the pleasure of her acquaintance. (12 FEB 1761)

To be sold at St.Mary's courthouse, the good Snow *BRENT*, a prime sailer, plantation built, 170 tons, square stern, mounting 7 carriage guns. Inventories to be seen on board or at Col. Abraham Barnes. At the same time will be sold a few pipes of choice Madiera. Thomson Mason. (26 FEB 1761)

Wanted: a woman as manager in a public house. James Marshall, Piscataway. (5 MAR 1761)

Charles Digges has for sale goods in his store in Alexandria. (5 MAR 1761)

Richard Barret, merchant in Alexandria, advertises goods for sale. (12 MAR 1761)

John Addison and Henry Addison are executors of the estate of Mrs. Eleanor Addison. (12 MAR 1761)

The horse *Young Traveller*, now in the possession of Mr. Henry Rozer, in Prince George's County, is covering mares this season. Bred by Col. Tasker from *Miss Colvill*, and *Traveller* in Virginia. (2 APR 1761)

On Monday or Tuesday next, the fencing around the Race Ground, in Annapolis, will be taken down, and made ready for coursing; the poles being already set up. (23 APR 1761)

On May 28th, on the usual race ground in Alexandria, a purse of £50 will be run for. It is a one-mile track. The managers are George Washington, John Carlyle, and Charles Digges. (23 APR 1761)

Ignatius Semmes, of Port Tobacco, seeks the return of a runaway servant. (23 APR 1761).

Mount Calvert, the house and 382 acres on the Patuxent, is to be sold. Lingan Wilson. (14 MAY 1761)

Champe & Hunter, Fredericksburg, advertise for sale slaves in Fredericksburg, Virginia, on June 1, on the ship *Alice*, Capt. Samuel Murdock, from Angola. (21 MAY 1761)

Daniel Jenifer advertises goods for sale in his store in Port Tobacco. (21 MAY 1761)

The ship *Alexander*, Daniel Curling, Master, is now lying at Piscataway landing, in Patowmack River, and has good accommodations for passengers. It will sail in about two months. (4 JUN 1761)

Along the Potomac River: **Extracts from the *Maryland Gazette*, 1728-1799**

William Clifton, in Virginia, attorney for the Hon. Charles S. Walmsley and his wife the Right Hon. Catherine Petre, have slaves of the estate of Henry Darnall (eight of them conveyed to them in 1740). (11 JUN 1761)

Champe & Hunter have two ships with slaves arriving in the Rappahannock. (11 JUN 1761)

The snow *Virginian*, John Marshall, Master, is now lying at Piscataway and is taking on tobacco consigned to Mr. Crosbies & Trafford, merchants of Liverpool. Send orders to Mr. John Baynes and George Hardy, Jr., in Piscataway. (18 JUN 1761)

Mules are advertised for sale in Queen Anne's County. (18 JUN 1761)

John Gody keeps a tavern in Port Tobacco, in the house where Mr. Doncastle formerly kept a tavern. (25 JUN 1761)

Daniel Dulany is sworn in as Secretary of the Province. He is going to London on July 2nd. (25 JUN 1761)

Alexandria. Richard Barrett wants to charter a vessel for the West-Indies, 80 to 100 tons burthen. (2 JUL 1761)

George Plater, of St. Mary's County, is arrived as a passenger on the ship in Potowmack, with Capt. Johnston. (9 JUL 1761)

Robert Brent, of New-Port, Charles County, seeks the return of a stolen dark grey horse. (16 JUL 1761)

Mr. George Hardey was a storekeeper for Stephen West, in Piscataway. West had other stores at Pig Point, Queen Anne, and Georgetown. West is issuing paper currency for the convenience of his customers: sixpence to half crown notes. Further description is given. (27 AUG 1761)

George Plater and Thompson Mason are among the judges in the race in Leonardtown. (27 AUG 1761)

George Washington seeks return of four runaway Negroes from his Dogue Run farm on August 9: Peras, Jack, Neptune and Cupid. The last two were bought from an African ship in August 1759. The middle two have tribal scars. (27 AUG 1761)

John Hanson, Jr., near Port Tobacco, seeks the return of a horse he lost. (3 SEP 1761)

Champe & Hunter advertise that the ship *Peggy*, Capt. Cuthbert Davis, is arrived from the Windward Coast of Africa, with a cargo of slaves which are to be sold at Fredericksburg. (17 SEP 1761)

Along the Potomac River: **Extracts from the *Maryland Gazette*, 1728-1799**

Just imported in the ship *Upton*, Capt. Samuel Pemberton, from river Gambia, on the coast of Africa, a cargo of fine healthy slaves to be sold on Wednesday, the 30th of September, at Boyd's-Hole on Potowmack, for sterling, bills of exchange, Maryland or Virginia currency, by Thomson Mason. N.B. Boats will be ready at Nanjemoy for convenience of all persons coming that way to the sale. (24 SEP 1761)

Port Tobacco. Robert Mundell is selling European and East-Indies goods. Samuel Hanson, of Charles County, is selling tobacco and Negroes, a house, and leasing lands. (1 OCT 1761)

John Patterson, agent for the Earl of Tankerville, advertises for sale the *Kittockton* tract, one on Difficult Run, and the lease of one on Four Mile Run, six miles from Alexandria. (1 OCT 1761)

A hound has been lost at Lower Marlborough. (1 OCT 1761)

Thomas Colville states that agent Patterson's advertisement for lands may not be valid, that the lands may have to be sold for debts to John Colvill's estate. (17 OCT 1761)

George Plater is made Representative from St. Mary's County. (22 OCT 1761)

The Ship *Upton*, a letter of Marque, carrying 17 carriage guns and 4 cohorns is now lying in Briton's Bay taking on tobacco for James Gildard, Esq., merchant in Liverpool. Inquire of the subscriber in Leonardtown. Also have white salt for sale. Thomson Mason. (22 OCT 1761)

Potowmack. William Digges offers for hire a Negro blacksmith. (22 OCT 1761)

Andrew Cranston offers for sale at Port Tobacco a parcel of slaves from the Windward coast. (29 OCT 1761)

Mr. Patterson warns others to not deal with Thomas Colvill on Tankerville lands. (5 NOV 1761)

Land tracts are for sale in Prince George's County: *Burbridge*, 280 acres, and part of *Land-over*, 320½ acres. Apply to William Turner Wootton. (5 NOV 1761)

John Addison seeks a man who can write and keep accounts to take charge of a ferry and public house in Prince George's County. (5 NOV 1761)

James Craik is one of the Commissioners for letting bids for a stone church and market house in Winchester. (3 DEC 1761)

Samuel Middleton Marlow seeks the return of a bay mare stolen from Piscataway on November 4th. (10 DEC 1761)

Along the Potomac River: Extracts from the *Maryland Gazette*, 1728-1799

Henry Crouch, carver, died at Annapolis. He was "As ingenious an artist at his business as any in the King's Dominions." A description of an over mantle that he carved, "which would be an ornament even in a palace." (7 JAN 1762)

Port Tobacco. Janet Kinsman, administratrix of the late John Kinsman, is going to move to Virginia. She wishes debtors to settle accounts, and keeps a tavern at The Sign of the Ship in Port Tobacco. (7 JAN 1762)

Alexandria, December 1. Yesterday being the feast of St. Andrew, was held for the first time, the election of the Lord Mayor, Aldermen and Council of this city, when Mr. William Ramsay, a Gentleman of Remarkable Probity and Benevolence, was unanimously voted to the chair; an honour doubly due him, as well as for his Virtuous Deserts, as for being first projector and founder of this promising city. The Office of Recorder was justly conferred on Mr. James Lawrie, M.D. ... who invested the Lord Mayor with a gold chain of metal, struck on that occasion ... [description of metal given]. A grand procession followed with drums, trumpet, etc. to different parts of the city. The Company wore blue sashes, crosses in compliment to the day. Crowds of spectators followed, many on horseback, some on tops of houses. Loud acclamations resounded from every mouth and a general joy sparkled on every face. Shipping ... displayed flags and fired guns the whole afternoon. Elegant entertainment is to be had at the Coffee House, where Lord Mayor, Aldermen and the Common Council dined. In the evening, a ball was given by the Scotch gentlemen ... bonfires, illuminations. (21 JAN 1762)

Notley Young, living near the mouth of the Eastern Branch, advertises that he seeks return of a runaway Mulatto named Billy Carroll, a Carpenter. He had on a pair of purple leather breeches, a light cloth coloured coat, a check shirt, etc. (21 JAN 1762)

Charles Wilson Peale is setting up shop as a saddler, harness maker, postering and repair of carriages in Annapolis. He says he is a young man just starting in business. (21 JAN 1762)

A lottery is to be held in Bladensburg for removing the shoals in Eastern Branch from the wharf at Bladensburg down, and from there to the bridge upwards, and for enlarging the wharf. Among the managers is Thomas Gantt, Jr., one of the first Commissioners for laying out Bladensburg. (21 JAN 1762)

John Pagan, Alexander Brown & Co., are merchants in Glasgow. (4 FEB 1762)

The announcement of the formation of a group to open Potomack River to navigation by small craft from Fort Cumberland to Great Falls. Col. George Mercer and Col. Thomas Prather, treasurers. Managers include William Ramsay, John Carlyle, Joseph Watson, Joseph Patterson, and Robert Peter. The gentlemen will view the Great Falls in the spring [further details given]. (11 FEB 1762)

Along the Potomac River: **Extracts from the *Maryland Gazette*, 1728-1799**

If James Tipper, butcher, who came to this place about 13 or 14 years ago and served his time with Daniel Wells, be living, and will apply to the printing-office, he will learn of something worth inquiring about ... he is supposed to live now not far from Alexandria. (11 FEB 1762)

James Marshall, of Piscataway, wants a 3,000 bushel capacity vessel to carry freight to Barbadoes. (25 FEB 1762)

Richard Bowes keeps a ferry on the south side of the Eastern Branch. (25 FEB 1762)

Janet Kinsman, of Port Tobacco, seeks the return of a strayed bay mare. Also, she has for sale a billiard table. (4 MAR 1762)

To be let in Alexandria, a riverside lot, whereon is a convenient house, 40 by 30 feet, with four rooms below (the largest of which, if any of the Mercantile appellation be inclinable to rent the said lot, is well adapted for the reception of a cargo of goods) and four above, a good dry cellar, and other convenient houses. Inquire of the subscriber living near Alexandria. Philip Alexander. (11 MAR 1762)

In Charles County, a few days ago, died suddenly at a very advanced age, Dr. Gustavus Brown ... a number of years a presiding magistrate of that county. (11 MAR 1762)

There is now living in Prince George's County, hearty and well, two venerable matrons, Mrs. Talbot and Mrs. Charter, who have lived to see their fifth generation. An instance of the healthfulness, as well as fertility, of that part of the Province. (11 MAR 1762)

Samuel Johnston now keeps the ferry formerly called Clifton's Ferry, and will take passengers at the same rates as are paid at Alexandria. Travellers will meet with private entertainment. C. Digges. (18 MAR 1762)

The horse *Young Traveller* is covering mares at Henry Rozer's. (1 APR 1762)

Joseph Watson is going to England. He is having a lottery to dispose of effects worth £2000 in Virginia currency, including eight tracts of land near Potowmack, books, goods, and maps. A drawing will be held on June 10th in Alexandria. For tickets, inquire of John Carlyle and George Johnston, Esq., Mr. William Ramsay, John Hunter, John Kirkpatrick, Robert Adam, Charles Digges, Managers. Also, Dekar Thompson, merchant, in Falmouth.; Col. Champe, in Fredericksburg; James Douglas, William Carr, Daniel Payne, Allen McCrae, merchants, in Dumfries; Hector Ross and Alexander Henderson, merchants, in Colchester, etc.; John Semple, merchant, in Port Tobacco, or John Baynes, merchant, in Piscataway. (1 APR 1762)

The famous horse *Aeriel* will cover mares at William Digges, on the Potomack. (15 APR 1762)

Along the Potomac River: **Extracts from the *Maryland Gazette*, 1728-1799**

The Alexandria annual race purse of £50 will be run for on May 17th. Managers are William Ramsay, James Lawrie and John Kirkpatrick. (15 APR 1762)

To be sold at public vendue, at Charles Robinson's, living near Broad Creek in Prince George's County, on April 28th, a parcel of young Negroes, among which is a good sawyer; cows, horse, hand millstones, and saws. John Tolson. (22 APR 1762)

Deserted from the subscriber, John Posey, at Annapolis, on April 22nd, at night: a recruit who said his name was William Davis, but his real name is John South; he is 5'8", of a thin visage, and is an assuming forward fellow. A reward of £6 will be given if returned to Alexandria. (29 APR 1762)

Lieut. Philip Love is recruiting for the Virginia Regiment. (6 MAY 1762)

Two servant men, who belong to John Tayloe, Esq., of Richmond County, and Col. Brockenbrough, ran away from the Neabsco Iron Works. Thomas Lawson. (6 MAY 1762)

The Rev. Theophilus Swift, of Port Tobacco Parish, died in Philadelphia of a consumption about a fortnight ago. (13 MAY 1762)

May 24th. To be let: a commodious and well accustomed tavern, with convenient outhouses, situate at the ferry landing at the town of Colchester, on the Post Road between Alexandria and Fredericksburg. Apply to the subscriber, living near the premises. Peter Wagener. (3 JUN 1762)

Notice is given of a meeting of the Potomack Company managers at Fredericktown, on July 26th. (10 JUN 1762)

Wanted: two or three journeymen cabinet makers, who are versed in their business. Also, wanted is two or three thousand feet of good mahogany plank. Apply to Mardun Vaghn Aventon, in Dumfries, about 20 miles above Port Tobacco, near Potomack River, in Virginia. (24 JUN 1762)

Just imported and selling by public vendue, on Monday, August 2nd, at Alexandria, a beautiful grey colt bred by John Holme, Esq., in the city of Carlisle. [genealogy of the horse is given]. Carlyle & Dalton. (24 JUN 1762)

Just imported in the ship *John & Presley*, from London, and the *Catherine*, from Glasgow, goods to be sold at Port Tobacco by Daniel Jenifer. (24 JUN 1762)

John Posey intends to leave Fairfax County in three or four months, and wishes to settle outstanding accounts. The subscriber keeps two good ferryboats and good attendants to carry over passengers from Pamunkey Neck, opposite Mr. Thomas Marshall's in Charles County, to Fairfax County in Virginia, which is much the nearest road for travellers going from the lower parts of Maryland to the upper parts, and no winds prevent their passing. Private entertainment is also kept at the subscriber's house for man and horse. (24 JUN 1762)

Wanted: John Barry, from Alexandria, one of the seven recruits who deserted from John Posey. John Dayly and Ezekial Magnett, from Port Tobacco. John Fitzpatrick from Westmoreland County. He was a soldier in my company in 1758 and 1760, and is often bragging of his courage. Reward offered. John Posey. (24 JUN 1762)

Leonard Town, June 26th. Imported from the rivers Gambia and Senegal, a cargo of choice slaves, which will be sold by the subscriber at his house near St. Mary's courthouse, on July 5th. Thomson Mason. (1 JUL 1762)

To be sold very cheap, the owner having no use for it, a chamber organ. It has five stops and is in good order, and is quite loud enough for a country church. Apply to the Printers. (1 JUL 1762)

To be sold at Upper Marlborough, a parcel of slaves. (1 JUL 1762)

To be sold at Port Tobacco, at the house of Ignatius Semmes, a tract in Charles County, near the dwelling plantation of Mr. Samuel Hanson, 400 acres with tobacco houses and a quarter. Edward, William or Henry Digges. (1 JUL 1762)

John Watson offers for sale at Georgetown, on August 19th, a tract of 400 acres at the upper falls of the Potomack in Virginia, and a tract of 280 acres at the lower falls, with run sufficient to carry a mill. (8 JUL 1762)

Notley Young, living at the mouth of the Eastern Branch, seeks the return of a runaway Mulatto named William. (8 JUL 1762)

The offices of the *Maryland Gazette* were broken into, but nothing was stolen. (15 JUL 1762)

On Wednesday, August 13th, will be sold a curious collection of books at Port Tobacco, belonging to the library of the late Rev. Mr. Swift. Daniel of Saint-Thomas-Jenifer. (22 JUL 1762)

Carlyle & Dalton offer for sale three colts and three fillies, arrived from Whitehaven on the ship *Christian*, Capt. Edward Stanley. (29 JUL 1762)

Strayed or stolen from Mr. Hunter's, near Port Tobacco, a gelding branded "H." Deliver to Ignatius Semmes in P.T. Henry Jernegan. (29 JUL 1762)

Along the Potomac River: **Extracts from the *Maryland Gazette*, 1728-1799**

July 24th. Alexander Henderson advertises that rum and sugar from Barbadoes are for sale at Colchester; also Archibald Henderson at Dumfries and Mr. John Orr in Alexandria. (5 AUG 1762)

A new printing press has arrived. (12 AUG 1762)

John Addison offers for rent a dwelling-house and kitchen, stable and pasture, also a good ferry boat to ferry over to Alexandria from the subscriber's landing. (12 AUG 1762)

Ignatius Digges, David Ross and John Brice offer for sale at Annapolis, Negroes from the Gold Coast, imported in the Snow *Favourite Polly*, consigned to Col. Tayloe, Col. Thornton, Mr. Richie and us. They are very fine healthy slaves. Capt. Thomas Campbell. (12 AUG 1762)

Nathan Hughes will offer for sale at public vendue in Alexandria on September 22nd, a house and lot, whereon the subscriber now lives. House is upward of 80 feet long, six rooms on the lower floor all with fire places, and vie above, with a very good cellar, kitchen, meat house, etc. Lots and garden all paled in, and the whole well calculated for a public house. (12 AUG 1762)

Alexandria, August 7th. Mrs. Lucy Washington, daughter of the late Mr. Nathan Chapman, and wife of Mr. Samuel Washington, died after a tedious and painful illness ... This is the third lady this gentleman has lost in eight years, all of great merit, and with whom he might promise himself much happiness, but Providence has ordered their stay to be so short here; this last not a twelvemonth ... (19 AUG 1762)

William Fitzhugh, of *Rousby Hall*, refuses to allow access through lands of which he is trustee at Shipping Hole, on Wye River, for a new ferry. (26 AUG 1762)

The Printer, William Rind, proposes to start a circulating library of new books. (2 SEP 1762)

Alexandria. Imported in the ship *Royal Charlotte*, Capt. Bartholomew Fabre, a parcel of Gambia slaves to be sold on September 13th. John and Thomas Kirkpatrick. (9 SEP 1762)

On September 21st will be sold a schooner. Also rum and molasses for sale. (9 SEP 1762)

The Snow *Virginian*, Henry McCabe, Master, is now lying at William Digges' landing, and taking on tobacco for Crosbies & Trafford, merchants in Liverpool. (23 SEP 1762)

Ran away from the Occoquan Iron Works, on August 26th, a servant named John Milborn, who, in order to discharge a debt of about £35 due by bond to the Hon. John

Along the Potomac River: **Extracts from the *Maryland Gazette*, 1728-1799**

Tayloe and Presley Thornton, Esq., indented himself as a servant for the term of three years. He is a forge Carpenter. Thomas Lawson. (23 SEP 1762)

Richard Bowes offers for sale at Alexandria court [day] on September 21st, three flats and a schooner. (23 SEP 1762)

John Posey seeks twelve recruits belonging to the Virginia regiment who deserted. Deserters are to be brought to the camp at Fredericksburg. (23 SEP 1762)

A lottery will be held at Bohemia, Md., for raising £150 for a library. (30 SEP 1762)

John and Thomas Kirkpatrick seek the return of a runaway servant, William Brookes, from the schooner *Industry*, lying at Alexandria. (21 OCT 1762)

The ship *Hicks*, John Smith, Commander, is 200 tons burthen, is daily expected round from New York to Alexandria, is available for charter. Carlyle & Dalton. (4 NOV 1762)

Alexandria. An English chestnut filly bred by John Holme is for sale. (4 NOV 1762)

November 2nd. John Stone Hawkins writes to the printers, Green & Rind, of the *Maryland Gazette*, from Prince George's County, "Gentlemen: Injured in so sensible a Part as I have been, and having such Palapable proof of the Infidelity of my wife that I have most tenderly loved, I hope I shall not expose myself to the Censures of Malignity itself, if I endeavor to avert the lesser evils it may still be in her power to make me suffer. Too long have I been blind to circumstances which amounted to the strongest conviction with every other person and not until the most open detection has removed every hope of excuse, it is that I declare to her and to the world that I remove her from by Bed, from my House, and need I add, my Affections; that I will never hereafter pay any debts of her contracting, and that it will ever give me pain to reflect she must still bear the name of Your Humble Servant, John Stone Hawkins." (11 NOV 1762)

George Plater, Esq., of St. Mary's, married Hannah Lee, daughter of the Hon. Richard Lee, on Sunday, in Charles County. (16 DEC 1762)

On Saturday, November 13th, died at her house in Stafford County, in the Colony of Virginia, Mrs. Anne Mason, widow and Relict of Col. George Mason, after a long and painful illness, in the 63rd year of her age [text continues]. (23 DEC 1762)

William Thompson, clockmaker, has moved from by Port Tobacco, to near Eversfield's chapel. (23 DEC 1762)

Prizes are listed for Mr. Joseph Watson's lottery. Tickets may be redeemed at Mr. Kirkpatrick, or Charles Digges, merchants in Alexandria. (30 DEC 1762)

Charles County school seeks a master. William Hanson, Registrar. (3 FEB 1763)

Along the Potomac River: **Extracts from the *Maryland Gazette*, 1728-1799**

John Hanson, Jr., in Port Tobacco, wants a captain for a large sea sloop. (10 FEB 1763)

The annual meeting of the Ohio Company will be held at Stafford Courthouse on March 1st. (17 FEB 1763)

Notice that a town will be layed off at Fort Cumberland by the Ohio Company. George Mercer. (17 FEB 1763)

Fifty eight lots of ½ acre each will be sold on May 9th, for enlarging the town of Alexandria. (24 FEB 1763)

Carlyle & Dalton offer for sale, on April 19th, two lots in Alexandria, known by the name of *Long Ordinary*, consisting of a dwelling house, 90 by 24 feet. Six rooms below with fire places, and six above. Cellar, kitchen, meat house, etc. Well paled in with garden distinct. Also one lot with a brick house, 36 by 24 feet, cellar, kitchen, etc., lot paled in. They are both well accustomed public houses. (24 FEB 1763)

The Port Tobacco Lottery, for the benefit of Mrs. Halkerston, will be drawn on May 12th. (17 MAR 1763)

Several of the store books of John Glassford & Co., formerly kept by William Gammell of Port Tobacco, were consumed by fire, and Gammell has left the country. Thomas Campbell, his assistant, is about to leave the country. Therefore, Campbell's deposition on the amounts which he has transcribed from the day books will be taken at Port Tobacco. Robert Mundell. (24 MAR 1763)

William Ramsay, of Alexandria, advertises six half-barrels of gunpowder, supposed to have been imported into Maryland in 1761 or 1762, marked "B.M." or "M.B." He also advertises for rent the *George Tavern*, near the courthouse, extremely convenient, has three rooms and a good bar below, and six rooms above, kitchen (two-story) adjoining, large dining room and good London billiard table above. Paled in garden, well, smokehouse, stable and necessary house. Late in the possession of Patrick Byrn, deceased. (31 MAR 1763)

Charles Wilson Peale has lately removed to Church Street [Annapolis], where Mr. Swan formerly kept his store. He carries on the saddlers business. Painting of signs is likewise performed. (7 APR 1763)

The horse *Aeriel* will cover mares at Mr. William Brent's, in Virginia, at £5 the season. Send mares to Mr. Brent's and only 20 miles from Piscataway, and 16 miles from Port Tobacco. John Casburn, groom. (7 APR 1763)

William Brown, just arrived from Britain, has opened a shop in Alexandria, where he does all kinds of taylors and staymakers work. (28 APR 1763)

Along the Potomac River: **Extracts from the *Maryland Gazette*, 1728-1799**

A lottery will be held in Annapolis for raising $2,400 to erect a building for balls, concerts, etc. Benedict Calvert, Esq., and Mr. Daniel-of-St.-Thomas Jenifer, etc., are managers. (28 APR 1763)

Mr. Calvert's horse *Jolly-C* won the race last Thursday. (28 APR 1763)

Mr. Thomas Posey seeks return of horse strayed from his plantation in Charles County. (28 APR 1763)

May 2. Bids will be taken on August 29th for building a brick church in Truro Parish, at or near the Old Falls church, now gone to decay, and to contain 1,600 square feet with convenient galleries. John West, Jr., Clerk of Vestry. (12 MAY 1763)

The horse *Traveller*, at Mr. Rozer's, in Prince George's County, is covering mares. Michael Walker, groom. (12 MAY 1763)

We have the following account from Aquia in Virginia: On Friday the 13th, about VIII in the evening, they had there a very severe gust with a very large hail; a neighboring planter's dwelling house chimney was struck with lightning. In the chimney stood an iron spit, and resting on the mantel piece and the other end pointing up the chimney, exactly under it stood the man's son, a boy about 7 or 8 years of age, who was instantly struck dead, and the mantlepiece shiver'd to pieces. (26 MAY 1763)

Notice is hereby given that the subscriber, from Dublin, living with Henry Rozer, Esq., near Broad Creek, Prince George's County, carries on the farrier's business in all its different branches; likewise nicking, docking and foxing. All gentlemen that please to favor him with their custom may depend on being faithfully served, by their most obedient humble servant. Michael Walker. (9 JUN 1763)

Mr. Walker, now moved to Piscataway, is carrying on the farrier's business. He has been regularly bred up to feeding and managing horses for racing, which has been his chief study and practise for 18 years past, and that with success. N.B. I have been under some of the most able hands in England, the greatest part of the time. (23 JUN 1763)

John Ballendine has a long notice about his new iron furnace at Shenando Falls, on Potomack River. (23 JUN 1763)

The subscriber has engaged a young man (from Scotland) to instruct 14 boys; he comes well recommended for his industry, sobriety and knowledge in the language. In order to make up this number the subscriber will engage for a few gentlemen's sons schooling, board, washing and lodging, for £25 Virginia currency per annum. The school shall be convenient to their lodging, and plenty of firewood provided, so long as may be necessary each season. William Ramsay. (14 JUL 1763)

Along the Potomac River: **Extracts from the *Maryland Gazette*,** 1728-1799

Alexandria. Charles Digges has a parcel of deerskins, which he will sell for 18 pence Virginia currency per pound, and deliver them ready packed for exportation. (14 JUL 1763)

Alexandria. Just imported from St. Kitts, in the schooner *Industry*, Joseph Thompson, Master, and to be sold by Lucas Gawey, who will be heard of at Mr. Kirkpatrick's store: very fine seasoned Negroes, molasses in hogsheads, rum in ditto, sugar in barrels, limes in ditto. (28 JUL 1763)

Piscataway. Found in possession of John Sullivan, who was committed on suspicion of felony on Wednesday, and who made his escape from the subscriber: a bay horse, saddle, and silver spoon marked "R.H." Richard Darkins. (4 AUG 1763)

On Monday last, as Thomas Mulliken was riding the road in Prince George's County, near the western branch, he got a fall from his horse, which killed him. (11 AUG 1763)

James Scott, in Prince William County, seeks the return of runaway mulatto with bandy legs named Bob. Return to him or Archibald Henderson, merchant in Dumfries. (25 AUG 1763)

An Aurora borealis is seen. (1 SEP 1763)

John Copithorn is selling in Alexandria, European goods. He intends to leave the country in a few weeks, and asks that bills be paid. George Johnston. (29 SEP 1763)

Hannah Plater, wife of George Plater, Esq., of St. Mary's County, and daughter of Richard Lee, Esq., died. She was in the full bloom of life and had not been ten months married. (29 SEP 1763)

The list of members of the Maryland Assembly: twelve in the upper house include Benedict Calvert, Philip Key. In the lower house, from Charles County, Mr. William Smallwood, Mr. John T. Stoddert, Capt. George Dent, and Mr. John Hanson, Jr. (13 OCT 1763)

Piscataway. James Marshall offers for sale at Upper Marlborough, slaves, 300 acres, the house in Piscataway where the widow Plasay formerly lived and kept a tavern. Well accustomed and known by most gentlemen who have travelled in this part of the country. The tavern is for rent. Marshall is leaving for Britain, and wants accounts settled for John Glassford & Co. The store of this firm will continue. (13 OCT 1763)

John Hanson Harrison is moving to Virginia. He offers for sale land in Charles County. [long advertisement, reflects his bitterness towards Maryland]. (13 OCT 1763)

William Ramsay offers for sale land in Frederick County. (20 OCT 1763)

Along the Potomac River: **Extracts from the *Maryland Gazette*,** 1728-1799

Four lots in the center of Port Tobacco are for sale; have two large houses, kitchen, stable, store house, etc. Francis Ware. (27 OCT 1763)

Bids are to be let for a brick house and prison in Alexandria, 36 by 20 feet, two stories high, the plan to be shown on December 12th. John West, John Carlyle, William Ramsay and Robert Adam. (3 NOV 1763)

George Plater seeks a bachelor to manage a large plantation in St. Mary's County. (10 NOV 1763)

Ignatius Semmes is stopping to keep a tavern. ·He wants accounts to be settled. (17 NOV 1763)

Walter Hanson offers for sale at his store near Port Tobacco, goods from Glasgow, from the ship *Fair Lily*, Robert Morrison, Master. (17 NOV 1763)

William Ramsay, sheriff, has a Negro in the jail at Alexandria. (24 NOV 1763)

An Act is passed to levy additional sums on inhabitants of Port Tobacco Parish for further support of an organist. Also, an Act is passed to levy on the inhabitants of St. John's (commonly called King George's) Parish, the sum of 56,000 lb. of tobacco for enlarging the church. (1 DEC 1763)

Piscataway. Francis King has taken over the widow Plasay's tavern. (15 DEC 1763)

A comet is seen. (22 DEC 1763)

Piscataway, December 14th. As a house of good entertainment is always well desired by gentlemen travellers, as well as others, and as I have taken the house in this place where the widow Plasay formerly lived and kept a tavern, and have made a beginning in that way of business; I take this method of acquainting the Public, that all Gentlemen who may please to Favor me with their custom, shall meet with good Entertainment for themselves and their horses, together with everything that may oblige, in the power of Their humble servant, Francis King. (12 JAN 1764)

The last will and testament of the Duke of Lancaster, judged to be as valid as "one that fills forty sheets of parchment" reads (12 JAN 1764):
*I, John of Gaunt
Do give and do graunt
To Roger Burgoyne
And the heir of his loyne
All Sutton and Potton
Until the world's rotton.*

Along the Potomac River: **Extracts from the *Maryland Gazette*,** 1728-1799

Broad Creek. The Vestry of King George's Parish, Prince George's County, will meet on February 22nd to receive plans for enlarging the church, in accordance with an Act of Assembly to levy £350 tax. John Sutton, Register. (26 JAN 1764)

For rent or for sale in Alexandria. An acre of ground, or ½ acre, on the river side, in the middle of the said town, whereon stands a dwelling house, 36 by 30 feet, four rooms below and four above (the largest below has been used as a store), and an excellent dry cellar. The house has every convenience, kitchen, etc. Enquire of the subscriber, living near Alexandria. Philip Alexander. (2 FEB 1764)

Charles Wilson Peale advertises his business of clock making and repair, watch cleaning, and also the saddler's business. (9 FEB 1764)

About ten days ago, died in Prince George's County, Mrs. Grace Cannon, in her 105th year. She was born in this county and within the last year was able to walk 10 to 12 miles a day. She was a widow. (23 FEB 1764)

To be sold or leased: The best and driest corner lot in the town of Alexandria, at a reasonable rate, with a large good dwelling house thereon, with six good rooms below stairs and a good fire place in each room, six good lodging rooms above stairs with a proper window to each room above and below, properly glazed, and the house extremely well built, and very well contrived, situate in the best part of the town, very suitable for any merchant or tavern keeper, with a large cellar, well walled with stone; the whole bigness of the house, near 7 feet deep, with proper apartments in the same, etc., a good kitchen and pantry with all the necessary conveniences to the same, with a good garden, etc., wellwalled up with stone and affords the best water in town, a good meat house and flour house, a good large stables sufficient for holding twenty horses, and a large Privy house with a partition therein. The above buildings are all well contrived, and covered with the best sort of shingles. Any person inclining to purchase or lease, to inquire of the subscriber living ont he lot, in the said town of Alexandria. Benjamin Sebastian. (23 FEB 1764)

A brewery is opened in Annapolis by John Jeudy. (1 MAR 1764)

For sale are 80 of his Majesty's seven-year passengers on the ship *Neptune*, Capt. Sommerville, on March 15th, in the Potowmack, in the ferry way to Alexandria. The sale was first advertised as being at Cedar Point, but was postponed. A three-day sale will be held on board. Includes farmers, taylor, weaver, silversmith, house painter, jeweller, and staymaker. David Ross. (8 MAR 1764)

A post rider is wanted from Annapolis to Alexandria, once a week. (15 MAR 1764)

The ship *Hicks*, now lying at Alexandria, is taking on tobacco. Carlyle & Dalton. (15 MAR 1764)

Along the Potomac River: Extracts from the *Maryland Gazette,* 1728-1799

Scotch coal, for smithys, is for sale on Wicomico River. (22 MAR 1764)

The Piscataway store of James Todd & Co. was broken up. They seek to settle accounts. (5 APR 1764)

Available is a lot in town with a storehouse and compting room, lumber house, stable and kitchen. Inquire at the house of Alexander Burrell. Ninian Mintier, attorney-in-fact. (5 APR 1764)

Mary Semmes seeks all persons who are indebted to the estate of Ignatius Semmes, of Port Tobacco, innkeeper, to settle accounts. (12 APR 1764)

The horse *Traveller*, at Mr. Rozer's in Prince George's County, covers at 2 guineas the season, and 5 shlilings to the groom; he was bred by the late Col. Tasker, and got by Mr. Morton's noted horse *Traveller*, out of *Miss Colvill*, is a fine strong horse, upwards of 16 hands high. Good pasturage for mares, and what should not prove with foal, to have the liberty of next season at half price. (12 APR 1764)

One acre of land with house for sale or rent in Piscataway; 32 by 28 feet with brick chimney and two fire places, and necessary outhouses are all new. Henry Queen, St. Mary's County. (26 APR 1764)

For sale, the estate of Benjamin Fendall. [Long advertisement lists] Individual pieces of furniture. The sale to be held on July 10th at his plantation on Patowmack, in Charles County, near the Naval Office. Also for sale 390 acres across from Hooe's Ferry [further details given]. (17 MAY 1764)

George William Fairfax and George Washington, churchwardens, seek a builder for a brick church at the falls, to be 1,600 square feet with galleries. A Vestry meeting will be held on the third Monday in June at what is commonly called the upper church of Truro Parish. (17 MAY 1764)

To be sold at the landing of William Digges, Esq., by William Graham, at his store at Georgetown, Md., and the landing, both near the head of Potomack, rum and sugar from the schooner *Virgin*, Thomas Jarrold, Master. (24 MAY 1764)

A dancing master is wanted at Bladensburg. (31 MAY 1764)

William Brent, of Stafford County, seeks the return of a runaway convict servant named John Fricker. He had on when he went away a white shirt, violet coloured waistcoat with yellow gilt buttons; it has a flap down the breast, over the button holes, and the skirts of it lined with white shalloon or tammy, a brownish color old superfine broadcloth coat ... It is suspected he has carried other clothes away with him. £10 reward offered. (21 JUN 1764)

Along the Potomac River: **Extracts from the *Maryland Gazette*, 1728-1799**

Piscataway. John Baynes wants to settle accounts for his employer Robert Waters, as Baynes intends to go to Britain at the end of October. (9 AUG 1764)

The George Tavern, is again for rent in Alexandria. It has been unlucky of late in having tenants that did not keep a good House. There is now a vacancy. William Ramsay. (9 AUG 1764)

William Ramsay, in capacity as Sheriff, has for sale horses, a watch, and pistols taken from felons. (9 AUG 1764)

The Hon. Philip Key has died at his seat in St. Mary's County. He was a member of the Governor's Council. (30 AUG 1764)

A white Negro is to be seen at the White House. This is thought by some to be a Specimen of what may be very common a few years hence, tho at present a great curiosity. (30 AUG 1764)

Patowmack. A ferry is to be started to Virginia, John Shirden's landing, as also across the mouth of Piscataway Creek to Mr. William Digges' landing. Mary Anne Noble. (30 AUG 1764)

Colvill lands are sale. (1 SEP 1764)

The estate of Colvill is in dispute. (6 and 27 SEP 1764)

A race is to be held at Piscataway on October 18, for £20. (6 SEP 1764)

The Virginia-built sloop *Nancy*, now lying in the mouth of Choppawansick Creek, is for sale. Also tar, pitch, rozin and turpentine. Inquire of Thomson Mason in Stafford County, or Col. Abraham Barnes in St. Mary's County. (27 SEP 1764)

John Manning, near Piscataway, has 200 acres for sale at Point Lookout. (27 SEP 1764)

William Brent, Stafford County, offers £10 reward for return of two English runaway servants: John Buckingham, took white fustian frockcoat, light colored bearskin coat lined with green, pink colored jacket richly trimmed with livery lace, etc. Also John Fricker. (11 OCT 1764)

To be sold at the house of Mr. John Doncastle, of Port Tobacco, a 800-acre tract called *St. Johns*. Samuel Hanson, Jr. (18 OCT 1764)

Daniel of St.-Thomas-Jenifer has goods for sale. (18 OCT 1764)

Along the Potomac River: Extracts from the *Maryland Gazette,* 1728-1799

James Lawrie, of Alexandria, seeks the return of a runaway Dutch servant. He took medical instruments, and treated Lawrie's patients. (1 NOV 1764)

The chimney on Governor Calvert's house, in Annapolis, caught on fire. The high house was old and made of wood, and located near the head of the dock. The chimney was very dirty, and is a hint to neighbors to clean theirs. (1 NOV 1764)

Ran away, from Benjamin Philpott of Port Tobacco, Margaret Cane. She is fond of drink and likes sailors' company much, and all masters of vessels are forewarned of carrying her off at their peril. (1 NOV 1764)

William Smallwood, John Hanson, John T. Stoddert and Mr. Dent are elected Representatives from Charles County. (13 DEC 1764)

The new dwelling-house of Thomas Fleming, shipbuilder of Alexandria, which was almost finished, caught fire. (13 DEC 1764)

Prince George's County Representatives included William Murdock. The Vestry at St. John's Parish, Prince George's County, will have a meeting on January 1st, to discuss enlarging the church. (20 DEC 1764)

The Prince George's County gaol lately was broke open. All prisoners escaped. (3 JAN 1765)

An epitaph in verse of an earthenware maker. (10 JAN 1765)

The bridge is now open over the Severn River, over which people pass. (10 JAN 1765)

Benjamin Philpott, in Port Tobacco, is giving up his public house on May 1st. (17 JAN 1765)

Small-pox is in the neighborhood of Piscataway and has proved fatal to many. One Mr. Marlow, in the height of that distemper, being much out of his senses, unhappily escaped his nurse, got out of his house, and was afterward found dead in Mattawoman, froze in among the ice. (24 JAN 1765)

A parcel of slaves is to be sold on February 2nd at Philpott's house in Port Tobacco. Francis Ware. (31 JAN 1765)

On Monday last, a very merry set of gents had a commodious tent erected on the ice between the town and Greenbury Point, where they had an elegant dinner, etc., and in the afternoon diverted themselves by dancing of Reels on scates, etc. (7 FEB 1765)

John Truman Stoddert died a fortnight ago in Charles County. He was a Representative from that county. (7 FEB 1765)

Along the Potomac River: **Extracts from the *Maryland Gazette*,** 1728-1799

Mr. Calvert has moved out of Annapolis. (14 FEB 1765)

Clish. Thomas Colvill offers for sale 6,300 acres in Frederick County. (14 FEB 1765)

Land in Fredericktown, Md., owned by John Colvill, deceased, will be sold by Thomas Colvill. (31 JAN 1765)

St. John's Church, at Broad Creek, Prince George's County, is to be enlarged. Bids are asked for. (14 MAR 1765)

Owner John Tayloe, Neabsco Iron Works, seeks the return of three Negroes who ran away from the Occoquan Iron Works. Also, a servant and boat. (14 MAR 1765)

Charles Digges, merchant, has returned from London on the ship *Jane*. (11 APR 1765)

A scurilous [sic] ad was posted in Church in Charles County, on March 19th. "This is to give notice to Mr. Winter and Justices of Charles County not to meet on Saturday next at Hugh McBride's & If judgment goes against one many they may be sure of being privately burnt up ... it hath pleased Almighty God to send a hard winter and scarcity by a desperate summer and we got agreeing to warranting-so much private rogery [sic] by malicious constables in striving to get half-crowns, William Compton Gill and Oliver Burch may be sure of being privately burnt up, if striving to get one man to justice. If Hugh McBride doth not call in all the warrants he has issued out and warrant no more he may be sure of being way Layd and shot. There is no less than 52 persons who ... will honestly pay debts but if warranted is fully bent to Do Murder to the Justices and Constables of Charles County." [Reward for author is offered by the Governor of Maryland]. (16 APR 1765)

The Ship *Trial*, Capt. Errington, arrived at Piscataway, on Potomac, with 100 servants; a sale will be held at Cedar Point on May 1st. (20 APR 1765)

Kingston, Jamaica. "On Sunday last the remains of the once prosperous, gay beautiful and almost irresistably engaging Miss Teresia Constantia Phillips were interred in the churchyard of this town, unattended by a single friend of either sex! While we hope no ungenerous Insult will be offered to her ashes we cannot forbear adding our wishes, that a Catastrophe so striking and melancholy may prove an advantageous lesson to many of the surviving Fair; and convince them, however flattering appearances may be, on their first Deviation from the Path of Rectitude & Honour, that no Admiration will be lasting, no happiness secure, which is not founded on the Basis of Rectitude." (18 APR 1765)

Bids are being taken for the building of a ballroom in Annapolis. (20 APR 1765)

William Triplett seeks the return of a runaway slave whose "back [is] much furrowed from Whipping," named Harry. (30 MAY 1765)

Along the Potomac River: **Extracts from the *Maryland Gazette*, 1728-1799**

An auction sale will be held for a tract on Occoquan River called *Belmont*. It was mortgaged to Hugh Blackburn & Co., Glasgow, by Benjamin Grayson, Gent. It contains 1,016 acres, near five sawmills, two forges, [nine] furnace, and the best grist mill on the continent. Also, an orchard, brick house, 24 by 18 feet, two rooms below and two above, a wooden house, 26 by 18 feet, three rooms below and cellar, new barn shingled, kitchen, dairy, meat house and fish house. Also three lots in Colchester, whereon a tobacco house was lately built, #6, 7, 29. Also, five other lots, a grist mill on Pohick [Creek], and two servants. (1 AUG 1765)

A stamp distributor's effigy was ridden backwards thru Dumfries on Monday last, halter tied around the neck, caned, whipped and burned. (12 SEP 1765)

On Wednesday, Col. John Baylis was killed in a duel [near Dumfries]. (12 SEP 1765)

For sale, a tract of 602 acres, with log dwelling-house, ten miles from Colchester, convenient situation to where a Church is intended to be erected in Truro Parish. (12 SEP 1765)

Because of the Stamp Tax, the *Maryland Gazette* is Expiring: In Hopes of Resurrection to life again." Another "Not Dead but Asleep, etc." Suspended until March 1766, as a regular publication. (10 OCT 1765)

Marlborough, 18 APR 1766. John Mercer offers for sale 20 slaves at the Fredericksburg fair on June 3rd, include house servants, watermen, laborers, etc., and three children. (22 MAY 1766)

The windmill in Annapolis is for rent. (31 JUL 1766)

George Johnston died on Friday last, after a very long and lingering indisposition. (4 SEP 1766)

For sale, three lots in Alexandria, belonging to George Johnston, deceased. A good dwelling-house upwards of 100 feet long, six fire places below stairs, another house 36 feet long with two fire places, stable, mill-house, meat house, office, other houses and a good garden, well, and the whole enclosed with poles and Brick. Front on the river of 70 yards, defended from the water by a stone wall, to which boats and other small vessels may come at moderate tide. Time will be given for Payment. (2 OCT 1766)

The Piscataway races will be run on the north side of town, ½ mile away. (2 OCT 1766)

Died, at *Clish*, Col. Thomas Colville, "that worthy good man," age 78, formerly a Representative from Cecil County. (30 OCT 1766)

Along the Potomac River: **Extracts from the *Maryland Gazette*, 1728-1799**

John de la Sumat, died in Fauquier County, age 130! He was banished from France in 1684, imported to Virginia to settle Brentown lands. He was a great-great-grandfather. (17 OCT 1766)

Advertisement for bids for [building] the Church in the town of Alexandria. (4 DEC 1766)

Bids sought for building a church at Falls Church and Alexandria. To be 2,400 square feet, walls high enough for galleries. Enquire of Wm. Adams, John Dalton, Churchwardens. (1 JAN 1767)

The "very melancholy influence of the Imprudence of Taking in a Passenger from a Convict Ship, lately happened a few miles from this city; Nine of the family have already died of the Jail Fever, and four more are in dangerous condition." Warning to be more cautious about admitting "these Wretches, doubly Nuisances from the Contagion of their Distempers, & of their Vices." (1 JAN 1767)

Daniel Jenifer offers for sale 260 acres on Zachia Swamp, part of *His Lordship's Favour*. There is a shell of a dwelling-house on the land. (1 JAN 1767)

Philip Alexander offers for rent or sale, one acre on the river side, in the middle of the town of Alexandria. It has four rooms below, four above, four fire places, cellar, kitchen, etc., a storehouse and balehouse. (8 JAN 1767)

Found left with William Digges, on Potowmack: A cask marked thus "N-F," containing tea kettles, etc. The owner please come for such. (22 JAN 1767)

Nonesuch plantation on the Eastern Branch [Anacostia River], belongs to Rev. Addison. He has a stray horse. Leonard Soper, overseer. (12 FEB 1767)

Walter Dulany, Esq., was sworn in as one of His Lordship's Honourable Council of State of this Province. (12 FEB 1767)

19 MAY 1767. The Glebe Lands of Truro Parish are for sale. 400 acres, with brick house, four rooms on a floor, passages above and below and cellars, kitchen, meat house, corn house, coach house and barn, other houses, yard and garden paled in, situation high, dry and healthy, good water. Some meadow, and a valuable peach orchard. Two miles to a navigable branch of the Potomack, and by having the great post Road from Alexandria to Williamsburg, passing through it at a proper stage between the former and the town of Colchester on Occoquan, it is rendered very convenient for a publican and might possibly suit a merchant or doctor. Plate of parish (before division) will be sold. Enquire of George Washington or William Gardner, Churchwardens. (12 MAR 1767)

The Annapolis races will be run May 19th. (12 MAR 1767)

Along the Potomac River: **Extracts from the *Maryland Gazette*, 1728-1799**

To be sold on the 3rd Tuesday in May, George Johnston's house in Alexandria. Sarah Johnston, Geo. Johnston, Executors. (19 MAR 1767)

Mr. Jonah Green, printer of the *Maryland Gazette*, died. He printed the *Gazette* for 21 years. Wife Catherine is carrying on. (16 APR 1767)

The horse *Traveller*, the property of Henry Rozer, will cover at *Notley Hall*, on Potowmack River, at 2 guineas the season. (14 MAY 1767)

Ignatius Middleton is keeping a tavern in Port Tobacco. (14 MAY 1767)

John Dalton and Robert Adam, Alexandria, seek return of runaway Irish convict servants. (18 JUN 1767)

The tract *Belmont* is to be auctioned on August 21st at Colchester. Lots in Colchester, #3 storehouse, stable and the lot enclosed, where Alexander Henderson formerly lived. Also, #19, 21 and 23, adjoining each other, with a dwelling house suitable for an ordinary or private family. Sale by David Lord of Essex County. (9 JUL 1767)

John Ralls offers for sale 700 acres of land in Stafford County, 8 miles from Aquia warehouse, 12 miles from Dumfries, convenient to church and mills. (6 AUG 1767)

To be sold on November 23rd by the executors of Thomas Colvill, deceased, 600 acres of land in Fairfax County, near the old courthouse. Frances Colvill, George Washington and John West. (3 SEP 1767)

Charles Digges, Merchant, is arrived on the ship *Swan* from London. (10 SEP 1767)

To be sold, land on Four Mile Run, six miles from Alexandria; 166 acres, a grist mill, and ¼ acre reserved from the sale for the cemetery of John Bale. (12 NOV 1767)

Thomas Addison, Jr. is married to Miss Rebecca Dulany, eldest daughter of the Hon. Walter Dulany. (31 DEC 1767)

The Ohio Company is to meet February 23rd at Stafford Courthouse. George Mason, Treasurer. (4 FEB 1768)

The 7,000-acre *Brenton* tract is to be sold on April 12th, by Robert Brent. (17 MAR 1768)

The Executors of George Johnston, offer again for sale a town house in Alexandria. Also, a very elegant silver teapot, milk pot and stand. (5 MAY 1768)

Notley Young's horse, *Gimcrack*, won the race at Upper Marlboro. (5 MAY 1768)

Along the Potomac River: **Extracts from the *Maryland Gazette*,** 1728-1799

William Rind is printing a revised edition of the *Laws of Virginia*. The price will be 40 shillings. (26 MAY 1768)

Charles Carroll is married to Mary Darnall at his father's home. (4 JUN 1768)

John Rhodes and John Medcalf have rented the Ship Tavern in Alexandria, and the ferry thence to Maryland to Mr. Addison's landing in Prince George's County. They offer cut rates on the ferry. (18 AUG 1768)

Thomas Belt, the 3rd, offers for sale 200 to 300 acres which are part of a tract, 5 miles from Georgetown, called *Chevy Chase*. (22 SEP 1768)

The Piscataway races will be held Thursday, October 18th, at 2:00. (29 SEP 1768)

Sampson Darrell seeks the return of a runaway convict servant named Thomas Fossit, a weaver, "who steps very high in his Walk." (29 SEP 1768)

The tract in Charles County, called *Nanjemoy*, is for lease; a good harbor. It offers a good place for a town, leasing lots for the town to be called *Elvira*; minimum of 50 shillings. Burditt Hamilton. (6 OCT 1768)

Michael Gretter, gaoler in Alexandria, has a runaway servant named John Hoget, who bears the mark of late whipping. Gretter seeks owner to claim. (6 OCT 1768)

At Charlestown, Cecil County, the day after the horse races, a fox hunt is proposed. (6 OCT 1768)

Thomas Addison, Jr., offers for sale 200 barrels of Indian corn. (27 OCT 1768)

On Friday, the 14th [October] instant, after a short illness at his seat, at Marlborough, in Stafford County, age 64, John Mercer, Esq. died. For many years a very eminent lawyer, and remarkable for his Assiduity, in his Profession. He was a Gentleman greatly esteemed, and of consequence is much regretted. (10 NOV 1768)

A race of $200 will be run on November 29th, between John Addison, Esq.'s horse *Dutchman* and Mr. Robert Hanson's *Fox*. (17 NOV 1768)

William Digges seeks the return of a runaway stonemason named Thomas Coreshil, who turns his toes in when he walks. (17 NOV 1768)

Daniel of St. Thomas Jenifer is appointed His Lordship's Agent and Receiver General in room of Mr. Bennett Allen. (1 DEC 1768)

Along the Potomac River: **Extracts from the *Maryland Gazette*, 1728-1799**

The half interest in a grist mill of James Edelin, deceased, is to be auctioned at the mill on the second Tuesday in January. The grist mill was built about 5 years ago, and is ½ mile from Piscataway. Also 10 acres. (29 DEC 1768)

The *Brenton* tract, 800 acres, is to be sold next April. It pays no quit rent. Inquire at the house of Scarlet Maddins on the premises. Robert Brent, William Brent, Daniel Carroll and Henry Rozer. (29 DEC 1768)

Ran away from the Neabsco Iron Works, on October 10th, a Negro slave named Billie, the property of the Hon. John Tayloe, Esq. He "puts on a sour look when taxed with anything amiss." Also Scipio. If found, return to John Calvert, manager, at Col. Tayloe's Mine Bank in Baltimore County, or to Thomas Lawson. (29 DEC 1768)

A master is wanted at the free school in Prince George's County, who is qualified as the law directs. (5 JAN 1769)

The tract *Bellair* is for sale, the former residence of the late Governor Ogle. Also, 21 slaves, furniture and 2,177 acres. The mansion is two-story, brick, and 60'x35'. An office nearby, two-story brick, is 40' square. Will be sold March 18th. (19 JAN 1769)

William Berry (called a liar by Andrew Beall in the issue of December 22nd), is called on to prove it. William Berry. (19 JAN 1769)

John Ballendine, in a lengthy advertisement, offers for sale at the falls of the Potomack, a stone building, 152'x36', three and a half stories high, containing a mill, bakery, store, etc. Also a dwelling house. (2 FEB 1769)

Susannah Patterson, living at Thomas Addison's ferry, seeks the return of a runaway servant. (16 FEB 1769)

John Hunter warns the public that he refuses to pay the debts incurred by his wife Jane. (16 FEB 1769)

Robert Brent and his father George offer for sale lands including *Brenton*, to pay debts. (9 MAR 1769)

Daniel Jenifer offers for sale three lots in Port Tobacco. One has a tavern now run by Mrs. Halkerston. Next where she formerly lived, a brick house with office below, 24'x18'; on the third lot is a brick house 32'x18' almost finished, with chimney in the middle. Also, 342 acres, part of *Haber Deventure*, and *Hanson's Plains Enlarged*. There are two tenements on the property. (9 MAR 1769)

John Addison advertises the horse *Jolly Roger* to cover. (6 APR 1769)

Along the Potomac River: Extracts from the *Maryland Gazette*, 1728-1799

For sale, the grist mill on Captain John's Run, 5 miles from Georgetown. (13 APR 1769)

Charles Digges, of Upper Marlboro, died on April 5th at Dumfries after an illness of two days. He was a young merchant. (13 APR 1769)

Counterfeit bills were passed at the ordinary in Todd's Bridge, Virginia. Mr. Payton, of Aquia, examined the bills, and remarked, "How can you thus attempt to impose on a stranger: these bills are every one of them counterfeit and so notoriously so you cannot be ignorant of it." (27 APR 1769)

Isaac Pierce, Jr., block and pump maker from Boston, has settled in Alexandria. (4 MAY 1769)

The trustees of the poor in Prince George's County intend to build an alms house. (11 MAY 1769)

Westmoreland County, Virginia has ordered for the courthouse there a portrait of the Earl of Chatham. It is done by Charles Peale of Maryland (formerly apprenticed to a saddler at Annapolis, but sent home to England by several gentlemen to study art). The portrait is like a Roman orator. (11 MAY 1769)

John Posey seeks creditors to meet him at Piscataway on the second Monday in August, Tuesday at Port Tobacco, and the third Monday in Alexandria, "where they will be thankfully paid." Anyone who owes him money is to come too. "Nothing but death will prevent his attendance." (18 MAY 1769)

The two following being paid advertisements, we insert them as such:
    Capt. John Posey, Esq., Fairfax County, Virginia, was married by Rev. Robert Reade on May 25, 1769, to Miss Elizabeth Adair of Chestertown, Kent County. She is a person of good family, considerable education and a large Fortune. Capt. Posey's Economy, Honour and Spirit must have been great. It is said that the lady, the Morning before she married, made her Estate, real and personal, over to Capt. Posey, though she has a Sister, and courted by many.
    One of Capt. John Posey's house wenches at his seat *Rovers-Delight*, Fairfax County, Virginia, had three sons at a birth, February 1766: two girls August 1767; and in March 1769, a son and a daughter. There was but two hours between the two, the boy is black with Wool, the girl is white with white hair like a white child. All the children are living. (1 JUN 1769)

Mr. Posey's wife and he, her sister Cassandra and husband John Moore, are owned money by brother Robert Adair. They are having his real estate sold. (8 JUN 1769)

James Handeser offers for sale a Saltpetre mine on the South branch of Potomac. (13 JUL 1769)

Along the Potomac River: **Extracts from the *Maryland Gazette*,** 1728-1799

For sale, a 100-acre tract, part of *Battersee*, on Broad Creek, Prince George's County, with several buildings on it; other small tracts for sale by James Marshall. (13 JUL 1769)

Land of 470 acres, lately the property of Col. Henry Peyton, is to be sold at Dumfries. It includes a grist mill. (20 JUL 1769)

Robert Adam, Alexandria, seeks the return of a runaway barber, named James Lowe. (27 JUL 1769)

Samuel Middleton has in his warehouse in Annapolis, a trunk, box and bundle of bed-clothes directed for Mr. John Lowrie to the care of Mr. Dalton, *Belhaven*. They came from England, 1767, on Capt. William Hambleton's ship. (3 AUG 1769)

Sarah Johnston offers for sale a ½-acre lot in Alexandria near the river, with a house 36'x24' with two fireplaces and a large dry cellar. Also, a genteel lodging-room, with fireplace adjoining, and a garden, the whole is enclosed with pales. (17 AUG 1769)

Whereas Mary Skinner my wife after all the Love and Tenderness which could possibly be shown by man to a woman, has polluted my Bed, by taking to her in my stead, her own Negro slave, by which she had a child, which has occasioned such disgrace to me and my family ... I have thought it proper to forbid her my sight any more. Walter Skinner. (12 OCT 1769)

Daniel McCarty's horse, *Volunteer*, raced last Tuesday at Annapolis for a purse of 50 guineas, and also his *Silverlegs*. The Piscataway races will be run on November 7th. Also, had a horse, *Little Driver*, running in the Ladies purse on Thursday in Annapolis. (20 OCT 1769)

Col. William Fitzhugh is sworn in as a member of Maryland Council of State. (16 NOV 1769)

Richard Graham, of Dumfries, seeks return of a runaway servant named William Powell. (30 NOV 1769)

To be sold on January 1st, all the land in Kent County of Mrs. Elizabeth Adair. Capt. John Posey is to attend the sale. Mrs. Posey, being indisposed, prevented his attending the sale of the 1st Tuesday of this month and the sale at Baltimore. (7 DEC 1769)

Samuel Hanson, in Charles County, offers for sale slaves, horses, and household furniture. (14 DEC 1769)

Mary Chapman, on Gunpowder River, had stolen a puppet Punch's head. (14 DEC 1769)

Along the Potomac River: **Extracts from the *Maryland Gazette,* 1728-1799**

John Baynes, seeks return of a runaway servant from Piscataway, a white servant boy named James Taylor, belonging to Mr. Rev. Boucher, of Virginia. (18 JAN 1770)

A master is wanted for the free school in Charles County. Walter Hanson, Thomas Contee, Samuel Hanson, and James Craik. (18 JAN 1770)

At Pig-Point, Prince George's County, Maryland, Demilion Kingsbury carries on the wheelwright business and runs a ferry. (29 MAR 1770)

Robert Hanson, of Charles County, died January 27th. About one year before, he leased to surgeon Joseph Aderton that part of his estate where his family graveyard is. Gerard Fowke asked that Hanson be buried there "to which he made a most unprecedented and unChristian-like Denial" and gave for Reason that his wife was timorous and fearful, and would by no means agree to have Mr. Hanson buried in the Grave-Yard (which Mr. Aderton has converted to, and made use of as a Horse-Pen). (5 APR 1770)

James Brown, of Piscataway, is going to Britain, and seeks to settle debts owed to Simpson, Baird & Co., Glasgow merchants. The firm has a store in Bladensburg and Piscataway. Alexander Hamilton. (19 APR 1770)

Sarah and George Johnston, Alexandria, advertise for sale a lot with house having two fireplaces, another room with a fireplace, and garden. To be sold May 21st. (3 MAY 1770)

A lottery will be held for clearing the channel in Patuxent River, 20 feet wide. This is prompted by a loss of navigation and the destruction of a breed of fish. (3 MAY 1770)

An alms house is to be erected in Prince George's and Charles counties. (7 JUN 1770)

Dumfries, Scotland. "The so long sought for perpetual motion has at last been found out by one Mr. Kirk. He got his first machine made by a Country Blacksmith and is at present preparing another in Brass, which will be sent to London." (28 JUN 1770)

Daniel of Saint Thomas Jenifer's house in Annapolis was robbed of silver with a mermaid engraved on spoons. [On October 4th, robbers were sentenced to death.] (5 JUL 1770)

The public grammar school is opened at Bladensburg. (5 JUL 1770)

Edward Rigden, Alexandria, seeks the return of a runaway servant. (12 JUL 1770)

The Johnston executors offer for sale in Alexandria, a house with two rooms above and a cellar below; also a small room proper for an office or accounting room. (16 AUG 1770)

Along the Potomac River: **Extracts from the *Maryland Gazette*, 1728-1799**

Hector Ross, in Alexandria, offers for sale 17 slaves, on September 17th, being Fairfax Court Day; also a tract on Pimmit Run near the falls, of 400 acres. Part of the estate of John Ballendine, will be sold for debts due Ross. (23 AUG 1770)

James Kirk seeks return of one William Mercer, a jobber on board a flat lying at Piles' Warehouse, Alexandria, who ran off and robbed the skipper of what cash he had to pay for inspection and also the sundry crop-notes at the warehouse [listed]. (23 AUG 1770)

Samuel Washington offers for sale a 878-acre tract in Westmoreland County on the Potomac and Machodock rivers. (6 SEP 1770)

Francis Mastin, of Charles County, has a ferry and an ordinary at Chickamuxon, over to Quantico. (20 SEP 1770)

The Schooner *George*, built in Alexandria in May 1767, will be auctioned at Alexandria. (11 OCT 1770)

The ferry lately kept by Capt. John Posey, from his landing over Potomack to the plantation of Capt. T. Hanson Marshall in Charles County, is still continued and travelers may depend on a ready passage. (11 OCT 1770)

Mrs. Christian Gordon, of the Wood Yard, died October 18th. (25 OCT 1770)

Charles Carroll is conveying 160 acres to form the town Carrollsburg on Anacostia; 261 lots. Trustees include Notley Young, Henry Rozer and Daniel Carroll. (22 NOV 1770)

Charles Leonard, of Alexandria, is publishing six elegant pieces of musick by subscription. Subscriptions of $2 will be taken in Alexandria by Dr. William Rumney, Mr. Henry Piper, James Stewart and Charles Turner: at Dumfries, Mr. William Grayson and Dr. Graham. Other towns listed. (22 NOV 1770)

Died. Thomas Addison, age 56, at his house on Potomac. Sometime Major of His Majesty's 35th Regiment of Foot. Having betaken himself pretty early in Life to the Honorable Profession of Arms he was present at some of the sharpest actions of the late and the preceding war, both in Europe and Spanish and British America ... If with the most amiable qualities some human frailties were blended, the Candid will not fail tenderly to draw the Mantle of Oblivion over them. The bulk of his considerable fortune he left to his nephew Thomas Addison, Esq., of *Oxen-Hill*. (6 DEC 1770)

Robert Adam & Co., Alexandria, offer for sale Jamaica spirits in hogsheads, Boston rum, sugar, coffee, ginger, allspice. They buy corn, wheat, and flour. (20 DEC 1770)

An organist is wanted for Port Tobacco parish. The parish has upward of 1,900 tithables. They offer a salary of 4 lb. tobacco per tithable. Rev. Thomas Thornton, and Theodore Hanson. (3 JAN 1771)

Along the Potomac River: **Extracts from the *Maryland Gazette*, 1728-1799**

For sale at Dumfries, on January 5th, by Thomas Montgomerie, the Brigantine *Brittania*, 140 tons, 4-5 years old, built in New England. (3 JAN 1771)

Wanted by Thomas Hanson Marshall, a woman qualified for managing a house, and bringing up Girls, in a genteel way. (21 FEB 1771)

A Presbyterian Church is to be built near Bladensburg at the present meeting house. (21 FEB 1771)

Thomas Stone died at his seat at Nanjemoy, on April 17th. He was Magistrate of the county for forty years, and Chief Justice of the county court. (2 MAY 1771)

The Upper Marlboro races were run on the 1st. William Fitzhugh's horse *Regulos* won £50. The next day, Daniel McCarty's horse *Silverlegs* won £30. (9 MAY 1771)

John Ballendine is to meet creditors on May 16th; offers for sale crops, wheat, tobacco, corn and land in Prince William County, and a house at the falls. (9 MAY 1771)

Wanted: a skinner and breeches maker. Contact through Mr. Charles Lansdale, Post rider from St. Mary's County to Annapolis, directed to William Sears, Tavern Keeper at Broad Creek, Prince George's County. (27 JUN 1771)

Thomas Triplett warns the public not to buy a bond of James Collet. (4 JUL 1771)

Henry Selkeld offers for sale an acre in Alexandria, near Royal and Cameron streets. (11 JUL 1771)

The Brigantine *Fairfax*, Capt. Samuel Brodus, is now lying at Alexandria, and is taking on tobacco for Liverpool, from both sides of Potomack river. Inquire of John Carlyle. (11 JUL 1771)

A statue of Lord Botetourt is to be erected at public expense at Williamsburg. (22 AUG 1771)

John Ralls offers for sale the tract *Beulah*, 780 acres with apple orchard, 8 miles from Aquia church and warehouse, Stafford County; he is selling for the benefit of younger grandsons. (22 AUG 1771)

Thomas Brereton has opened in Baltimore an insurance office for ships, vessels and cargo. (22 AUG 1771)

Trinity Parish, in Charles County, is to build a brick church. (29 AUG 1771)

Along the Potomac River: **Extracts from the *Maryland Gazette*, 1728-1799**

Mr. Lomax, at the ferry in Alexandria, will take $1 subscriptions for a book written by Peter Egerton, living near Piscataway, for the benefit of the injured unfortunate. (5 SEP 1771)

Thomas Stonestreet, of Prince George's County, age 98 (but may be 105 or 106), died last week (12 SEP 1771)

George Scott, deputy commissioner of Prince George's County, died. (12 SEP 1771)

Last Monday, Daniel of St. Thomas Jenifer and Col. Plater were sworn in as members of His Lordship's Council of State. (26 SEP 1771)

The Proprietor's Agent, John Jordan, died in Bermuda of the flying gout. He had an enterprizing temper "the sallies of which, even when he was on the brink of the grave, often filled his friends with Astonishment." Daniel of St. Thomas Jenifer, Esq., was appointed in his place. (26 SEP 1771)

John Dalton, of Alexandria, lost two black horses. (26 SEP 1771)

George Hunter is laying out a town on Chapel Point, called Edenburg (near Port Tobacco), and near the mouth of Port Tobacco Creek, for 3/4 miles along the creek and 80 perches from the waterside. 100 acres are divided into 196 lots. Lots are for sale by lottery at £10 a ticket. (3 OCT 1771)

John Schneider, a musician of Annapolis, cut his own throat. (31 OCT 1771)

Mary Mason, wife of Thomson Mason of Loudoun County, died. "A mistress whose servants were more afraid of offending her than of receiving correction," etc. She died at *Westwood*, Prince William County, the seat of Rev. Scott, on her return home from a visit to her father on Monday the 21st. Poem. (14 NOV 1771)

Mr. Stephen West, of the Wood Yard, tutor, advertises for a new place. He teaches Latin, Greek, English, and arithmetic. (14 NOV 1771)

A tract on Aquia Creek, 1,200 acres, 6 miles from the warehouse, is to be sold according to the will of Henry Brent, of Maryland. Auction will be on April 22nd. Apply to Mr. John Gibson, merchant, at Aquia. Clare Brent, Executrix. (12 MAR 1772)

On Saturday last, at 12:00, the foundation of the State House was laid. (2 APR 1772)

The Brig *Betty* is now on stocks in Alexandria, and ready for charter May 15th to any part of Great Britain. She will carry 320 hogsheads of tobacco. Inquire of William Wood. (2 APR 1772)

Piscataway. John Baynes offers for sale cloth, coarse and fine hats, clothes, nails, etc. (15 APR 1772)

William Carr, is a merchant in Dumfries. (23 APR 1772)

The horse *Ranger* will cover this season at William Digges, on Patowmack. (30 APR 1772)

A slight earthquake shock was felt in Maryland. (30 APR 1772)

Goods for sale at Robert Adam's store in Alexandria [long list]. The Brig *Swift*, is to be sold at Alexandria, on August 17th. Apply to Carlyle & Dalton, or Robert Adam. (16 JUL 1772)

Counties in southern Maryland want to sell free school lands and combine them to form an Academy. £1200. is already subscribed. Benedict Calvert, William Fitzhugh, Henry Addison and Mr. Boucher are among the signers. (30 JUL 1772)

The theatre in Annapolis is to be remodelled [description given]. (30 JUL 1772)

Mr. McCarty's horse *Achilles* will be in the races at Annapolis. (7 OCT 1772)

It is proposed an Academy be built at Cool Springs. (5 NOV 1772)

Notley Young, living at the mouth of the Eastern Branch, seeks the return of a runaway Mulatto. (26 NOV 1772)

A convict servant named Samuel Gasford, who belonged to Rev. Brooke in Stafford County, has runaway from Mr. Boucher's. (26 NOV 1772)

All those who are indebted to Alexander Burrell at his store at Piscataway, Pig Point, or Elk Ridge Landing, are asked to settle accounts. (26 NOV 1772)

October 18th. John DeButts offers for sale 800 acres in St. Mary's County; 499 near Dumfries; 194 near Great Falls; 92 on Cedar Run; and part of a tract in Fauquier County that was patented to Rev. Lawrence DeButts. (3 DEC 1772)

For sale by John Wynn, near Piscataway, *Wynn's E. & W. Littleworth*, 143 acres; *Littleworth*, 50 acres; *Addition to Littleworth*, 53 acres. These three adjoin and are about 4 miles from Piscataway. (3 DEC 1772)

Nails are for sale. (10 DEC 1772)

A letter from the Rev. Boucher to William Paca and Samuel Chase questions their rights as vestrymen. It begins a lengthy controversy. (31 DEC 1772)

Along the Potomac River: **Extracts from the *Maryland Gazette*,** 1728-1799

By an act of Assembly, 1692, the Church of England was first established in Maryland. County justices are required to lay out the counties into parishes. Freeholders voted for six vestrymen. The majority in Maryland were Catholic until 1689. (28 JAN 1773)

For sale at the plantation of Thomas Contee near Port Tobacco, where Dr. Joseph Aderton now lives, Negroes [detailed description], household furniture, etc. Jane Aderton. (18 FEB 1773)

John Moss, William Hutchinson, churchwardens, are taking bids on the second Monday in March at the land of Joshua Evans in Loudoun County, near the falls of Potowmack, for building a brick church, 53'x42', walls to be raised 28' from the surface. £150 Virginia currency to be paid on the day work is let, £350 in June, and other payments will be discussed. (18 FEB 1773)

Members of the Lunatick Club are meeting at the coffee house in Annapolis on March 8th. (25 FEB 1773)

February 19th, Alexandria. Horse *Bay Bolton*, imported last October, will stand at *[Torthorwald]*, my plantation about three miles from Alexandria. Covering mares. John Carlyle. (25 FEB 1773)

All persons indebted to the estate of William Willett, pewterer, late of Prince George's County, are asked to settle debts. Mary Willett. The pewterers business is still carried on at his house by his wife. (4 MAR 1773)

A grammar school in Bladensburg is run by James Hunt [further details given]. (4 MAR 1773)

Port Tobacco. All persons indebted to John Jamieson & Sons' store in Port Tobacco are asked to settle debts. George Gray. (11 MAR 1773)

A fishery is started at the mouth of Mattawoman Creek by Basil Smith. (11 MAR 1773)

Thomas Hanson Marshall, has at the plantation on Pomonkey Neck, a stray gelding. (11 MAR 1773)

John Addison advertises a sale to be held on April 22nd of 700 to 800 acres, including a dwelling plantation, on which are very good buildings. (25 MAR 1773)

The creditors of Mr. Robert Harmer are requested to meet at the house of Mrs. Halkerston, in Port Tobacco, at August court week. (25 MAR 1773)

David Stone died at his seat in Charles County. (1 APR 1773)

Along the Potomac River: **Extracts from the *Maryland Gazette*, 1728-1799**

The Custom house on South Potowmack has been removed from *Lee Hall* where it was for many years and moved on January 29th to [*Harmony*] *Hall*, the seat of the late Col. James Steptoe, which is on the river and the second house above Sandy Point. Joseph Lane, deputy collector. (22 APR 1773)

Whereas Henrietta, wife of the subscriber, has committed adultery with a Mulatto man and now has a Mulatto child, for which most atrocious crime I have put her away, and do forewarn all persons dealing with her I am determined to pay no debts. Henry Pratt, Talbot County. (22 APR 1773)

On Sunday the 9th, after a short illness, in her 52nd year, Mrs. Elizabeth Hanson, wife of Walter Hanson, Esq., of Charles County, died. (20 MAY 1773)

James Marshall asks all to meet on June 28th who have complaints against him while he did business in Piscataway. (20 MAY 1773)

Representatives appointed include William Lyles, Calvert County, and Thomas Contee, Prince George's County. (27 MAY 1773)

Barnes and Ridgate had a store in Port Tobacco which was operated by Zephaniah Turner. (27 MAY 1773)

For sale, a house in Piscataway, occupied by Mrs. Mary Hawkins. The dwelling-house is commodious for traveller's entertainment, garden and yard paled with locust posts, adjoins the main road. Thomas Dent. (27 MAY 1773)

Representatives appointed include Richard Barnes and Philip Key from St. Mary's County, and William Smallwood from Charles County. (3 JUN 1773)

The Gentlemen's Subscription Purse of £50 at Nottingham on Tuesday last was won by His Excellency's Governor Eden's bay horse *Why Not*; beating Dr. Hamilton's bay *Harmony* and Mr. Baynes' grey horse *Regulus*; both of whom were outdistanced on the first head, by the superiority of *Why Not*, who had run three very hard 4-mile heats at Philadelphia, on that day fortnight, and had since travelled from thence, in very hot weather, which was supposed to be much against him; nevertheless he won very easily and the knowing ones were greatly taken in. (3 JUN 1773)

To be sold at Port Tobacco on June 28th, the sloop *Ranger*, of 3,000 bushels. It lies off Capt. Laidler's. Inquire of J. Rogers, Th. Stone, Phillip Fendall or J. Laidler. (3 JUN 1773)

On the last day of July will be sold the plantation on Hanson's Branch, six miles from Potomack, at Alexandria, on which is a fine apple orchard and tenant buildings, containing 208 acres. There is a fine spring issuing from a rock. Zachariah Scott. (10 JUN 1773)

Along the Potomac River: **Extracts from the *Maryland Gazette*, 1728-1799**

Stolen or seduced from Emmanuel Kent, Queen Anne's County, two Negro girl slaves, formerly the property of Elizabeth Adair of Kent County, who intermarried with John Posey, and were purchased from Posey by Sarah Flower (Kent's wife). (17 JUN 1773)

James Mercer offers for sale tracts in Fairfax County: 1) on Pohick Run, 5 miles from Colchester and the same distance from Pohick warehouse, containing 957 acres; 2) 1,225 acres on Four Mile Run, 4 miles from Alexandria. Col. George Mason, of *Gunston*, has plats and titles. (8 JUL 1773)

William Aikman, bookseller in Annapolis, has opened a circulating library. (19 AUG 1773)

George Washington offers for rent the plantation whereon William Clifton formerly lived, lately possessed by Mr. Samuel Johnston, and at present occupied by his daughters. It contains 200 acres, also one of the largest and best springs this side of the Blue Ridge, within 20 yards of the door. One and a half miles on Potowmack River, has a ferry on the most direct road from Annapolis through Colchester, Dumfries, Fredericksburg to Williamsburg. The dwelling-house has two brick chimneys and 7 rooms, kitchen, smoke house, etc. (9 SEP 1773)

July 15th. George Washington offers for sale 20,000 acres of land on the Ohio, part of 200,000 acres granted by proclamation in 1754; dividing them for tenants. (9 SEP 1773)

James Craik offers for sale 6,000 acres of land in Ohio for the same purpose. (9 SEP 1773)

The Hon. Walter Dulany, Esq., died on Monday last in Annapolis. The Hon. William Fitzhugh has been appointed Commissary General in his place. (23 SEP 1773)

For rent on January 1st, in Leonardtown, a large convenient house in good repair, well suited to public-house keeping; the property of Col. Abraham Barnes. Manager wanted. He has six constant boarders for the year. (23 SEP 1773)

William Buckland seeks return of runaway indentured servant named Thomas Holkins, bricklayer. (23 SEP 1773)

On Monday last, William Fitzhugh, Esq.'s grey filly won the sweepstakes. (30 SEP 1773)

Piscataway, September 23rd. Alexander Hamilton has imported about £400. of goods, including green hams, sheeting, Irish linen, rugs, etc. (7 OCT 1773)

October 10th. Part of *Mattapony* is for lease in St. Mary's County, "a remarkable place for trade, fish and oysters, large sea vessels lay within a pistol shot of my door, etc." William Rogers. (28 OCT 1773)

Daniel of St. Thomas Jenifer wants a manager for 12 hands, who understands farming and making meadow, and who can bring proper recommendation of his knowledge and fidelity. (4 NOV 1773)

Lucas Garvey offers for sale a house and lot in Alexandria. (4 NOV 1773)

The *Royal American Magazine* is to be published. (4 NOV 1773)

Members of the Upper Marlborough assembly are desired to meet on Wednesday the 17th at 11:00 in the morning. (17 NOV 1773)

A sober man, that hath been bred to the principles of gardening, who has been employed in that way by the first families of Great Britain, and is well assured he can give satisfaction to any gentleman that shall choose to employ him, and as he is well versed in mathematics, would be glad to be employed by some gentleman that is going to carry some grand design into execution as he can execute any plan in the art of gardening. Inquire of Mr. Roberson at Governor Eden's, or Mr. Andrew Wales, brewer, in Alexandria. (17 NOV 1773)

Daniel of St. Thomas Jenifer offers for hire three slaves: a carpenter, blacksmith, and collier. (2 DEC 1773)

Joseph Delaforce, cabinet maker, was a convict servant brought to this country upwards of 2 years past, in the ship consigned to Messrs. Davenport, Strather & Lane, merchants in Prince William County, Va. News of his whereabouts is desired. (9 DEC 1773)

November 28th. A boat was taken on October 19th from Thomas Hanson Marshall's landing. It had a 16' keel, frame all mulberry, and white bottom, gunwale painted blue on the outside and red on the inside, as are her seats, stepboard red and white ... keel made of gum ... $6 reward for its return. (9 DEC 1773)

Charles County. Leidler's Ferry on Potowmack; all gentlemen and ladies that pass from [Mr.] Howe's to Leidler's ferry may depend on the best usage and good accommodations. Elizabeth Leidler. (16 DEC 1773)

William Buckland seeks the return of a runaway named Thomas Hall, a carver. (16 DEC 1773)

Mr. John Leidler, on Thursday, was riding an unruly horse, and was unfortunately thrown and killed on the spot. (16 DEC 1773)

Along the Potomac River: **Extracts from the *Maryland Gazette*, 1728-1799**

A blacksmith shop is for rent with dwelling-house. Inquire of Capt. Zachariah Wade, within 2 miles of Piscataway. (30 DEC 1773)

Joseph Horatio Anderson, architect in Annapolis, has an employee Samuel Rusbatch who paints frescoes, etc. (30 DEC 1773)

Piscataway. Charles Lansdale is carrying on the staymaking business here, under direction of Richard Littlemore. N.B., I still continue to ride as a [by-Oist?] from Leonardtown to Annapolis. Orders may be left at way stations. (13 JAN 1774)

Piscataway. To be sold on the 3rd Monday in March at the house of Mr. Carne, in Piscataway, tracts of 1 or 2 miles of town: part of *Hawkins Lot*, 184 acres; *Something*, 49 acres; *Merry Thought*, 40 acres; part of *God's Gift*, 117½ acres; the whole being 390½ acres. Includes orchards of peach and apple. Also, 16 acres in the town of Piscataway, part of *Hazard and Never Fear*. George F. Hawkins. (13 JAN 1774)

Joseph Noble, near Piscataway, will offer for sale on February 17th, part of a tract *Nick'd Him* of *Deer Range and Meadows*, containing 264 acres. Includes a new house, 30'x20', four rooms above and below, two chimneys at each end, etc., and an apple orchard. (27 JAN 1774)

William Hicks, Esq., merchant in Whitehaven [England], is settling north American affairs. He is selling in St. Mary's County lands that were once the metropolis of Maryland, and flourishing city of St. Mary's; adjacent to each other: *St. Mary's Freehold*, 7 acres; *Governor's Field*, 200 acres; *Squire's Purchase*, 37 acres; part of *St. Peter's*, 100 acres; the old chapel land, 27½ acres; all totalling 371½ acres, on which are a good dwelling house, 54'x20', etc. Inquire of William Aisquith, attorney for Hicks. (3 FEB 1774)

A teacher is wanted for the Charles County free school. (17 FEB 1774)

George Washington will offer for sale in Alexandria on March 28th, the Brigantine *Ann & Elizabeth*, four years old, which may be seen at Mr. Adam's wharf. (10 MAR 1774)

The horse *Bay Bolton*, hunter, will stand at *[Torthorwald]*, my plantation in Virginia, about halfway between Alexandria and Georgetown, at 1 guinea the leap, and 5 shillings to the groom. "Most compleated horse that has been imported for this county ... last season we had 20 odd mares at a time, some stayed near a month, some were lost or hurt, and all returned in better order than when they came." John Carlyle. (17 MAR 1774)

Port Tobacco. David Walker is leaving the province, and seeks to settle accounts due Alexander Cunningham & Co., of Glasgow. Mr. John Craig is now carrying on. (24 MAR 1774)

Along the Potomac River: **Extracts from the *Maryland Gazette*, 1728-1799**

On Friday, April 22nd, at the new church near Pohick, Truro Parish, will be let by the vestry the building of a brick vestry house, 24'x18', and the inclosing of the said churchyard, 158' square, with posts and rails, the posts to be of sawed cedar and the rail of yellow pine, clean of sap, with three handsome palisaded gates, the whole to be done in the neatest and most substantial manner. George Mason and Thomazin Ellzey, churchwardens. (24 MAR 1774)

William Buckland seeks the return of three runaways: Richard Sadler, plasterer; John Wakefield, plasterer; and Croasdale Sprotson, joiner. (7 APR 1774)

Constitution Hill, Piscataway. The horse *Ranger* is standing this season at $2 the leap, one guinea to the season. Inquire of Edward Edelin, Jr. (14 APR 1774)

Prince George's County. John Bowie offers for sale a tract of land called *Riley's Discovery*, 210 acres. (14 APR 1774)

An act is passed for the support of an organist in King and Queen parish, St. Mary's County; and an act to unite free schools in St. Mary's, Charles, and Prince George's counties. (21 APR 1774)

Charles Calvert, the eldest son of the Hon. Benedict Calvert, died at *Eton*, on January 30th. (28 APR 1774)

Joseph Watson, Alexandria, had a horse stolen out of his stable. (5 MAY 1774)

February 10th. Notice is hereby given, if Capt. John Posey is living who married Miss Elizabeth Adair in 1769, and will apply to me the subscriber living in Charleston, S.C., he will hear of something greatly to his advantage. If Capt. Posey should be dead, and has any children living, it would be kind of their friends to apply as soon as they can, to take care of the estate left Capt. Posey and children. Inquire of Jonathan Waddle. (12 MAY 1774)

April 25th, Prince George's County. To be let to the highest bidder, the building of an assembly room of wood near the free school, 50'x24', 10' pitched and arched. Give proposals at Queen Anne on May 26th. (12 MAY 1774)

George Washington announces that in March he sent out carpenters to build houses on his Ohio lands, and seeks settlers there. (19 MAY 1774)

To be let to the lowest bidder, at the house of Robert Bland in Loudoun County, Virginia, on the 3rd Thursday in June, the building of a brick church for Cameron parish in said county, 53'x42', 28' pitch with galleries, plan will be shown. George Summers, Samuel Love, churchwardens. (26 MAY 1774)

Along the Potomac River: **Extracts from the *Maryland Gazette*, 1728-1799**

On Wednesday the 11th inst., was run for at *Nottingham*, in Prince George's County, a purse of £50, weight for age, which was won by His Excellency Gov. Eden's bay horse *Why Not*, aged, at four heats, beating Dr. Hamilton's *Primrose*, Col. Barnet's young *Tanner*, and two others. Mr. Lyle's filly ran the next day. (26 MAY 1774)

On Tuesday the 17th, a purse of £50, weight for age and blood, was run for at Baltimore-town; and won by His Excellency Gov. Eden's bay horse *Why Not*, aged, at two heats, beating Col. Nicholson's horse, and Mr. Gough's horse [*Ganky*]. *Why Not* and *Slim* have gone to Philadelphia. (26 MAY 1774)

Norfolk. Vessels are needed to transport 6,000 tons of stone from Mr. Brook's quarry on the Rappahannock, to Cape Henry for the lighthouse. (9 JUN 1774)

On June 6th a meeting was held at Dumfries, wherein it was resolved that no person ought to be taxed but by his own consent; until said acts are repealed all importation and export ought to be stopped [5 resolves]. Evan Williams, clerk. (16 JUN 1774)

Charles County. At a meeting of June 14th at the courthouse at Port Tobacco, Walter Hanson was chosen as chairman [9 resolves]; James Craik, Walter Hanson, William Smallwood, Thomas Stone, George Dent, Gustavus R. Brown, Thomas Hanson Marshall, and Daniel Jenifer, the committee of correspondence. (16 JUN 1774)

John Clifford seeks the return of a runaway servant Thomas [Breaton?], at Alexandria Ferry on the Maryland side. He took a forged pass with him which I expect has Mr. John Bayne's and Capt. Alexander Hayes' names signed in it, wrote by himself. (16 JUN 1774)

May 26th. William Lyles seeks return of a runaway servant named Thomas Columbine. Lyles is living near Piscataway, Potomac River. Runaway took a brown coat, old red cloth jacket, pale blue jacket, striped blue and white damask jacket with lapels, etc., "he has a watch in his pocket, which I believe does not go." (16 JUN 1774)

Col. Abraham Barnes is on the committee of correspondence in St. Mary's County. (30 JUN 1774)

Upper Marlborough. To be sold on the premises at the fork of the road, about three miles below Piscataway, between there and Port Tobacco: 46 acres in three parcels, called *Barker's Lot, Barker's Hazard,* and *Girls Delight*. On the land is an apple orchard and bricked well; new house now rented to Zachariah Wade as a tavern, with 7 convenient rooms, blacksmith shop and smith's house. In trust for William Barker's creditors. Ralph Forster, Sheriff. (30 JUN 1774)

For sale, a tract in Prince William County, Va., of 500 acres of high land, 90 acres of marsh on Quantico Creek, between the mouth of said creek where 9 or 10 ships load yearly, and the town of Dumfries, where are inspected near 2,000 hogsheads of tobacco yearly, and the court of Prince William County is held monthly, about 3 miles from each. Apply to Andrew Leatch who lives in Dumfries, and the subscriber who will be at the tavern near the bridge in the aforesaid town on the 1st Monday in August. John Boone Luckett. (30 JUN 1774)

Thomas Montgomerie seeks the return of runaways George and John Allen, from his plantation near Dumfries. (30 JUN 1774)

Trustees who have been appointed by the Assembly to sell free school land in Prince George's County, for the purpose of erecting a school at Cool Springs, St. Mary's County, called *Charlotte Hall*, give notice that they will meet at the free school on September 1st to survey the land; 215 acres of level land. (14 JUL 1774)

To be sold at *Belvoir*, the seat of the Hon. George William Fairfax, Esq., in Fairfax County, on Monday, August 15th (pursuant to his directions), all his household and kitchen furniture of any kind, consisting of beds and their furniture, tables, chairs and every other necessary article, mostly new and very elegant. Francis Willis, Jr., Berkeley County. *Belvoir* is for rent. (14 JUL 1774)

George Washington and John Tayloe offer for sale on behalf of Col. George Mercer, now in London, 3,500 acres in Loudoun County, 6,500 acres on Shenandoah River opposite Snicker's ordinary. The first tract is near West's ordinary. (21 JUL 1774)

For sale, in Alexandria, a few modern law books, in good order. William Ramsay. (11 AUG 1774)

Andrew Leitch, in Dumfries, seeks return of a runaway deaf and dumb servant named Thomas Jones. (11 AUG 1774)

Piscataway. John Baynes offers for sale goods from the snow *Norfolk*. The snow can now be chartered. (11 AUG 1774)

For sale, two lots in the town of Philee at the falls of Potowmack, with storehouse, 36'x25', has store-room, two accounting rooms with fireplaces, cellar, stable. Also goods, cattle, furniture. Thompson & Magruder. (18 AUG 1774)

Fredericksburg. At the last meeting of the Jockey Club, races at this place in October next were fixed. George Weedon, President. (18 AUG 1774)

Marking instruments, by which initials, names at length, or a verse, are impressed on silk, muslin, paper, etc., are for sale by William Aikman, stationer. (25 AUG 1774)

Strayed or stolen from Mr. Thomas Addison's ferry, opposite Alexandria, a roan mare. Deliver to William Herbert, merchant at Alexandria. Grafton Dulany. (25 AUG 1774)

Along the Potomac River: **Extracts from the *Maryland Gazette*, 1728-1799**

The Charles County free school lands are to be sold on October 1st. 100 acres. The situation commands a find prospect of the Patowmack River, where the house stands is a high hill, within 1 mile of Port Tobacco. 70 acres are low ground, 44 of which are in woods. (1 SEP 1774)

Bids are being taken for the building of an overfloat watermill at Cool Springs, for the trustees of *Charlotte Hall*. (1 SEP 1774)

Queen Anne's Parish, Prince George's County, is petitioning the Assembly to levy a tax for finishing and completing the inside of the church and the building of a new vestry house. Samuel Tyler, registrar. (8 SEP 1774)

Piscataway. To be let in this neighborhood, a small piece of land with dwelling house, smith's shop and coal wood. Also wanted in the neighborhood is a schoolmaster. Inquire of Josias Beall. (8 SEP 1774)

Falls of Patowmack. John Ballendine just arrived from Great Britain with a number of engineers to remove obstructions to navigation on the Patowmack and at and below the lower falls. He wants a meeting of subscribers to be held in Georgetown on September 22nd where a plan and estimate are to be shown. (8 SEP 1774)

James Hendricks, of Alexandria, seeks the return of a runaway named Daniel Kennedy, 16 years old. (15 SEP 1774)

On Friday last, died at his seat on Patowmack, greatly lamented, Thomas Addison, Esq. He left a widow and small children. (29 SEP 1774)

On September 26th, Mrs. Mary Swift, widow, died at her seat near Port Tobacco, age about 90 ... attributed her good health to Peruvian Bark, which she at first took on the advice of Dr. Gustavus Brown, and continued to take every morning a small dose for the last 40 years. (6 OCT 1774)

Mr. ELIE VALLETTE, pay me for painting your family picture. Charles Peale. (6 OCT 1774)

To be sold on October 17th, part of the tract called *Northampton*, in Prince George's County, 226 acres on the main road from Upper Marlborough to Bladensburg. Includes a dwelling house, tobacco house and apple orchard. Inquire of William Pile living on the premises. (6 OCT 1774)

Bids for an alms and workhouse are to be let at Leonardtown. Inquire of George Plater or Abraham Barnes, etc. (13 OCT 1774)

William Lyles, Jr., offers a reward of £5 for the return of a horse stolen out of Mr. Edward Odell's meadow near Piscataway. (13 OCT 1774)

Along the Potomac River: **Extracts from the *Maryland Gazette*, 1728-1799**

The brig *Peggy Stewart* is arrived in Annapolis with tea. The owner Antony Stewart went aboard and set fire to his ship voluntarily. (20 OCT 1774)

Alexander Hamilton, merchant in Piscataway, has seized a Negro wench and boy in possession of William McPherson. He warns others to not purchase. (20 OCT 1774)

Mrs. Rachel Addison, wife of Rev. Mr. Henry Addison, died Wednesday the 19th. She was the second daughter of the late Hon. Daniel Dulany, Esq. — the worthy daughter of a worthy father. (27 OCT 1774)

John Ballendine's plan is approved. Trustees are as follows: George Washington, George Mason, Thomson Mason, Bryan Fairfax, Daniel McCarty, John Carlyle, John Dalton, William Ramsay, Robert Adam, William Ellzey, etc. He is now at work on the locks at the lower falls on the Maryland side of the river. (3 NOV 1774)

The Jockey Club has canceled races in accordance with the resolves passed by the congress in Philadelphia. (3 NOV 1774)

Joseph Leitch, in Dumfries, seeks the return of a runaway named Joseph Fisher, a tailor, in a small boat. He went with Patrick Fisher, William Booth. (10 NOV 1774)

A reward of £15 is offered for the return of a runaway from Alexander Henderson, of Colchester, on October 8. He was a serving man named Pooling Horne, calls himself John Horne. He came into Patowmack on the ship Tayloe last September. Richard Henderson. (17 NOV 1774)

Andrew Leitch, in Dumfries, is disposing of an engraver. (24 NOV 1774)

Belvoir is offered for rent. (1 DEC 1774, 2 FEB 1775)

The storehouse belonging to Col. Fitzhugh caught fire, almost burning his dwelling which was a few feet from the store. (1 DEC 1774)

John Ballendine is hiring 50 slaves to start work on cutting a canal around Great Falls. (12 JAN 1775)

The deputies for Charles County are listed for the next provincial convention. (19 JAN 1775)

John Baynes, in Piscataway, is selling goods imported in the ship *Ocean*, Capt. Dixon, from Whitehaven. (26 JAN 1775)

John Carlyle advertises that the horse *Bay Bolton*, is at stud. Colts have been sold at one month old for $100; if the weather is good, he will send it to Prince George's County, March Court. Selling the horse after this season. (2 FEB 1775)

Along the Potomac River: **Extracts from the *Maryland Gazette,* 1728-1799**

Neabsco Furnace. Thomas Lawson has for sale barrels of flour. (16 FEB 1775)

William Lyles, Jr., has the noted horse *Regulus* standing this season at his plantation near Piscataway. For rent, 3 or 4 fishing landings on the Patowmack, opposite Alexandria, now in possession of Mrs. Verlinda Fraser. Apply to Allen Bowie. (9 MAR 1775)

William Allison, jailer of Fairfax County, has Irishman John Connell who is suspected of being a runaway. (6 APR 1775)

George Washington seeks the return of a runaways named Thomas Speers, a joiner, and William Webster. (27 APR 1775)

Mr. Patrick Graham, of Port Tobacco, has an anchor found near Poplar Island. (27 APR 1775)

The horse *Othello* will cover at *Belmont*, Fairfax County, near Colchester, at 4 pistoles and a dollar to the groom. Inquire of John Casturn, groom. (4 MAY 1775)

April 18th, Alexandria. To be let on June 1st, the building of a brick church in Alexandria, of the following dimensions, 60'x50', with 26' pitch. Inquire of John Carlyle or William Ramsay. (11 MAY 1775)

April 1st, Alexandria. William Allison, jailer, has two Scots, Dan Munrow and John, suspected of being runaways. (25 MAY 1775)

For rent, houses and ferry opposite Alexandria. Apply to Rev. Jonathan Butcher or Mr. John Addison, living near the premises. This being a place much frequented and likely to become daily more so with the rising importance of Alexandria, renders it fit for a tavern. (1 JUN 1775)

To be sold on July 3rd, the dwelling house of the late William Buckland, on Bloomsbury Square in Annapolis. There are two lots belonging to the said house, and are leased for 99 years, 2 years of which have expired. Inquire of Denton Jacques. At the same time, the remaining part of the household furniture will be sold. (22 JUN 1775)

A tombstone which was sent around from Patowmack to Benedict by John Baynes was imported contrary to the continental association in the ship *Mary & Anne*, Capt. Ball. It is resolved that it be broken into pieces. (13 JUL 1775)

A horse has strayed from *Poplar Hill*, the seat of Robert Darnall, Esq., in Prince George's County. (21 SEP 1775)

The Rev. Boucher, having sailed last Sunday in the *Choptank* frigate for England, with the hope of returning next summer, desired that Overton Carr, who has power of attorney to give notice that if in his hurry he had left any accounts unsettled, all should apply to Carr. (21 SEP 1775)

The Lower Marlborough Academy chooses trustees. (9 NOV 1775)

Elizabeth Courts has for sale slaves and furniture at her present dwelling plantation in Durham Parish. (23 NOV 1775)

Charles County. Francis Meek has sold his land at Maryland Point to Daniel Jenifer, Esq. (28 DEC 1775)

The noted half-blooded horse, *Frederick Jones*, a full 15½ hands high, a fine dapple grey, 8 years old, strong active and boney, stands at *Notley Hall*, in Prince George's County, and will cover at 30 shillings the season. Inquire of Henry Rozer. (25 APR 1776)

The horse *Bay Bolton* is at stud at *Constitution Hill*, near Piscataway. "I think it needless to describe him as he is generally known, he stood last season at Col. John Carlyle's plantation in Virginia." Edward Edelen. (2 MAY 1776)

Mrs. Young, being so unfortunate at Hooe's Ferry, to lose her boats, I will send over my boats for any passengers crossing to Virginia, who will hoist the flat or make a smoak at the usual place. Gerard Hooe. (22 AUG 1776)

John Hesselius, near Annapolis, seeks the return of a runaway English gardener named Samuel Griffith. (29 AUG 1776)

Rebecca Addison, opposite Alexandria, wants a teacher of reading, writing and arithmetic. (5 SEP 1776)

Capt. Robert Conway, of the *Protector* rowgalley, went down to Yeocomico to recruit men about five weeks ago before August 10th. Lieut. John Thomas, of this galley, gave deposition: "On Tuesday, July 23rd, about 9 a.m., near Sandy Point, seven of us with 2 boats landed on the Maryland shore within half a mile of the enemies' fleet, consisting of 4 ships, 2 tenders, and 1 rowgalley. Expecting as soon as we landed to have been guarded by a party of Maryland militia, having no arms ourselves, expecting to pass the fleet the following night we conveyed our luggage to an adjacent house where on inquiry we were informed that the troops were opposite the Roebuck .. from whence we observed the fleet manning their boats, with the intent, (we thought) to land on the Maryland shore ... when a gentleman they called Col. Harrison said, 'Let us march down,' to which several militia replied 'I can't bear to shoot a man'; others that their guns were out of order." (Militia gave their guns to Virginians who marched to the shore under Col. Harrison). "After we came down to the shore the enemy gave three loud huzzas, and rowed over to the Virginia side with 2 tenders, 1 gondola, and 10 rowboats, from which they landed and burnt Mr. Brent's house, from whence they returned in

Along the Potomac River: **Extracts from the *Maryland Gazette*,** 1728-1799

about an hour to their vessels." (400 militia had collected on the Maryland side but would not help Conway save his boats by dragging them up into the marsh. Sentries ran.) "Col. Harrison called 'Come back, boys.' 'No,' says I,' they will not come back until they get to Port Tobacco,' at which he laughed. They would peep at the enemy when they rowed close to our boat, but never offered to fire. (The men and the colonel retreated). When the enemy saw them (from the Roebuck's masthead) running off they hollowed at them and called them sundry names; then made signs for the rowgalley to pull ashore, which they did, and launched our boat off, then gave three huzzas and fired shots both small and great, at the house where our baggage was stored, then returned to their ships with their booty without one shot having been fired at them." Sworn to before William Ramsay, J.P., Alexandria.

When Capt. Conway got back to Alexandria, advertisements had been posted at several public places in that town saying that this was all a lie, and signed S. Hanson. Depositions were also taken of Messrs. Finlay, Hunter and Lawson of Alexandria, who had been sightseeing in the vicinity and retreated behind a hedge when the action started. Also that of Rev. Fendall and Mr. Warren Dent. (7 NOV 1776)

Alexandria. Jennifer & Hooe offers for sale on February 13th the schooner *Anne Maria* and cargo. (13 FEB 1777)

Daniel of Saint Thomas Jenifer is chosen President of the Maryland senate. (13 FEB 1777)

For sale, a lot in Port Tobacco, with 40'x20' house, 5 rooms below and 6 above, cellar of 20'x16', kitchen of 20'x16' with brick chimney, meat house, stable, 2 other houses on the lot, suitable for a tailor or tradesman, a well accustomed public house, or a convenient place for a store. Said lot fronts the courthouse. In the lot stands a large elm tree, very valuable for shade in the summer. For sale on March 1st, at the house of Rachael Furry. Joseph Simms. (20 FEB 1777)

Thomas Johnson, Jr., Esq., is elected governor. Thomas Stone and William Paca are elected to the Continental Congress. (20 FEB 1777)

March 1st. On Saturday last, the lady of his excellency General Washington arrived in town, and Monday morning set out for Baltimore on her way northward. (13 MAR 1777)

Piscataway. Deserted on the 15th inst., from Capt. Deen's company, William Gilpin, 5'8", 21 years old, "he is a talkative fellow and has a long drone to the word yes, which he often makes use of in his discourse." (3 APR 1777)

All persons indebted to Christie & Stone for dealings with the subscriber at Port Tobacco, are asked to settle accounts. J.H. Stone, Col. 1st Md. Reg. (10 APR 1777)

The horse *Othello* is at stud at *Constitution Hill*, near Piscataway. Last season it was at *Belmont* in Virginia, and is the property of Benjamin Dulany, Esq. (10 APR 1777)

Along the Potomac River: **Extracts from the *Maryland Gazette,* 1728-1799**

All persons having books of Rev. Boucher, are asked to return them to Overton Carr, who will put up his library for sale. (17 APR 1777)

The death of John Dalton has dissolved the partnership of Carlyle & Dalton of Alexandria. There will be sold on Monday, May 13th, on Fairfax Court Day, 8 Negro men, 6 of whom are good smiths who do all sorts of ship and planters' work, and shoe horses; one understands a good deal of gun work and making nails, another is a waterman and pilot in the river and bay. Also for sale, smiths tools, steel, iron, and 2 tobacco flats. (24 APR 1777)

King George County, Va. For sale on June 2nd, 500 acres where Mr. Richard Fowke formerly lived, on Patowmack River, near *Pasbetansay*. Includes a dwelling house with 2 brick chimneys. Inquire of Thomas Bunbury, Jr. (8 MAY 1777)

Benedict Calvert, living at *Mt. Airy*, seeks the return of a runaway tailor named Hugh Morris. (15 MAY 1777)

The schooner, *Saltana and George*, is to be sold on the 23rd in Alexandria by Jenifer & Hooe. (15 MAY 1777)

Rev. Boucher's library is for sale. Also beds, tables, chairs, etc. (5 JUN 1777)

Williamsburg, Wednesday May 30th. Thomas Davis, late adjutant, and six other torries and traitors, mounted in a wagon, under a proper guard, making a very decent appearance, passed down the street on their way to the public gaol, from Alexandria, where they are to remain for trial. (12 JUN 1777)

Jenifer & Hooe advertise for sale goods imported in the ship *Molly*, Capt. Robert Conway, from Martinico; they have blankets, molasses, waistcoat patterns, etc. (12 JUN 1777)

Port Tobacco. The partnership of Dr. James Craik & Walter Hanson having expired on June 10th, by reason of Dr. Craik having accepted a military appointment, seek to settle accounts, for practice of physic and surgery. Many accounts have been outstanding since the partnership began. (26 JUN 1777)

The noted and well frequented tavern in Port Tobacco where Mrs. Halkerston now dwells is to be sold. Inquire of Daniel Jenifer. (26 JUN 1777)

Jenifer & Hooe, Alexandria, offer for sale the schooner *Lucy* and its cargo. Also a pilot boat. (26 JUN 1777)

Prince George's County. Whereas a report prevails somewhat to the prejudice of the character of Mrs. Margaret Hutton, which report says on the 9th of April 1776, at her own table, Mrs. H. called on a lady for a toast, and on "General Washington" being given

Along the Potomac River: Extracts from the *Maryland Gazette*, 1728-1799

preemptorily refused to drink it. This I swear to be a malicious lie ... according to Mrs. Hutton this is the true account: Mrs. Hutton was visited that day by several ladies, one a wife of a general, preference was given that lady; she gave "General Washington," which was by all the company, without exception, drunk. Mrs. Hutton was then called on, her reply was "We will leave politics and public toasts to the gentlemen, and wish for "Peace and Quietness," for I hate spinning. Hezekiah Magruder. (3 JUL 1777)

Rev. Boucher's library is to be sold on July 22nd at the lodge near the ferry house, opposite Alexandria. (3 JUL 1777)

Alexander Hamilton offers for sale his lot in Piscataway, including a dwelling house, 2 storeys high, 30'x18', 2 rooms below and 2 above, a stone cellar, stable of 30'x14', 1½ storeys high, and an old storehouse, newly covered three years ago. 1 acre. (10 JUL 1777)

Charles County. Mrs. Sarah Dent, wife of John Dent, Miss Anne Wilkinson, Miss Elizabeth Tyler, made oath on the holy evangelists of the Almighty God that on the 9th of April 1776, they in the company with Mrs. Mary Magruder, Miss Polly Cox and Miss Nancy Maxwell, dined with Mrs. Hutton ... after dinner Mrs. H. gave for her toast "Peace and Plenty," that after sitting some time, Mrs. Hutton said "Ladies, Let us finish the toast," on which Mrs. Sarah Dent said she hoped it would not be disagreeable to give a little addition to it, and drank "General Washington" as her toast, which Mrs. Hutton instead of pledging drank, "a safe return to General Dent from the mouth of the Patowmack." (24 JUL 1777)

Mr. Magruder has not signed the articles of association or enrolled in the militia. Is he a Tory? "Such as being I cannot in good conscience believe Mr. Magruder naturally to be, for these reasons: he is a native of America, a branch of a family that has not been backward in our present conflict against Great Britain, in possession of a tolerable share of property in this state, and if the said Margaret Hutton should not marry again (which I believe will not happen), he in all probability enjoys all she possesses." John Dent. (24 JUL 1777)

Prince George's County. Notice is hereby given to all gentlemen traveling that I have undertaken to keep a ferry about a mile above Clifford's Ferry on Patowmack, opposite Alexandria. Allen Hodskin. (7 AUG 1777)

William Hanson offers for sale his dwelling plantation, near Port Tobacco. The house has 7 rooms and 2 passages on the lower floor, 5 rooms and a passage above, kitchen with brick floor, brick milkhouse, etc. [further description is given of outbuildings]. The situation is high, dry, and healthy; the prospect delightful, having a fine view of Patowmack River, Virginia, Port Tobacco Creek and the neighborhood all around you; very close to two places of public worship, a protestant church and a Roman Catholic chapel, which last is an elegant building, full in view and adds to the other beauties of the place; two grist mills within a mile and a half, Port Tobacco warehouse almost at the

Along the Potomac River: **Extracts from the *Maryland Gazette*, 1728-1799**

door, plenty of fish in their season and frequently opportunities in the winter for getting oysters ... in short, this seat has every advantage to make life delightful and happy. (14 AUG 1777)

Williamsburg, August 3rd. Last Tuesday, Mrs. Washington arrived in this city, amidst ringing of bells, several discharges of artillery ... and the cordial good wishes of all the inhabitants, who have the greatest regard for her ladyship's own personal merit. (21 AUG 1777)

Annapolis, August 21st. Between two and 300 sail of British ships of war, transports, etc., passed the mouth of the harbour about 9 o'clock. They are still sailing up the bay. (Howe is going to Philadelphia). (21 AUG 1777)

Calvert County, Lions Creek. To be run for, near my house on Friday and Saturday, October 3rd and 4th, any quantity of good stall fed beef, not exceeding 1,000 weight. If the gentlemen racers should not think it proper to make up for any beef, there will be a purse of £10 free for any horse, mare or gelding, carrying weight for size, 120 to be the standard, and to raise and fall according to the rules of racing. Horse, to be entered the same day of the races, with the subscriber at one o'clock. Same races to be run every week until December 19th. Inquire of Benjamin Lane, of Richard. N.B. Good entertainment for many, and horse at my house, where they may always find good swamp oysters. (9 OCT 1777)

Port Tobacco. Agreeable to the will of Mrs. Anne Halkerston, will be sold on November 12th, a variety of furniture, 2 slaves. John Halkerston. (6 NOV 1777)

Piscataway. For sale at the house of Mr. Richard Carne, of this place, agreeable to the will of George Hardy, two tracts of 446 acres on Mamazink on the road to Port Tobacco, about 4 miles from Piscataway. Thomas Dent, Thomas Hardy. (11 DEC 1777)

Last Issue. The printer has run out of paper. The next issue will be April 30th, 1779. (25 DEC 1777)

Kent Fort Manor is for sale by William Brent. It is bounded by east and west bays. On the lower end of the island. Doesn't know the exact amount of acreage. Apply to the subscriber near Dumfries. (7 MAY 1779)

Runaway from St. Mary's County, the Negro Monica. Had with her a jacket and petticoat made of striped country cloth, of cotton and wool, the stripes of yellow, blue and black, the stripes crossways the cloth; took a woman's black furred hat and a silk bonnet. Abraham Clarke. (10 SEP 1779)

Lost by the subscriber, the ancient proceedings of the Tuesday Club, bound in parchment, several of the leaves are loose. Frederick Green, printer of the *Gazette*. (10 SEP 1779)

Along the Potomac River: **Extracts from the *Maryland Gazette,*** 1728-1799

The Port Tobacco races are to be run on October 12th. Enter horses with Thomas Reeder in Port Tobacco. (1 OCT 1779)

Nanjemoy. To be sold on October 20th, *Woodberry's Harbour*, half of the tract, on the banks of the Patowmack, at that once famous seaport called Nanjemoy. Contains 175 acres, having a large peach orchard, 2 houses, 2 kitchens, 2 meat houses, stable, chair house, etc. Both dwellings have glass windows and one has brick chimney. Also, horses, 2 riding chairs, furniture, sheep. Inquire of Burditt Hamilton. (8 OCT 1779)

Dr. Benjamin Fendall, dentist, has left this city for his seat in Charles County. (14 JAN 1780)

Our bay and rivers continue to shut up ... several persons have gone from Kent Island on the ice, which has not been known before even by our oldest inhabitant, nor had the like ever happened, we believe, in the memory of man. (11 FEB 1780)

A fire has burned the printing office. (18 FEB 1780)

The horse *Ovid*, raised by William Fitzhugh, Esq., of *Marmion*, of whom he had lately purchased, stands at stud this season at my plantation near Piccawaxon Church. William Courts. (7 APR 1780)

J.P. Custis has horse *Leonides* at stud at *Abingdon*, near Alexandria. (5 MAY 1780)

The coffee house in Annapolis is for rent. It contains 24 rooms plus garrets. (12 MAY 1780)

For sale, a fire engine ... also useful for watering gardens. John Shaw. (19 MAY 1780)

September 29th. The Hon. William Smallwood, Esq., is promoted to major general. (6 OCT 1780)

Small armed enemy vessels have been on the Patuxent. Col. William Fitzhugh's house, *Rousby Hall*, near its mouth, was burned. (24 NOV 1780)

Found: A stray bull on the plantation of John Bruce, near Piscataway church. (15 DEC 1780)

On the death of Rev. Arthur Hambleton, Port Tobacco parish is vacant. (22 FEB 1781)

Warehouses for the reception of tobacco, on St. Mary's river, were set afire by a party of British ships in the river on the 7th. 200 hogsheads of tobacco were destroyed. (22 MAR 1781)

Along the Potomac River: **Extracts from the *Maryland Gazette*,** 1728-1799

W. Lyles has an Arabian horse covering at his plantation near Piscataway, Patowmack, Prince George's County. (29 MAR 1781)

There is a stray black bull at the plantation of James Craik. (29 APR 1781)

By resignation of Rev. Joseph Messenger, the parish of Port Tobacco is again vacant. (21 JUN 1781)

For sale at Port Tobacco, houses and lots, late the property of John Glassford & Co., formerly occupied by Robert Mundell; also those at Benedict, occupied by Robert Young. Office of Preservation and sale of forfeited estates. (12 JUL 1781)

Three persons in the characters of peasants, on Tuesday evening the 14th, stopped the northern post on his way down, and robbed him of his mail. (9 AUG 1781)

The property of Rev. Henry Addison, in Frederick County, is confiscated and for sale. (27 SEP 1781)

William Lyles, in Alexandria, offers for sale on December 19th, at his plantation near Piscataway, 25 slaves. These Negroes are sold for no fault. It is necessary to observe that they are equal to any Negro in the state, many of which are likely young breeding women. Also for sale, sheep, horses and cattle. For lease, two valuable plantations on Patowmack River, on one which is a commodious distillery with several large stills and a large iron boiler. (22 NOV 1781)

November 22nd. General Washington arrived in the city yesterday afternoon on his way north ... on Friday last, our illustrious and beloved commander in chief left this city ... A few Torries, to expiate their crimes, feebly joined in applause. (29 NOV 1781)

> You would have thought the very windows spoke
> So many greedy looks of young and old
> Through casements darted their desiring eyes
> Upon his visage; and that all the walls
> With painted imagery, had said at once,
> God save thee, Washington.

The estate of Dr. Joseph Adderton, of Piscataway, to be sold on December 18th, according to his will. (6 DEC 1781)

Congress is to erect a marble column at Yorktown; a horse and sword to be given to Col. Tilghman; and Rochambeau to be given 2 ordnance field pieces. Two stands of the colors taken of the British Army are to be given Washington, a sword to be given Col. Humphrey, his aid-de-camp, to whose care the standards were consigned. (15 DEC 1781)

Along the Potomac River: **Extracts from the *Maryland Gazette*, 1728-1799**

John Addison will offer for sale on January 29th, 24 Negroes, stock, 9 years of a lease of 600 acres in Maryland, within 3 miles of Alexandria. Also, plantation utensils at his plantation near Broad Creek, Prince George's County. Overton Carr, trustee, offers for sale the horse *Roebuck*, got by Benjamin Dulany, Esq.'s horse *Othello*, who was bred by William Fitzhugh of *Chatham*. (27 DEC 1781)

Stafford County, December 11th. William Brent offers for sale the horse *Tamerland*, brother to his mare *Stella*. (17 JAN 1782)

S. Hanson, of Samuel, offers for sale in Charles County, lands, including his dwelling plantation of 329 acres, including a tolerable dwelling house. Also, the noted horse *Curious Dentalus* and other stock. (17 JAN 1782)

Port Tobacco, February 20th. Land for sale, part of *Poynton Manor*, 300 acres on Nanjemoy Creek. Robert Doyne. (24 JAN 1782)

Prince William County. John Hammitt seeks return of runaway Bob, who "has a large dent in one of his cheeks and is remarkably fond of playing on the fiddle." (7 MAR 1782)

The real and personal estate of Rev. Boucher will be sold as confiscated property. (28 MAR 1782)

The horse *Traveller* stands to cover mares at my estate on Patowmack. The horse is the property of Col. Edward Lloyd. Henry Rozer. Also, the horse *Cyprus* is standing at William Court's plantation near Piscataway. (4 APR 1782)

An Arabian horse stands at Edward Edelen's plantation near Piscataway, "in high perfection." Four other horses are also announced in this issue. (18 APR 1782)

The horse *Comet* is covering at *Rural Hall*, within 3 miles of the Wood Yard, Prince George's County. John Brown. (2 MAY 1782)

To be sold, a 460-acre plantation in Prince George's County, near the Brick Church, part of it formerly the free school, 4 miles from Upper Marlboro, part on Collington Branch. Singleton Wootton. (2 MAY 1782)

The horse *Cub* is at stud, a "thoroughbred from the best stock in England," a fine bay now in his prime, at my house in Westmoreland County, Va., 20 miles below Hooe's Ferry and nearly opposite Lieweiler's Warehouse in St. Mary's County. Daniel McCarty. (9 MAY 1782)

John Read Magruder has various items for sale within 1 mile of Upper Marlboro [further description given]. (16 MAY 1782)

Along the Potomac River: **Extracts from the *Maryland Gazette*, 1728-1799**

Col. Otho H. Williams is made Brigadier General by Congress. (30 MAY 1782)

On Saturday evening last, about 7 o'clock when the post rider was passing Gravelly Hill, in the forest between Onion Iron Works and Harford town, upon his way to Philadelphia, in company with Mr. William Matthews and a young lady from Baltimore, they were suddenly rushed upon and made prisoners by six armed desperadoes, who instantly seized the mail, which they sent off by one of the gang on horseback toward the water side, which was contiguous, detaining the captives in an adjacent thicket, about three quarters of an hour until he returned, when they were liberated without further molestation. (20 JUN 1782)

On Monday, July 19th, that valuable and well-known farm at the mouth of the Eastern Branch of the Patowmack River called *Gisborough*, late in the possession of Mr. John Hawkins, deceased, together with slaves, stock, household furniture, will be sold. Immediate possession will be given except for the dwelling house and kitchen. William Bayly, administrator. (11 JUL 1782)

On Friday, the 5th inst., at one in the morning, the Brigantine *Ranger*, Capt. Thomas Simmons, mounting 7 carriage guns and 20 men (which sailed from Alexandria on the 2nd), was attacked off St. Mary's near the mouth of the Patowmack, by the noted Anderson and Barrett, commanders of two refugee barges, with 30 men each, and after an obstinate engagement for 3 glasses, the latter were obliged to steer off with the loss of 15 men killed and 34 wounded; the barges rowed off to St. George's Island with their mangled crew, where they have buried two and left two others mortally wounded. Capt. Simmons is wounded in the leg, and his 2nd Lieut. in both arms; 1 private is wounded and one killed. Nothing could exceed the bravery of the captain and crew, having 3 men to 1 opposing, and the night being dark, the barges could not be discovered until they were nearly alongside, which gave them but a moments warning. The brig returned to Alexandria on the 8th inst., having no surgeon on board. (18 JUL 1782)

Samuel Hanson, of Samuel, offers for sale his dwelling plantation of 829 acres, 6 miles below Piscataway on the main road leading from there to Port Tobacco. (25 JUL 1782)

Port Tobacco. To be sold on Saturday, September 22nd, 175 acres, part of a tract called *Cain's Purchase*, near the mouth of Port Tobacco Creek, adjoining the land of Mrs. Slye. The soil is good, the water fine, and the situation beautiful. Daniel Jenifer, attorney in fact. (1 AUG 1782)

For rent, a good storehouse, public house with other necessary houses, and on an excellent lot for grass of 3 or 4 acres, apple orchard which may be made 7 or 800 gallons of cider, a good fives yard and skittle alley in good order. This place answers extremely well for a store and public house, there being in the neighborhood a set of considerable and good planters, and is within a small distance of Broad Creek warehouse, which in good times annually receives 1,000 hogsheads tobacco. The public main roads from the lower counties run through this place, and close to the store and public house doors, and near the fowling and fishing landings, and with a convenient landing near the store for landing goods. Edward Magruder. (8 AUG 1782)

At Piscataway, confiscated property for sale on September 2nd: 100-acre tract called *Duncaster*, and a 200-acre tract called *Convenience*, late the property of Massey's heirs. (15 AUG 1782)

On Saturday, arrived in this city on a visit to the governor, his excellency Count Rochambeau, commander in chief of the auxiliary army, accompanied by Count Dillon and others, and on Monday, returned to Baltimore. (15 AUG 1782)

For sale, a Negro blacksmith who is a very good workman, excellent horseshoer, has worked two years at anchor business, can make good grain and grass sithes, understands every kind of plantation work, 26 years old, sold for no fault, is employed in shipwork by Mr. Caverley of Alexandria. For terms apply to Josiah Watson, Esq., of Alexandria. Samuel Love, Jr., Loudoun County. (5 SEP 1782)

The Annapolis races are to be run October 1st. (5 SEP 1782)

The ferry over South River has been run by the same family since 1737. (26 SEP 1782)

Prince George's County. For sale, the subscriber's tract called *St. Elizabeth*, containing 600 acres by patent and lying on the Eastern Branch of Patowmack, 6 miles above Alexandria by water, and the same distance to Georgetown and Bladensburgh. Soil is excellent for Indian corn, tobacco or small grain. Several tenant buildings, tobacco house, and many other necessary houses. Walter Hoxton. (26 SEP 1782)

Walter Hanson, "being desirous of contracting his affairs into a narrow compass," is offering for sale his plantation near Samuel Hanson's; including slaves, cattle, furniture, kitchen and plantation utensils. (17 OCT 1782)

Dr. Fendall, operator on the teeth, will be in Annapolis. Dentifrice always available at his residence in Charles County near Port Tobacco. The sooner ladies and gentlemen apply, the better, as the doctor's stay in town will be uncertain; he proposes at least to continue during the races and perhaps longer. He transplants natural teeth, has false ones, etc. (31 OCT 1782)

G.B. Causin, at Port Tobacco, offers for sale breeding mares with foals by a large horse belonging to Rev. Ignatius Matthews of Port Tobacco, and got by a horse called *Othello*, formerly belonging to Benjamin Dulany, Esq. (31 OCT 1782)

A few copies of "Case of the Episcopal Church in the U.S. Considered," are available for sale at the printing office. (7 NOV 1782)

Along the Potomac River: **Extracts from the *Maryland Gazette*, 1728-1799**

The United States in Congress Assembled set apart Thursday, November 27th, as the day of Solemn Thanksgiving to God for all his mercies. (14 NOV 1782)

Green Hill, Charles County. Samuel Hanson offers for sale for tobacco, should any purchasers incline to pay money, I will take it at the rate of 2 silver dollars per cent, a neat and fashionable assortment of London plate, among which are candlesticks, coffee pot, mahogany silver mounted case with one dozen silver handled knives and forks, etc. Also, a quantity of London mahogany furniture, spinet, tables, chairs, etc. Theodolite. (19 DEC 1782)

On Thursday, January 9th, will be rented to the highest bidder, the well known ferry opposite Alexandria, commonly called Clifford's [sic] Ferry, with the houses and 39 acres. Thomas H. Hanson. (26 DEC 1782)

The horse *Chatham* shall run with any horse, mare or gelding in America; for 500 pounds, on the following terms: To run over the course at Alexandria, on the 1st Tuesday in May. H. Belt and T. Hanson. (27 FEB 1783)

On March 19th, 1783, Capt. Gerard Fowke, of Charles County, died in the 59th year of his age. He was taken ill from home and his death was surprisingly sudden. He was a gentleman of great humanity, honesty and hospitable beyond what is common ... (3 APR 1783)

A proclamation declaring the cessation of arms, as well as by sea as by land, is agreed upon between the United States and his Britannic Majesty. (17 APR 1783)

The horse *Dauphin* is at stud for not more than 20 mares at *Benfield*, the seat of Benjamin Contee, Esq., within two miles of Port Tobacco. George Nayler, Jr. (17 APR 1783)

The Upper Marlborough races was run on May 1st for a purse of 50 guineas. In 4th place was N. Young's bay horse *Why Not*. Next day was won by Ben. Dulany's sorrel horse *Slim*. (8 MAY 1783)

Annapolis, June 10th. On Wednesday, the 18th inst., at four o'clock p.m. will be sold at public sale for ready money, at Mr. Middleton's 's tavern on the dock, the schooner *Why Not*, a strong new well built vessel, burthen 83 tons, completely fitted and well founded with every necessity for sea. An inventory will be shown at the time of sale. Wallace & Muir. (12 JUN 1783)

Goods imported from France and Portugal by the brig *Marquis de la Fayette*, will be sold in Alexandria on reasonable terms for cash, tobacco or flour, by M. Terrasson, at the store of M. Perrin. Includes wines, millstones, tea, etc. (19 JUN 1783)

Along the Potomac River: **Extracts from the *Maryland Gazette*, 1728-1799**

The sheriff of Charles County has a runaway Mulatto who "has a scar above his left eye, and says he got it by a knife being thrown at him," and that his name is Jerry. He belongs to Col. Ramsay of Virginia, but some say he belongs to William Lindsey of Colchester. (3 JUL 1783)

All persons with claims on the estate of William Digges, late of *Warburton*, Prince George's County, deceased, are to send them in. George Digges, executor. Also, I have a grist mill on a good stream of water, near Piscataway, for rent. G. Digges. (10 JUL 1783)

Philadelphia. Commencement at the university featured a debate on dueling — calling it *Gothic phrenzy*. (10 JUL 1783)

Near Port Tobacco. William Dodson offers for sale eye water; it restores sight, etc. Those who apply are requested to bring phials, as the subscriber has none to furnish them with. Includes testimonials by Baker Brooke and Robert Brent, Jr. (14 AUG 1783)

Alexandria. William Lyles, Jr. will offer for sale at Piscataway, on September 15th, a tract of 304 acres, being at the mouth and south side of Piscataway Creek on Patowmack River, and in full view of his excellency General Washington's seat *Mount Vernon*; within 4 miles of Piscataway and 7 of Alexandria. 4/5ths entirely level, 1/5th high ground. No land on Patowmack exceeds it for fishing and fowling, and in its elegance of situation. (21 AUG 1783)

A petition by sundry inhabitants of Charles County for an act to pass for building of a courthouse at the place formerly laid out for a town by the late Rev. Mr. George Hunter at the mouth of Port Tobacco Creek, and to condemn the land necessary to build a town providing the present proprietor should refuse or delay to sell. (28 AUG 1783)

Ignatius Matthews will petition the Assembly to lay out a town at Chapel Point, at the mouth of Port Tobacco Creek. (11 SEP 1783)

On Wednesday, July 29th, Mr. John Blate, from Essex County, Va., shot himself through the head with a pistol, in the compting room of Col. John Fitzgerald of Alexandria, with whom he had acted as clerk, and whom he had never mentioned but in terms of gratitude and affection. He had had the measles, and had gone two months ago to a house in the country for 5 weeks to recuperate, but disliked company, and would lower his head and become depressed, etc. He had been offered a partnership. (18 SEP 1783)

Daniel of St. Thomas Jenifer, Intendant, offers for sale at Annapolis, soldiers' uniforms, etc., just arrived from France. (9 OCT 1783)

Nanjemoy. Thirty or 40 slaves to be sold from the estate of the late Capt. Gerard Fowke. (9 OCT 1783)

Along the Potomac River: **Extracts from the *Maryland Gazette*, 1728-1799**

A counter petition from Charles County inhabitants to not condemn lands of the Roman Catholic Church formerly intended to be laid out for a town by Rev. Hunter, not for building a courthouse, nor for altering the place of holding court.

On the 2nd day of November court, will be sold at Port Tobacco a lot on the west side of the road that leads through the said town, occupied by Mr. John Halkerston, whereon is an exceeding good dwelling house, 56'x20', fronting the fourth side of the courthouse, hip-roofed, 3 rooms and a fireplace in each on the lower floor, and the same on the upper floor, with a slip partition for the purpose of a ballroom, large dry cellar, kitchen of 16'x20', in between which and the mansion is a passage of 16'x14', corn house of 16'x14', framed stable of 20'x16', and addition. The whole of the grounds is paled in and partitioned ... yard, garden and horse yards (horse yard in which a stable stands is 60'x100'), etc. There is a large and beautiful spreading elm in the garden which provides shade, garden 230' square. Soil of which is equal to any on the continent. Rents for £125 per year. Inquire of Charles Mankin. (16 OCT 1783)

John Halkerston offers for rent in Port Tobacco where he now keeps a tavern, fronting on the courthouse. (23 OCT 1783)

On September 24th, a Negro named George, en route from Chester County gaol, escaped from Thomas Hanson's at *Oxen-Hill*, Prince George's County. Samuel Hanson. (6 NOV 1783)

November 22nd. On Saturday last, departed this life, at *Oxen-Hill*, the seat of Mr. Thomas Hanson, in the 63rd year of his age, the Hon. John Hanson, Esq. This gentleman had long been a servant to his country, in a wide variety of employments, the last of which was President of Congress. He had been ill since he returned home, sick then for several months, then had a relapse while on a visit to *Oxen-Hill* ... Amidst lingering torments, he steadily persevered the fortitude of a man, with the temper of a philosopher ... (27 NOV 1783)

Paris, November 20th. A report of the first balloon ascension to 3,000 feet, aloft for 20 minutes, "when they descended they said they had never been so hungry in their lives, and that they had been astonished at the awful silence which reigned in the high regions." (19 FEB 1784)

Warburton, February 8th. Notice is hereby given that a petition will be referred to the next General Assembly, praying that a law may be passed to prevent the putting down of hedges or weirs adjoining the town of Bladensburg. George Digges. (26 FEB 1784)

Alexandria, February 26th. The ship [*Sampson*], Capt. Joseph Greenway, from this port, with tobacco from Amsterdam, struck on the Goodwin sands on November 16th, and by the violence of the weather soon beat into pieces. The captain and crew, after suffering extreme hardship during a night and a day, on a part of the wreck, which was driven into the North Sea, were miraculously saved (except for one of the people) by a French fisherman ... and landed at Dunkirk. (11 MAR 1784)

Along the Potomac River: **Extracts from the *Maryland Gazette*, 1728-1799**

Last Sunday, in the afternoon, as a man was coming over Patowmack from Maryland to this town, with three horses, two of the horses broke in, and were lost. The man with difficulty saved his life. (11 MAR 1784)

Daniel of St. Thomas Jenifer, Intendant, seeks a skillful architect to repair the Stadt House in Annapolis. (18 MAR 1784)

Thomas Hanson offers for rent Clifford's Ferry, opposite Alexandria. (25 MAR 1784)

Alexandria, March 18th. Sunday last the ice in the river Patowmack began to break up, and on Monday ran very rapid, exhibiting an appearance of such vast bodies of ice and timber as was never known by the oldest inhabitants here. (1 APR 1784)

Fairfax County. George Mason seeks a person to build a dwelling house of about 1,200 square feet; "he will either furnish materials or not, at the option of the undertaker." (1 APR 1784)

Alexandria, March 25th. On Monday evening last, the brigantine *Ranger*, Capt. Peabody, arrived here from St. Martins ... ; the brigantine *Fortitude*, Capt. Gardner, arrived a few days ago. (8 APR 1784)

Alexandria, April 8th. Yesterday, sailed for London, the ship *Two Friends*, Capt. Street, in which went passengers Mr. John Muir, merchant of this town, his sister, and several gentlemen. (27 MAY 1784)

Annapolis. Last Friday morning his excellency Gen. Washington arrived here from Philadelphia, and the next day set off for his seat at *Mount Vernon*. (27 MAY 1784)

Ariana Calvert, the youngest daughter of Benedict Calvert, Esq., died at *Mt. Airy*, on Monday the 24th [long obituary continues]. (10 JUN 1784)

A balloon is to be built in Philadelphia, by subscriptions; envision its use for travelers crossing the desert in war. (1 JUL 1784)

Thomas Hanson will offer for sale on September 18th, at *Oxen-Hill*, 40 slaves; also horses, cattle, furniture and an "elegant chamber organ, very elegant coach with harness for four horses." (24 JUL 1784)

George Mason, Jr. seeks the return of a runaway slaves: Dick, a stout lusty Mulatto fellow, about 22 years of age, has large features and eyes, has a roguish down look. He beats a drum pretty well, is artful and plausible, and well acquainted with most parts of Maryland and Virginia, having formerly waited upon me. Clem, a well set black Negro lad, of about 19 years, has a remarkable large scar of a burn, which covers the whole of one of his knees. Tis impossible to describe their dress, as I am told they have stolen a variety of cloaths since their elopement. Ten pounds reward offered. (24 JUL 1784)

To the Public-Warm Springs, at Bath, in Berkeley County, Va. On June 13th, James Rumsey and Robert Throgmorton propose the opening of a very commodious boarding house for the residence of ladies and gentlemen who may honor the Bath, at the sign of the Liberty Pole and Flag. (5 AUG 1784)

Edward Digges, executor of the estate of Edward Digges, seeks debtors to discharge their outstanding accounts. (5 AUG 1784)

The Charles County sheriff has a Negro man by the name of Kitt who belongs to Mr. Daniel Tebbs of Prince William County, Va. (5 AUG 1784)

Tracts of land in St. Mary's City are under litigation. (26 AUG 1784)

On Tuesday morning last, the Marquis de la Fayette arrived in this city on his return from a visit to General Washington at *Mount Vernon*, and in the afternoon set off for Baltimore. (2 SEP 1784)

The ship *Notley*, Capt. White, arrived from Virginia. (2 SEP 1784)

The Piscataway races will be run for on October 7th; a purse of 30 pounds, heats will be 4 miles. The following day a purse of 15 pounds will be run, 2 mile heats. (16 SEP 1784)

To be sold on November 18th, the beautiful plantation in Charles County known by the name of *Middleton*, formerly the property of Dr. Gustavus Richard Brown. It runs along a branch of Nanjemoy Creek about 2 miles, verged in most parts with a valuable and improved marsh; containing 1,288 acres. Also, a large dwelling house with brick chimneys, 4 rooms below with fireplaces, a large passage; 4 rooms above, one of which has a fireplace. The house is in good repair, a part of the plaister excepted; framed kitchen with brick chimneys, good milk, meat and corn houses, stable, 2 new tobacco houses, new barn and 2 quarters, orchard and cherry trees [additional variety listed]. Robert Furguson. (23 SEP 1784)

London, July 6th. They write from Aix-la-Chapelle that a young lady named C__r, married to M. de E__, Jr., President of the parliament, was found dead in her bed with her throat cut. She was not 24 years of age. As her purse only was missing and her jewels had not been touched, it was suspected that the murder had been done by some robber; the lady's woman and the domestics have surrendered themselves prisoners. But now letters from Provence have cleared up this matter. A domestic confessed the whole; he cut off the head of the unfortunate lady, by order of his master who forcibly held her during the barbarous operation, after having attempted in vain to strangle her with three handkerchiefs. Eight days before, he had attempted to poison her ... The

Along the Potomac River: **Extracts from the *Maryland Gazette*, 1728-1799**

parliament have resolved not to break up for vacation in order to attend solely to that affair ... The president, de E__, is but 26; he lived publicly with a widow, whom he wished to marry. This is the sole reason that induced him to commit the horrid deed. (16 SEP 1784)

Alexandria, October 1st. To be sold at Port Tobacco, on November 9th, the land where the subscriber lived on Patowmack, 700 acres, large elegant brick dwelling house, completely finished, etc. Commands an excessive view up and down the river. Philip Richard Fendall. (14 OCT 1784)

William Fitzhugh offers for sale 6,000 acres of land on Aquia Run, not more than 1 mile from Aquia warehouse, 6 miles from Dumfries. Inquire of the subscriber opposite to Lower Marlborough, or Col. [Bailey] Washington, near and adjoining the premises. (14 OCT 1784)

To be sold on November 8th at the subscriber's mill, near Port Tobacco, slaves, horses, and cattle. T. Stone. (14 OCT 1784)

Leeds, Yorkshire, June 25th. The following curious advertisement was stuck up last week in Lorton, near Cockemouth. "To all my lovin frins my wife has for some time past been rather Cowdy and like to get the upper hand of me, I am at last firmly resolved to pock her off some way or another, therefore if any of my lovin frins want to borrow or buy a wife they shall be supplied upon the most reasonable terums. N.B. They must apply soon or she will be disposed of." (4 NOV 1784)

Alexandria. The schooner *Hope*, from this port, lately mentioned to have been quitted at sea by the captain and crew, was some time after taken in tow by an Irish cutter, and the mate was put on board to steer her; in a heavy gale of wind the captain of the cutter was obliged to cut her loose, but, on his arrival, dispatched some pilot boats in quest of her, who found her. Unhappily, some disputes arose between the mate and pilots, when the former was killed. The schooner is brought in to the eastern shore. (18 NOV 1784)

Ship News. The schooner *Hope*, Capt. John Christie, belonging to Alexandria in Virginia, sprung a leak at sea, which overpowered the utmost exertions of captain and crew, whose lives were providentially saved by Capt. Reuben Clarke in a whaling sloop from Boston, where they arrived on the 4th ult. (23 NOV 1784)

By the *Journal*, we learn that a meeting is proposed at Mr. Lomax's in Alexandria on the 15th inst., at 10 a.m., of gentlemen of the states of Maryland and Virginia, especially those who live contiguous to the Patowmack, and wish to see an attempt made to extend navigation of that river. Desire to form a company. (23 NOV 1784)

William Smallwood, Thomas Johnson, and Gustavus Scott, Esq., are elected delegates to Congress. (9 DEC 1784)

Along the Potomac River: **Extracts from the *Maryland Gazette*, 1728-1799**

Port Tobacco. The subscriber is desirous of taking an apprentice to surgery and physic. James Craik, Senior. (9 DEC 1784)

Peregrine Fitzhugh offers for sale a 2,150-acre tract in Prince William County, 2 miles from Dumfries, 8 miles from Colchester, and 24 miles from Alexandria. (16 DEC 1784)

William Smallwood, T. Johnson refused to serve as congressmen; others elected. (23 DEC 1784)

Robert Darnall seeks a skillful architect to build a genteel country villa the ensuing summer. Apply to the subscriber near Upper Marlborough. (27 JAN 1785)

John F. Mercer, delegate to Congress for Virginia, was married on the 3rd to Miss Sprigg of Annapolis. (27 FEB 1785)

The Patowmack Canal Company is offering for sale subscriptions. (27 FEB 1785)

Died at *Cedar Hill*, the seat of her affectionate husband, Dr. Benjamin Fendall, Charles County, Mrs. Anne Fendall, aged 26 years and 9 days [long obituary continues]. (27 FEB 1785)

Benedict Calvert seeks return of runaway Mulatto named Archibald, who ran off during the "holydays." (26 MAY 1785)

Alexandria, May 19th. Last Tuesday, at Lomax's Tavern, was held the first meeting of the Patowmack Canal Company. George Washington, President; George Gilpin, John Fitzgerald, Thomas Johnson and Thomas Lee, Directors. (26 MAY 1785)

William Fitzhugh will offer for sale on September 20th, a tract in Stafford County, southern boundary, 9 miles from Fredericksburg; northern boundary 5 miles south of Dumfries; "both considerable and growing towns." Bounded on the east where it crosses Aquia Run at the fork (1 mile from Aquia warehouse), where the north and south branches divide. Next to Col. [Bailey] Washington. (26 MAY 1785)

T. Stone will offer for sale at Port Tobacco on June 15th, being the Thursday of Charles County Court, a number of valuable Negroes. (9 JUN 1785)

To be rented on August 1st, the store rooms, cellar, and counting rooms now in possession of Col. John H. Stone, in Port Tobacco. William Layman. (9 JUN 1785)

Washington College, State of Maryland. On Tuesday and Wednesday, June 7th and 8th, 1785, the third anniversary commencement was held in this seminary, where the following degrees were conferred: [list], Master of Arts to John Scott. (23 JUN 1785)

Along the Potomac River: **Extracts from the *Maryland Gazette*,** 1728-1799

A group is applying to the next session of the Virginia legislature for the formation of a new state to be called Kentucky, and by computation contains at this time 30,000 souls. (7 JUL 1785)

Gentlemen interested in the formation of a college on the western shore of Maryland will meet in Annapolis. (7 JUL 1785)

To be rented, storerooms, cellar and counting room now in possession of John H. Stone ... being in Port Tobacco and in a most convenient stand for any merchant who proposes to carry on the purchase of tobacco, or any other produce of this part of Maryland. (7 JUL 1785)

We hear that the Congress on the 4th inst., resolved that the dollar would be the money unit, and the 1/200 part of the dollar the smallest copper piece. (21 JUL 1785)

Daniel of St. Thomas Jenifer offers for sale 1,181 acres of limestone land in Berkeley County, Va., on the Patowmack. He is still Intendant of the Revenue. (21 JUL 1785)

Alexandria. A hail storm and lightning struck the conductor on the house of Wm. Herbert, Esq. (21 JUL 1785)

Gentlemen in possession of subscriptions for a book proposed to be printed by the late Rev. Isaac Campbell, now in the press, will return them to Dr. Gustavus R. Brown, of Port Tobacco. (21 JUL 1785)

Stolen or strayed from the subscriber's plantation, *Mount Azile*, in Prince George's County, two and a half miles from Alexandria ferry, 2 mares. P. Savary. (4 AUG 1785)

Hezekiah Wynn offers for sale his plantation on Mattawoman, within 3 miles from Piscataway; 200 acres with a large dwelling house. (4 AUG 1785)

J.H. Beans offers for sale a 304-acre plantation on the south side of Piscataway Creek; "this beautiful and fertile spot is almost surrounded with water where fish and fowl in their different seasons may be taken in abundance through the year. (8 SEP 1785)

Three houses and lots in Pig-Point, in Anne Arundel County, on the Patuxent R., are for sale. Two are stone houses and perhaps superior to any other in this place as they are new ... needless to say much of this place as it is so generally known as one of the first inspections for tobacco on that river. Henrietta Walker. (6 OCT 1785)

Marsh M. Duvall seeks return of a runaway named Christopher Seahorn, a well looking man about 23 years of age, from Queen Anne ... he is a young fellow who professes dexterity of hand and has been with a woman he calls his mother, and one Thomason, with Bailey's puppets. (20 OCT 1785)

Along the Potomac River: **Extracts from the *Maryland Gazette*,** 1728-1799

George Digges is among those elected to the Assembly from Prince George's County. (20 OCT 1785)

To be sold on November 28th, at the house of the subscriber, opposite Alexandria, the personal estate of George Frazier Hawkins, Esq., deceased. Includes Negroes, animals and furniture. Susanna J. Hawkins, Executrix. (27 OCT 1785)

To be sold on the premises on December 6th, part of the tract called *Major's Choice*, lying near Piscataway; 108 acres. Elizabeth Wheeler. (3 NOV 1785)

The subscriber takes this method of informing the public that a report which has been in circulation about six years of his being married, is groundless. Walter Dyer. (3 NOV 1785)

The races will be run at Queen Anne on November 24th. Marsh M. Duvall. (10 NOV 1785)

Stolen out of the house of the subscriber, on Wednesday, November 2nd, three elegant coats, one of superfine blue broadcloth, quite new, with very elegant yellow buttons, the pockets on the outside pretty high under the arms; the others were drab coloured: one had a crimson velvet cape, the buttons were covered with the same as the coat; the other had a cape the same as the coat with mohair buttons. George Mann. (10 NOV 1785)

The Hon. William Smallwood is elected governor. Gabriel Duvall is elected one of the council. (24 NOV 1785)

John Hancock was elected president of the Congress, on November 23rd. (8 DEC 1785)

On Friday the 16th, after a short illness, departed this life at his house in Port Tobacco, Walter Hanson Jenifer, Dr. of Physic [obituary continues]. (22 DEC 1785)

A lottery will be held for disposing of 50 lots in La Fayette village at the Cool Springs. Charlotte Hall school is now building within 200 steps of this place. (5 JAN 1786)

This is to inform my customers in general, that I hope they will all come and settle with me by the 28th inst., which will enable me to discharge my debts; for this is the last time of asking, so I wish you all a happy new year and plenty of money. Joseph Brewer. (5 JAN 1786)

S. Abell, late sheriff of St. Mary's County, has a runaway Negro named George Green, but since says his name is Harry and that he belongs to the widow [Tebbs] in the state of Virginia. (12 JAN 1786)

Along the Potomac River: **Extracts from the *Maryland Gazette*, 1728-1799**

Letters remaining in the post office at Annapolis include those for Chancellor Brent of Port Tobacco; Charles Pye, *Notley Hall*; Thomas Rozer, *Notley Hall*. (9 FEB 1786)

An act is passed which authorizes Maryland and Virginia to lay out a road through Pennsylvania between the Potomac and Ohio rivers. (16 FEB 1786)

The flour that is branded "Beason," as mentioned in a letter from Barbadoes (and inserted in our last paper) as little inferior to Philadelphia superfine, was shipped from Alexandria. (16 FEB 1786)

An act is passed for investing in George Washington, Esq., a certain interest in companies established for the opening and extending the navigation of the James and Patowmack rivers. "These great works for its improvement ... will be durable monuments of his glory, may be made monuments also of the gratitude of his country." Fifty shares of James River stock and 100 shares of Patowmack stock were to be given him. He declined with thanks, and donated them to the public welfare. (16 FEB 1786)

Alexandria. Servants who were hired to work on the navigation of the Patowmack, and tried to run away, were sentenced to have their heads and eyebrows shaved every week during servitude. (16 FEB 1786)

Sotterley, St. Mary's County. George Plater seeks return of runaway Negro named Towermill, "well made and of a soft, insinuating manner." (16 FEB 1786)

The estate of the late Ignatius Digges asks that claims against it be presented. To be sold at *Mellwood Park*, the plantation of the late I. Digges, on March 14th, hay, wheat, molasses, brown sugar, looms, chariot and harness, cider, casks, etc. Mary Digges, Executrix. (23 FEB 1786)

The subscriber, living near Port Tobacco, offers for sale eye water. Testimonials from Robert Brent, Walter Pye, Henry Hammersley and Mary Brent. Wm. Dodson. (23 FEB 1786)

An act is passed for erecting a lighthouse on Patowmack River. Also, an act is passed for more effective preservation of the breed of wild deer. (16 MAR 1786)

Henry Stonestreet offers for sale a healthy farm of 215 acres, 9 miles from Alexandria, and 2 miles from Piscataway, with a good dwelling. (15 JUN 1786)

Alexandria, May 8th. Last Monday afternoon, a number of disorderly people assembled near *Cameron* where they attacked and unmercifully beat with clubs all who came in their way. They were with difficulty quelled, not before they had been fired on, with several badly wounded. The principal ringleaders were brought to town and committed to prison. (15 JUN 1786)

Prince George's County. Runaway Negro named Bob, a criminal who got from the constable as he was carrying him to prison on the 15th inst., was brought home by one of the neighbors the evening before and made an attempt to kill one of my sons by twice stabbing him with a knife. Henry Boon. (22 JUN 1786)

Nathaniel Greene, Esq., died on June 19th, Monday, at his seat near Savannah. On Tuesday morning, his remains were brought to town to be interred ... (20 JUL 1786)

A proclamation by the governor results from a number of disorderly persons entering the courthouse at Port Tobacco while the court was sitting, and obliged Mr. John Allan Thomas, attorney, to strike off several actions which he had brought for recovery of British debts. Governor warns persons to refrain from such actions. (20 JUL 1786)

During a hailstorm, lightning struck the conductor on the house of William Herbert, in Alexandria. (21 JUL 1786)

Details on coinage are published; values to be mills, cents, dimes and dollars. Coins of half dollar, double dime, and dime. Coopers will be cents, half-cent. Gold will be the eagle ($10) and the half-eagle. (7 SEP 1786)

William Bowie, 3rd, seeks return of runaway Negro named Charles; had been purchased from Notley Young, Esq., by the present owner. (21 SEP 1786)

Lost in September, on the main road from Broad Creek to Port Tobacco, within three miles of Piscataway, a black leather pocket book. Jason Jenkins, living near Piscataway. (21 SEP 1786)

A petition is filed with the general assembly praying that part of the main road which leads from Port Tobacco to the old courthouse, may be moved up a valley through the Rev. Mr. Leonard Neale's plantation. (28 SEP 1786)

George Mason, and George Mason, Jr. seek the return of runaway slaves Dick and Watt. Dick "beats a drum pretty well and has formerly been a waiting man." He took with him a light lead-colored country cloth coat with white metal buttons, short green ditto, round hat, white cloth waistcoat, red ditto, faced with black velvet. (5 OCT 1786)

The Bladensburg races will be run on October 19th. (12 OCT 1786)

[A series of lengthy letters between Daniel of St. Thomas Jenifer and Gabriel Duvall, on the topic of selling lands]. "I have been obliged to defend my public character and conduct against the attacks of others; but this has not been done by censure and abuse but by facts and arguments." Jenifer. (19 OCT 1786)

Mr. Peale, ever desirous to please and entertain the public, will make a part of his house a repository for natural curiosities ... (2 NOV 1786)

An act is passed to establish a U.S. mint. (9 NOV 1786)

William Smallwood is re-elected governor. Benjamin C. Stoddert is elected to the senate in room of Richard Barnes; Samuel Hughes in place of Thomas Johnson. (14 DEC 1786)

The play "The Rivals" was acted last night by the American Company. (14 DEC 1786)

Whereas the business of the Charles County court has been greatly retarded and delayed by the non-attendance of Thomas Stone, Esq., practicing attorney of said court, whereby the docket has been loaded and swelled to a most enormous size, we therefore think it proper to give public notice that from this time on, no action or suit will be delayed on account of the non-attendance of the gentlemen of the bar ... (21 DEC 1786)

Thomas Stone writes a letter in protest, saying he has practised in Charles County court for 18 years, and was always present. This time he went to Annapolis to a meeting of commissioners from several states, got sick; plus the weather was bad. (28 DEC 1786)

A late *Martinique Gazette* contains the following: "When the American ambassadors obtained an audience with the dey of Algiers, he addressed them in these words, 'You Americans are a new people; you are too poor to make the presents which I want, and too far off for me to be afraid of you'." (11 JAN 1787)

Port Tobacco. To be rented, a large and commodious store house with good cellar and counting room, lately in the occupation of Mr. Nicholas and Valentine Peers. Daniel Jenifer, Jr. (11 JAN 1787)

Charles County. Whereas William Copher, of Washington County, sold Thomas Courtney Reeves a part of two tracts called *Betty's Delight*, containing 62 acres, and part of a tract called *Mistake*, with 45 acres in Charles County; the lands were conveyed by mistake in the name of Thomas Charles Reeves, and since the said William Copher has since moved to Kentucky (he will petition the next assembly to have the correct name put on the deed). (11 JAN 1787)

Calvert County, January 4th. Will be sold at public sale on Wednesday the 31st, at the dwelling house of Thomas Johnson, late of the county aforesaid, deceased, sundry Negroes, horses, and cattle. Estate asks that claims be brought in. Mary Cleaverly Johnson, Executrix. (11 JAN 1787)

Alexandria, January 1st. The subscriber will taken an apprentice in physic and surgery. James Craik, Sr. (17 JAN 1787)

Newport, Charles County. Robert Brent complains about fences pulled down, and fruit trees injured by trespassers. (17 JAN 1787)

Along the Potomac River: **Extracts from the *Maryland Gazette*, 1728-1799**

H. Addison, of Prince George's County, clerk, and son, will petition to the next session of the Maryland Assembly concerning certain confiscated property of the said Addison. (1 FEB 1787)

A big fire has occurred in Richmond, Va. A list of destroyed buildings is given. A total of 43 burned last Monday at 4 a.m. (1 FEB 1787)

An act for the benefit of Rev. Henry Addison is passed. (1 FEB 1787)

Robert Brent, Jr., when living near Port Tobacco, found a red steer on his land. (1 FEB 1787)

Marmaduke McCain is building a pile-driving machine. (1 FEB 1787)

Peregrine Fitzhugh lost a boat, 25' long [further description given] from his landing on Kent Island. (15 FEB 1787)

Died, at *Blenheim*, Charles County, on January 26th, the Hon. Richard Lee, in his 81st year [long notice continues]. (15 FEB 1787)

Prince George's County. The subscriber will petition the next assembly for an act to sell *Berry's Enclosure*, 347 acres; *Oxen Hill*, 70 acres; and *Holly Spring*, 50 acres; all late the property of William Berry, Prince George's County, deceased. William Berry Warman. (1 MAR 1787)

Belain Posey will petition the assembly to obtain title to a tract in Charles County, called *Grub's Venture*, or *Crane's Low Grounds*, which he purchased from George Crane. (1 MAR 1787)

A petition will be made to make valid a deed dated September 19th, 1759, from Henry Rozer and Eleanor his wife, to Edward Neale, and to vest the real estate in the persons who ought to possess the same. Henry Rozer, Eleanor Rozer, Francis Hall, Martha Hall, Benjamin Young. (1 MAR 1787)

October 5, 1786. George Mason, Jr., seeks return of a runaway named Dick, in the latter end of September last. Very lusty Mulatto fellow, 25 y ears of age, has bushy hair or wool, which he generally combs back, large features and eyes, a grum down look, and frowns when spoken to; he is a subtle artful fellow, and well acquainted with Virginia and Maryland, having formerly been a waiting-man; he is fond of dress and took with him a variety of clothes ... he worked on board a vessel by the name of *Thomas Webster* in his last runaway trip ... George Mason, Jr. (1 MAR 1787)

London, December 15th. In Norfolk, a man was tried on a charge of bigamy. Two wives had already proved their titles to his person, when a third stood up for the same purpose and a fourth appeared in readiness. "Why you fellow," exclaimed the judge,

Along the Potomac River: **Extracts from the *Maryland Gazette*,** 1728-1799

"at this rate, where did you intend to stop?" "To stop, my lord," replied the other," I was only going on til I could find a good one." (8 MAR 1787)

The quarrel between Daniel of St. Thomas Jenifer and G. Duvall continues in lengthy letters being published in the newspaper. Duvall says "his last public [letter], however, will induce me once more to expose his vanity, baseness and folly, to do justice to his character, he is one of the most shameless and abandoned imposters that ever disgraced human nature." (15 MAR 1787)

Mount Vernon. *Royal Gift* and *Knight of Malta*, two valuable Jack-asses will cover mares and jennies at *Mount Vernon* this spring, for 5 guineas the season. (22 MAR 1787)

The horse *Magnolio*, is standing at stud. Pasture at half a dollar a week for mares. John Fairfax, overseer. (22 MAR 1787)

The horse *Chatham* is at stud at *Mt. Asaph* in Charles County, about 6 miles below Piscataway, about ten miles above Port Tobacco. T. Hanson. (22 MAR 1787)

Died at Upper Marlborough, on March 11th, Mary Contee, wife of Richard, and third daughter of David Craufurd, Esq., age 19 years [on her birthday; long obituary continues]. (22 MAR 1787)

All those having subscription papers for the first volume of the "Origin of Civil Government" by the Rev. Isaac Campbell, deceased, of Charles County, are asked to please return to Walter Stone, Esq., merchant, at Port Tobacco. William Campbell. (29 MAR 1787)

John Ashton, Sr., offers for sale a tract in King George County, Va., near the head of Machodock Creek, where he lived [further details given of house]. (5 APR 1787)

William M. Wilkinson has horse *Roebuck* at stud at Port Tobacco. (12 APR 1787)

The Patowmack Company is selling 46 shares in the company at auction at the courthouse in Alexandria on May 14th, and 9 shares at Suter's Tavern in Georgetown (these are delinquent shares which have not been paid for by the proprietors). John Potts, Secretary. (12 APR 1787)

A stray horse is at William Craik's, at *Strawberry Hill*, near Port Tobacco. (19 APR 1787)

A stage is to be run between Annapolis and Alexandria. From Annapolis on Monday and Friday, and from Alexandria on Tuesday and Saturday. William Clark. (19 APR 1787)

Along the Potomac River: **Extracts from the *Maryland Gazette*, 1728-1799**

Piscataway. For sale on Tuesday, June 12th, at the house of Mr. Charles Lansdale, in Piscataway, part of the tract called *Major's Choice*, 108 acres ... within a half mile of said town [dwelling described]. Elizabeth Wheeler, Charity Wheeler, Benedict Edelin. (19 APR 1787)

Mount Vernon, May 8th. In consideration of the scarcity of cash, the price for stud is now 5 pounds, or 8 barrels of corn. John Fairfax. (24 MAY 1787)

An act is passed for the relief of Belain Posey. An act is passed for the appointment a commission to make a correct survey of Upper Marlborough. An act is passed for the relief of William Berry Warman. (31 MAY 1787)

The convention in Philadelphia is to revise the constitution; has assisting: J. McHenry, Daniel of St. Thomas Jenifer, Daniel Carroll, John Francis Mercer and Luther Martin, Esq. (31 MAY 1787)

On June 1st, int., Margaret Stone, wife of the Hon. Thomas Stone, departed this life [long obituary continues]. (7 JUN 1787)

Georgetown. Will be sold at Col. John H. Beane's tavern in Piscataway, a house and lot in Piscataway where Mr. George Dent Hardey now lives, also 15-20 acres adjoining or near said town. The above has for many years been occupied as a tavern. Benjamin Reeder. (26 JUN 1787)

John Petty & Co. has a store at Port Tobacco. (12 JUL 1787)

The *Columbian Magazine* for July 1787 is embellished with a perspective view of the state house in Philadelphia. (23 AUG 1787)

The Constitution of the United States is published. (27 SEP 1787)

John Halkerston, a prisoner in Prince George's County, is an insolvent debtor. (27 SEP 1787)

About 6:00 on Tuesday morning last, the Stadt House was discovered to be on fire, because of the fire left in the chimney. It was distinguished without much damage. (1 NOV 1787)

Port Tobacco, October 24th. Offered £100 reward. The inhabitants of Port Tobacco, reflecting with horror the attempt made to destroy the town on Tuesday night the 16th inst., by setting fire to the store of the subscribers; do offer the above reward for the discovery and convicting the perpetrators of that infernal act; and any accomplice becoming states evidence shall receive the reward on the conviction of his associates. Nicholas and Valentine Peers. (1 NOV 1787)

Along the Potomac River: Extracts from the *Maryland Gazette,* 1728-1799

Notice is given by Elizabeth Dulany, wife of Walter Dulany, Esq., that she proposes to petition for restitution of the confiscated property of her former husband, Lloyd Dulany, remaining unsold. (1 NOV 1787)

George Digges, Esq., is elected to the House of Delegates for Prince George's County. (15 NOV 1787)

Port Tobacco, November 2nd. J.H. Stone & Co. seek the return of a runaway Negro named Bob. (15 NOV 1787)

William Smallwood is re-elected Governor. (15 NOV 1787)

Annapolis, November 23rd. John F. Mercer wants a carpenter "who will live on a country estate," who will receive 25 guineas per annum, and be himself and family provided with a good house, room and provisions [pencilled in margin, J.R. Sprigg]. (29 NOV 1787)

Richard Potts, Esq., is chosen a member of the senate in room of the Hon. Thomas Stone, deceased. (6 DEC 1787)

A lecture on Poetry, being the last of this course, will be delivered with permission, this evening in the ballroom by a Lady. (6 DEC 1787)

Port Tobacco. A call to the Brethren of Charles County; they are requested to meet at Mr. Simpson's tavern, on Friday, December 28th, to concert measures for obtaining a warrant to hold a lodge in Port Tobacco. Jonathan Anderson. (6 DEC 1787)

Philip Heidy, of Alexandria, is one of a list of those to receive hogs' bristles to be saved for John Fisher in Lancaster, Pennsylvania, who is carrying on the brush-making business. (13 DEC 1787)

Part of *White Hall* is for sale, 246½ acres, 11 miles from Annapolis. (13 DEC 1787)

A petition is filed to annul the marriage of Winn Winship of Talbot county to his wife Maria. (13 DEC 1787)

Rules for pilots per a recent act of Assembly. Rates from the mouth of Patowmack River to Georgetown are 5 shillings and 6 pence; for every half foot of water the vessels draw and 1/5 of this sum for less distance in the same proportion. (3 JAN 1788)

A remedy for gout is described. (10 JAN 1788)

A letter is in the post office for Notley Young, 3rd, of *Newport*, Maryland. (10 JAN 1788)

Richmond, December 23rd. Mrs. Tabb, of Kingston parish, in Gloucester County, has in her possession a small stone that has the efficacy of suction so powerful as to extract poison. Two trials have been made on bitten persons. (17 JAN 1788)

Sotterley, January 7th. George Plater will apply to the next court of Calvert county to mark the lines of two tracts, called *Mile's End* and *Mill Run*. (2 FEB 1788)

All ships may be entered and cleared either at the naval office in Alexandria, or at Yeocomico. (2 FEB 1788)

To be sold on April 16th, the revenue office with the ground it stands on. Daniel of St. Thomas Jenifer. (6 MAR 1788)

John Addison, of Prince George's County, intends to petition the assembly to enable him to collect fees due him as sheriff in 1769, 1770 and 1771. (27 MAR 1788)

George Plater is president of the Maryland Constitutional Convention. (24 APR 1788)

To be sold on May 13th, on the premises near Port Tobacco, a tract of 500 acres called *Rozer's Refuge*, taken in execution as the property of Walter Pye, and to be sold for the benefit of John Cooke, assignee of George Mason. (24 APR 1788)

Mount Airy, March 14th. Elizabeth Calvert, executor of Benedict Calvert deceased, will petition to mark the bounds of *His Lordship's Kindness*, the other part of *The Lodge*, commonly called *Darnall's Lodge*. (24 ARP 1788)

April 16th. Henry Rozer will apply to the assembly to mark the bounds of part of a tract called *Admirathoria Manor*. (8 MAY 1788)

The estate of John Semple, deceased, for payment of his debts, will be sold on September 8th; a tract in Prince William County, about 22 acres, on which is a forge, grist mill and saw mill, commonly known by the name of Occoquan Works; on navigable water. The other tracts are here and at Great Falls. (22 MAY 1788)

Robert Darnall will apply to the assembly to mark the bounds of the tract *The Addition*. (22 MAY 1788)

Some time in December last was stolen out of the home of Mr. John B. Turner, in Port Tobacco, a very small pinchbeck watch with a tortoise shell case, the under part of the rim that confines the cristial and prevents its going through, was near one half broken off, the number and maker's name unknown. Thomas How Ridgate. (5 JUN 1788)

Joseph Barnes, as per Mr. Rumsey, writes concerning the experimental fire engine he is developing. (12 JUN 1788)

Fredericksburg, June 5th. Extracted from a letter from Richmond, June 2nd. It was today agitated, whether the shorthand gentlemen should be suffered to take down the business of the House, for public information. Opposed by Henry, Mason, Grayson and White, with success. Mr. Mason rested his opposition upon the ground, that these gentlemen were strangers; that it was an important trust for anyone; for not only the people at large might be misinformed, but a fatal stab might be given by a gentleman of the House from a perversion of his language; that it was a breech of privilege, and had been frequently been determined so by the house of commons; that to show the member who moved this question, that his objection proceeded from those principles, and not from a wish to again be a member of another con-elade [sic] he had given his voice for an adjournment to the theatre, where, surrounded by his countrymen, he would endeavor to speak the language of his soul. (19 JUN 1788)

Mr. Rev. Thomas Hopkenson, between 30 and 40 years of age, at *Cedar Hill*, in Charles County, the seat of Dr. B. Fendall, departed this life [obituary continues]. (19 JUN 1788)

For Rent. Valuable tract of about 600 acres on Port Tobacco Creek, some 2 miles below the town of Port Tobacco. A good dwelling house, 38'x28', good kitchen, 2 tobacco houses, outhouses; the land is rich, produces good crops of Indian corn and tobacco, and is allowed to be preferable to any other in the neighborhood of Port Tobacco for grazing. The subscriber is now residing on the said plantation. G.B. Causin. (17 JUL 1788)

Wants Employment. A young man who has been regularly bred to the mercantile business, is a good accomptant, writes a fair hand and can be well recommended. Apply to John Gwinn, Esq., at Annapolis, or Messrs. Nicholas and Valentine Peers, merchants, Port Tobacco [pencilled in margin J. Betton]. (17 JUL 1788)

A letter remains in the post office for Miss Rozer, of *Notley-hall*. (17 JUL 1788)

Richmond, June 27th. Amendments to the proposed constitution and a proposed bill of rights. (24 JUL 1788)

Warburton, June 27th. George Digges will apply to mark the bounds of *Warburton Manor* and *Frankland*. (24 JUL 1788)

Sundry inhabitants of St. Mary's, Charles and Prince George's counties will petition for the establishment of a new county from parts of these remote from the courts thereof. (24 JUL 1788)

Thomas Rutland, near Annapolis, offers for sale a phaeton, chariot [description given], an elegant double harpsicord with inlaid front, patent swell, celestina stop and machine pedal, with turning instruments, strings, and a genteel collection of the most modern and approved music. (31 JUL 1788)

Along the Potomac River: **Extracts from the *Maryland Gazette*, 1728-1799**

George Mason, on June 8th, 1788, Stafford County, certified that: "Being informed that by Col. John Mercer that a rumor in Maryland (that Mercer wrote to his brother James Mercer that people in Maryland were against the constitution and would take up arms; that Mason had so told the Virginia Convention, who sent investigators to Maryland to take depositions; and it untrue), Mason says 'my attendance at the convention ... was very constant, from the beginning to the end of it.'" (7 AUG 1788)

Prince William, July 23rd. Fifty-four lots in the town of *Newport*, on the Patowmack River, at the mouth of Quantico Creek, about 3 miles below Dumfries, are for sale. Most lots lay either upon the river or the creek, the streets extending at right angles from one to the other, the harbor is equal to any on the river and the banks sufficiently high for making wharves for ships of almost any burthen to lay along side; at present ships carrying 500 hogsheads of tobacco may load safely within twice their length of the shore ... 6,000 hogsheads have been taken at Dumfries the previous inspection; the grain trade if carried on to any advantage from this part of the country, must be from the mouth of this creek; as at present it can only be navigated but by very small craft, and is daily growing worse. Cuthbert Bullet. (7 AUG 1788)

Charles Mankin, of Charles County, says slander has been said of him as collector of taxes, that "my being in arrears to the state was caused by my converting the public money to my use in making large purchases and improving the same, in the town of Dumfries in Virginia." Not so. (21 AUG 1788)

Messrs. J. Stone and Gustavus R. Brown want to settle the estate of Thomas Stone, deceased. (28 AUG 1788)

On the 20th, died of a deep decline, at Mrs. Dent's near Piscataway, Mrs. Henrietta Beans, wife of Col. John H. Beans [obituary continues]. (28 AUG 1788)

August 26th. New acquisitions to Peale's Museum included an American Pelican, entire and in good preservation, killed on the Chester River, Maryland, and presented by Col. Tilghman. (4 SEP 1788)

For sale on October 18th, by B. Reeder, a house in Piscataway town on a lot of near 2 acres, in an advantageous part of town, for any kind of public business; also 10 or 15 unimproved lots of 1 acre each. (17 SEP 1788)

Alexandria. Subscribers to shares in the Patowmack Company are to pay the treasurer William Hartshorne 5 pounds per cent on each share. G. Washington, President; T. Johnson, Thomas S. Lee, George Gilpin and John Fitzgerald, Directors. (17 SEP 1788)

Proclamation from Governor Smallwood about Nathan Soper, of Prince George's County, that his tobacco house was burned, and the night before a tobacco house in which he had an interest (belonging to Notley Young, Esq.) was burned. Soper was manager for Young. On August 28th last, he lost 7 stacks of wheat and rye in the same

Along the Potomac River: **Extracts from the *Maryland Gazette*,** 1728-1799

manner, and at the same time he had a new tobacco house set on fire which he extinguished. A $60 reward is offered for the perpetrators of this outrage. (2 OCT 1788)

A £20 purse will be run for on October 22nd, over a good course near Piscataway. (9 OCT 1788)

October 6th. G.B. Causin offers for sale Negroes, horses on December 2nd at *Benfield*, the place of his present residence. At *Causin-Manor*, on January 2nd, will be sold Negroes. (16 OCT 1788)

George Digges is elected a delegate to the Assembly from Prince George's County; Henry H. Chapman, George Dent., etc. are elected from Charles County. (16 OCT 1788)

The clergyman, W. Stoy, of Lebanon, Pennsylvania, had a cure for hydrophobia. (23 OCT 1788)

Thomas Johnson is elected governor. (13 NOV 1788)

Rachel Brooke, late of Prince George's County, had lived at *The Vineyard*. T. Brook[e] is administrator of the estate. (27 NOV 1788)

Patowmack, November 29th. I have to rent the ferry opposite Alexandria, lately occupied by Mr. Lowe, with the house and ground annexed. Susannah T. Hawkins. (4 DEC 1788)

An act is passed to encourage the destroying of wolves. (4 DEC 1788)

Lost between Annapolis and South River church, wrapped up in a piece of newspaper, about the sum of twenty eight pounds in gold. Reward [pencilled in margin, Daniel of St. Thomas Jenifer]. (4 DEC 1788)

John F. Mercer lost in the city a clouded cane, with a gold head, the workmanship of the head of gold of different colors, with a coat of arms engraved on the top and the motto *Non Nobis Solum*, the letters I.A. the initials of the maker's name stamped on the side. (12 FEB 1789)

The Patowmack Company urges its shareholders to pay for their shares. (12 FEB 1789)

William Grayson is elected senator from Virginia. (12 MAR 1789)

A poltergeist story is published from Fishkill, New York. (19 MAR 1789)

Along the Potomac River: **Extracts from the *Maryland Gazette*, 1728-1799**

Notice is given that a petition will be made to the court to mark the boundaries of a tract in Prince George's County, called *Landover*. Jonathan Simmons. (26 MAR 1789)

The horse *Ajax* will cover mares at the subscriber's plantation within five miles of the Alexandria ferry and ten miles of Piscataway. Francis Tolson [pencilled in margin, John Craggs]. (26 MAR 1789)

The horse *Venetian* will stand at Francis Tolson, Esq.'s plantation in Prince George's County. John Kirton is *Venetian's* jockey, and Thomas Coates is the trainer. (26 MAR 1789)

The horse *Hyder Alley* will stand this season at *Mt. Arrarat*, my dwelling plantation, six miles below Piscataway. Thomas Marshall. (16 APR 1789)

The ferry buildings at *Rock Hall* ferry are described. (16 APR 1789)

New York, April 7th. George Washington is elected President. (23 APR 1789)

For sale, part of the tract called *Harwood*, 596 acres, near Port Tobacco, the property of Mungo Muschett, taken for debt. [Many debtors and insolvents all through this year. — Eds.] (30 APR 1789)

An apothecary shop has opened in Annapolis, by Reverdy Ghiselin. (30 APR 1789)

New York, April 25th. George Washington arrives in New York. The venerable old gentleman at landing when the barge arrived, said "I have beheld him when he commanded the army, I saw him at the conclusion of the peace, retiring to his primeval habitation." (7 MAY 1789)

J.H. Stone, of Port Tobacco, wants to charter a ship for Europe, for tobacco. (7 MAY 1789)

Life estate of 150 acres is to be sold on May 27th; part of *Durham Freehold*, and two lots in Charles-Town, commonly called Port Tobacco, with improvements thereon, on which Mr. Henry Barnes now lives, the property of Henry Barnes to be sold to satisfy debts. (7 MAY 1789)

The plantation of the Rev. Addison has two stray steers. C. Thompson, overseer. (7 MAY 1789)

A lot in Charles-Town, commonly called Port Tobacco, on which Matthew Blair now lives, will be sold for debts. (28 MAY 1789)

To be sold on October 20th at the house occupied by Edward Jenkins, in Charles County, 180-acre tract of *Batchelor's Hope*. (11 JUN 1789)

Along the Potomac River: **Extracts from the *Maryland Gazette*,** 1728-1799

Alexandria, May 29th. James Craik, Sr. will take an apprentice in physick and surgery. (25 JUN 1789)

John F. Mercer wrote a pamphlet, "Introductory Discourse to An Argument in Support of the Payments Made of British Debts Into the Treasury of Maryland During the Late War." Copies 15 pence. (16 JUL 1789)

For Dumfries, including Newport, Richard Scott is collector of revenue [see list]. (13 AUG 1789)

On December 3rd, will be sold a seat of 400 acres on Zachia Swamp, 5 miles from Port Tobacco. John Hanson, Jr. (27 AUG 1789)

A 125-acre part of the tract called *Taylortown* will be sold at the dwelling of Nicholas Blacklock, Esq.; located 2 miles of Piscataway. (27 AUG 1789)

The partnership of Nicholas and Valentine Peers, on the 1st inst. [August], seek to settle debts. Nicholas Peers, Port Tobacco. (3 SEP 1789)

The estate of Capt. Thomas Dent, deceased, is to be sold. Includes slaves, furniture (also a mahogany bookcase). Elizabeth Dent, executrix. (3 SEP 1789)

The inhabitants of Charles Town, Charles County petition to lay out said town and ascertain lots and bounds, to open a street on the east side of Lot 4 on the town plot, bounding on the west. Ware's lot on the said plot is now of Charles Mankin [pencilled in margin, Dr. John Chapman]. (10 SEP 1789)

Charles Jones, Montgomery County, will petition to mark the bounds of tract *Clean Drinking.* (10 SEP 1789)

Port Tobacco. Dr. Gustavus R. Brown seeks a young gentleman who is well inclined to study medicine. (24 SEP 1789)

A petition is presented to the assembly for erecting a bridge (want further levy for it) over the eastern branch near the town of Bladensburg. (24 SEP 1789)

St. Mary's County. Found adrift in February last, at the mouth of Wicomico in Patowmack, a [batteau], 30' long, 7' wide, painted on the stern with lampblack the word "Maurlbourgh." Inquire of George Locke. (24 SEP 1789)

The Bladensburg races will be run on October 29th. Inquire of Mr. Thomas Rose. (24 SEP and 15 OCT 1789)

Rinaldo Johnson is forced to sell a part of *Brooke Court Manor* and part of tract *Joseph and Mary*, between 700 and 800 acres, because of having acted as security for Thomas

Along the Potomac River: **Extracts from the *Maryland Gazette*, 1728-1799**

Williams, deceased, tax collector, "to the hard condition of being obliged to answer for the failure, mismanagement and indiscretion of his principal." (15 OCT 1789)

William Craik is elected Burgess for Charles County, and George Digges is elected Burgess for Prince George's County. (15 OCT 1789)

Died, on the 16th, at *Blenheim*, Mrs. Grace Lee, relict of the Hon. Richard Lee, aged about 76 years. (29 OCT 1789)

Thomas Oston warns trespassers on land belonging to the Port Tobacco mill. (29 OCT 1789)

Being directed by the governor and council to dispose of property lately purchased for the use of the state, I will sell on November 16th, at the plantation of Nicholas Blacklock, near Piscataway, tracts near Bladensburg; on November 18th, at Port Tobacco, 54-acre tract called *Mankin's Venture*, 144-acre tract *Mankin's Folly*; in Charles County, near Port Tobacco, some Negroes, furniture and riding chair and harness. Three lots in Port Tobacco, #3, 5 and 6, with small tenements and three other lots in the town with large dwelling houses, late the property of Charles Mankin. On November 19th, at Port Tobacco, will be sold the 115-acre tract *Hawkins' Barrens*; 60-acre part of tract *Come by Chance*, adjacent to Port Tobacco, and two Negroes; 44-acre *Luckett's Benefit*; 186-acre part of *Moisditch*, near Port Tobacco, lately the property of Thomas Hussey Luckett, security of Mankin, etc. (5 NOV 1789)

Josias Hawkins died October 30th, at his seat in Charles County, in his 54th year [obituary continues]. (12 NOV 1789)

Piscataway. By virtue of a deed of trust from Win Jenkins, will be sold on December 7th at Piscataway, 51 acres, *Oxmon-Town*; 87 acres, *Strife*; 120 acres, *Maiden Bradley* — adjoining tracts are within 3 miles of Piscataway. Also, 8 acres adjacent to Piscataway, 2 lots in town, 10 horses, 14 head of black cattle, 38 hogs and 2 feather beds. Henry Hardy. (12 NOV 1789)

Long list of lands for sale for delinquent taxes for 1780, 1781, 1782. "No consideration, short of the payment, will prevent the sale." Rinaldo Johnson. The Oxen list includes 100-acre part of *Geeseborough Manor*, Thomas Bayne; 100-acre part of *Geeseborough Manor*, Thomas Bayne, Jr.; and another 100-acre part of the same, John Barrick; Rock Creek: 265-acre part of *Barbadoes*, William Conn; Piscataway: 172-acre part of *Swan Harbour*, John Addison Smith heirs; 100-acre part of *Lordship's Manor* rev. in Benedict Calvert; 150-acre part of *Lordship's Manor* rev. in Benedict Calvert and Jonas Galwith. Entire page of listings is signed by Henry Hardey, Sr. (12 NOV 1789)

All those who are indebted to Gustavus R. Scott are asked to settle. Payment can be made in wheat, corn or pork, at market price, or credit in any store in Port Tobacco. (19 NOV 1789)

Along the Potomac River: **Extracts from the *Maryland Gazette*, 1728-1799**

On Wednesday the 11th, St. John's College opened [long article]. (3 DEC 1789)

On Tuesday, January 5th, will be exposed for public sale in Port Tobacco town, a Negro carpenter and several Negro women and children. M.J. Stone, Gr. R. Brown, executors of Thomas Stone, Esq. (24 DEC 1789)

An act to continue the act passed June 1752, to prevent disabled and superannuated slaves from being set free, or the manumission of slaves by a last will and testament. (31 DEC 1789)

Daniel of St. Thomas Jenifer has a no trespassing notice on his property in South River, or Beard's Creek. (31 DEC 1789)

Fredericksburg, January 21st. About a fortnight since a dead cow supposed to be drowned by the preceding sudden fresh, was cast ashore a little about Falmouth, at this side of the river. She was skinned, opened and four perfect calves, of about 1 foot long were taken from her. (28 JAN 1790)

On February 22nd, will be sold near Port Tobacco, on the dwelling plantation of Walter Pye, 29 Negroes mortgaged by Thomas How Ridgate. (4 FEB 1790)

Debtors to the estate of the late Rev. Richard Brown, of Charles County, are asked to settle accounts. (4 FEB 1790)

A high bred horse is in great perfection, and horse *Hyder Ally* is standing this season at *Mount Arrarat*, the seat of Dr. Thomas Marshall, 6 miles below Piscataway. Peter Corneil, groom. (1 APR 1790)

The state house at Annapolis caught fire [details given]. (1 APR 1790)

The horse *Royal Gift* and [jack-ass] *Knight of Malta* are covering. (1 APR 1790)

J. Addison seeks the return of a lost pointer dog named *Ponto*, on Saturday last, from the subscriber living at Mr. Stevens' in Annapolis. (8 APR 1790)

Benjamin Ogle gives notice that he will mark contiguous tracts in Prince George's County: *Bell-Air, Woodcock's Range*, part of *Larkin's Forest, Ridgely's Addition*, and part of *Enfield Chase*. (8 APR 1790)

Port Tobacco. Died on the 2nd inst., at his seat on the Potomac River, in Charles County, in his forty-fifth year, the Hon. Robert Hanson Harrison, Esq., Chief Judge of the general court of the State of Maryland [prose continues]. (8 APR 1790)

Died, on Friday, March 26th, between the hours of 2 and 3 o'clock, in the 56th year of his age, Thomas How Ridgate, merchant, in Port Tobacco [obituary continues, and mentions he was a most merciful creditor]. (8 APR 1790)

Dr. Gustavus Brown offers for sale 15 to 20 slaves at his plantation near the Patuxent River, St. Mary's County, about 2 miles from the Queen-Tree. (15 APR 1790)

Dr. John Chapman has died at his house in Port Tobacco. (10 JUN 1790)

John Halkerston, Prince George's County, petitions for the relief of debts. (10 JUN 1790)

All indebted to the estate of the late Hon. Robert H. Harrison, Esq., are asked to bring in their accounts to Hooe & Harrison, in Alexandria, or to the subscriber. Walter H. Harrison. (17 JUN 1790)

Letter from Salem, New Jersey. Farmers are now cutting their hay without the use of rum. "In a few years we are in hopes it will be entirely out of use amongst the farmers here, as much as the practise of giving rum and wine at funerals is now, which is a practise much used till within a few years past, and now there is no such a thing seen at a burial in this county, these several years, and would be looked upon at this time to be scandalous piece of conduct (as it really is) to have strong drink handing about on such solemn occasions by people professing Christianity." (8 JUL 1790)

To be sold on order of the general court, at Port Tobacco, at the house of Mr. Thomas Crackles, on August 30th, a 195-acre tract called *Littleworth*; 415-acres, *Wilkerson's Throne*; and 55-acres part of *Thomason's Chance*. (22 JUL 1790)

At the house of Mr. John Beans, tavern keeper, in Piscataway, on September 1st, will be sold a 216-acre tract called *Exeter* where Mr. Nicholas Blacklock, Esq. now lives. (22 JUL 1790)

The subscriber will petition the assembly for a divorce from her husband, Thomas Boylan. Mary Boylan. (5 AUG 1790)

To be sold on August 23rd, at the house of the late Thomas How Ridgate, in Port Tobacco, the personal estate and goods appraised to £1600; several slaves, including 5 valuable house servants, 4 horses, one phaeton and harness, sulkey and harness, furniture. John Forbes, attorney for Elizabeth Ridgate. (5 AUG 1790)

To be sold on September 20th, at the dwelling of the late Robert Brent, Sr., near Newport: horses, oxen, bulls, sheep, furniture. Robert Brent, Executor. (12 AUG 1790)

Notley Young and George Digges are Executors for the estate of the late Daniel Carroll, Jr., of Montgomery County. (12 AUG 1790)

Along the Potomac River: **Extracts from the *Maryland Gazette*, 1728-1799**

An act of Congress is passed for providing for the enumeration of the inhabitants of the United States. (26 AUG 1790)

The subscriber will apply to the assembly for allowance to be made him from the public levy in Prince George's County, of certain hogsheads of tobacco which were lost out of Broad Creek Warehouse, and which he as inspector was obliged to make good to the owners. Zachariah Wade. (26 AUG 1790)

The sheriff will sell at the dwelling of Col. John Addison, near *Oxen Hill*, on September 8th, eight Negroes, to satisfy judgment in the suit of *John Hall vs. Addison and Wife*, administrators of Thomas Watkins, deceased. (2 SEP 1790)

A few days ago, died in Yorkshire, an old man supposed to be near 130 years old. He was born in Wales ... he well remembered Charles II ... he had one daughter when age 90 ... He had never accustomed himself to eat any breakfast. (16 SEP 1790)

By deed from Gerard Blackiston Causin, of Charles County, will be sold on December 30th, Negroes and a 918-acre tract on Patowmack River at the mouth of Port Tobacco Creek. Includes a very large genteel dwelling house, within 4 miles of Port Tobacco, in a good neighborhood. Apply to Alexander Hamilton, Piscataway. (23 SEP 1790)

A petition by sundry inhabitants of Prince George's County is sent to the Maryland Assembly to levy for building of a gaol and gaol yard. (7 OCT 1790)

P. Savary seeks the return of Negro named Antony who ran away from his plantation, 3 miles from the Alexandria Ferry, in Prince George's County. (14 OCT 1790)

To the House of Delegates were elected George Plater, Jr. and Philip Key from St. Mary's County, etc.; William Craik, John H. Stone, George Dent and John Parnham from Charles County; and Robert Bowie, Charles Clark, Walter Bowie and Fielder Bowie from Prince George's County. (21 OCT 1790)

Members of the Maryland Society of the Cincinnati will meet at Mann's Tavern on October 28th. William Smallwood. (21 OCT 1790)

John Petty & Co. has a store in Port Tobacco. (4 NOV 1790)

On Saturday morning, the 30th, departed this life after a short illness at *St. Bernard's*, in Charles County, in the 32nd year of her age, Mrs. Dorothy Brent, amiable consort of Robert Brent. (11 NOV 1790)

Died in this city, early in the morning of the 16th ult., in his 67th year, the honourable Daniel of St. Thomas Jenifer, Esq. A man so well known and distinguished by his country that an eulogium on his character is altogether unnecessary. We cannot, however, forbear to express our regret at the loss which the community at large, as well as his particular friends and connections have sustained by the death of this accomplished gentleman, citizen and friend — in an eminent degree he possessed every useful and social virtue, the many and important offices which he held under the former and present government were discharged with the highest reputation, and his benevolence, disinterestness, patriotism and attachment to the rights of man, were conspicuous during the whole course of a long active and well spent life. (18 NOV 1790)

Alexandria. Beer. I have just received a quantity of this highly esteemed Beer, which in order to accommodate the citizens of Annapolis, I will sell by the barrel or gallon. William Alexander. (25 NOV 1790)

An elegant chariot and a pair of bay geldings is for sale. Daniel Jenifer. (25 NOV 1790)

Charles County. The subscriber has for sale, in Port Tobacco, medicine and books of the late Dr. John Chapman, with the necessary instruments and shop-furniture. To be seen at Col. Stone's store. Henry H. Chapman. (2 DEC 1790)

A plea to forbid the firing of guns in the streets at Christmas. (9 DEC 1790)

January 21st. All persons having claims to the estate of the late Daniel of St. Thomas Jenifer are asked to present them. Daniel Jenifer, Sr. and Daniel Jenifer, Jr. (27 JAN 1791)

We hear that Thomas Johnson and Daniel Carroll, Esq., of this state, and Dr. Stewart, of Alexandria, are the three commissioners appointed by the President to lay off the District of ten miles square for the permanent seat of the government, agreeably in his directions. (3 FEB 1791)

January 25th. To be sold, at Ware's Tavern, *Allen's Fresh*, Charles County, on March 14th, 20 Negroes and furniture. Philip Richard Fendall, Alexandria. (10 FEB 1791)

To be sold, March 7th, at Dumfries, the noted thoroughbred horse *Rockingham*. Lawrence Taliaferro. (24 FEB 1791)

Nathaniel Hagan seeks the return of a runaway named Henny. She has a sister named Daphne, lately set free by the Rev. Mason Weems, of Anne Arundel County, where she formerly lived. It is supposed her sister has passed her for a free woman. (3 MAR 1791)

The horse *Royal Gift* and [jack-ass] *Knight of Malta* are standing at stud at *Mount Vernon*. Inquire of Anthony Whiting, manager. (17 MAR 1791)

Sotterly, March 6th. Ran away on the 19th of February, a likely young Negro man named Joe. George Plater. (17 MAR 1791)

Along the Potomac River: **Extracts from the *Maryland Gazette*, 1728-1799**

Dumfries, March 8th. Negro Frank is committed to the gaol at Dumfries. He says he belongs to Charles Carroll of Carrollton, Maryland. Inquire of Colin Campbell, keeper of the said gaol. (17 MAR 1791)

Early on Friday morning last, this city was honoured by the arrival of the PRESIDENT, attended by only his private secretary Major Jackson. He was expected on Thursday. The vessel, which contained the chief treasure of America, did not enter the river Severn until ten p.m., on a dark tempestuous night, she struck on a bar, or point, within about a mile of the city, and although she made a signal of distress, it was impossible before daylight to go to her relief. The guardian angel of American was still watchful, and we are happy in assuring our countrymen that the health of the dearest friend has not been at all affected by the accident far more distressing to those who were apprised, or rather apprehensive of his situation, than to himself. At ten the same day he visited the college ... on Saturday his presence enlivened a ball, at which was exhibited everything which this little city contains of beauty and elegance ... On Sunday, he rode out of town at eight on an arduous patriotic journey southward. (31 MAR 1791)

Port Tobacco, March 7th. To be sold on June 15th, on the premises, that valuable seat of land, the property and place of residence of the late Daniel of St. Thomas Jenifer, known and distinguished by the name of *Stepney*, Anne Arundel County, 4 miles from Annapolis, containing 750 acres. There are on the premises a small framed dwelling, kitchen, stable, new large barn, orchards, from which may be made, in a favorable year, 15,000 gallons of cider. Beautifully situated on the road from Upper Marlborough to Annapolis, within one mile of the South River, binding on a creek. Also 229 acres, part of a tract called *Puddington*, or *Puddington Harbor*, on the South River, one mile away. Also, 100 acres, part of a tract called *Townhill*. (14 APR 1791, *Stepney* again on 9 AUG 1792)

Phillip R. Fendall, of Alexandria, seeks the return of a runaway Negro named Marcus. (2 JUN 1791)

On August 20th, will be rented the noted farm called *Gisborough*, lying at the mouth of the eastern branch, opposite the Federal city. The dwelling and outhouses are sufficient for the accommodation of a large family. John Addison, Jr. (30 JUN 1791)

President Washington pointed out places for the Capitol and Executive department buildings. (7 JUL 1791)

Port Tobacco. $100 reward offered. On Saturday, August 13th, between 10 and 11 at night, as my Negro man Benjamin was going from this place to *Haberdeventure*, as soon as he reached the top of the hill, commonly called *Theobald's Hill*, ½ mile distant from this town, he was met and accosted by a white man who had on a dark coat and rode a small black horse. The man stabbed him. H. Stone. (7 JUL 1791)

Along the Potomac River: **Extracts from the *Maryland Gazette,* 1728-1799**

References are found to the City of Washington, in the territory of Columbia. (15 SEP 1791)

On the 6th ult., at Sweet Springs, Botetourt County, Virginia, Walter Stone, of Charles County, merchant, departed this life. (6 OCT 1791)

According to the census, Virginia has 747,610 population; Alexandria 2,748, and Fredericksburg 1,485. Other towns listed, and a breakout by category. (13 OCT 1791)

Richard H. Courts offers for sale 20 Negroes at Broad Creek, Prince George's County. (20 OCT 1791)

On Monday last, the Honorable George Plater was unanimously elected Governor of Maryland, and the Hon. Henry Lee was elected governor of Virginia. (10 NOV 1791)

John Cragge, of Londontown, is sailing for England in March or April, and will order horses for gentlemen. (17 NOV 1791)

An act is passed in the assembly for erecting a bridge over the Patowmack River. Also, an act is passed to enable justices of Charles County to order a levy for repairs of the courthouse and to build a record office. (5 JAN 1792)

A 562-acre part of a tract called *Rozier's Refuge* is for sale on Port Tobacco Creek, about two miles below the town. It is on navigable water and near the Patowmack River, not far distant from the city of Washington. Anything may be readily brought to and from this place, it is near Nanjemoy on Patowmack. This place must be the harbour for the navy of the United States ... a large and commodious dwelling house with two brick chimneys on each end, large kitchen with good brick chimney, etc. Also for sale, another 17-acre tract, called *Tomsonton*, which adjoins. Thomas Contee. (5 JAN 1792)

On Friday, the 10th, died in this city, his Excellency George Plater, Esq., Governor of this state ... "In private life, he lived an amiable, and died an honest man." Details of funeral procession to *Sotterly* for burial. (16 FEB 1792)

George Digges will apply to the assembly to mark the bounds of *Clarkson's Purchase, Darketh, The Addition, Hanson's Progress, Addison's Folly, Frankland,* and *Warburton Manor.* (1 MAR 1792)

On Sunday evening, the 4th, departed this life, age 32, Mrs. Mary Stone, amiable consort of the Hon. John Hoskins Stone, Esq., of this city ... "her white robed innocence is contrasted by the driven snow," ... "how vain the lustre of her spritely eye" ... (8 MAR 1792)

The horse *Hyder Ally*, now the property of Peter Emmerson, of Herring Bay, stands this season at the seat of Richard Chew, Esq. (22 MAR 1792)

Along the Potomac River: **Extracts from the *Maryland Gazette*, 1728-1799**

An advertisement for Mr. Bowen's WAXWORKS, now showing in Annapolis. The display figures include "the unfortunate Baron Trenck who was confined to a Dungeon upward of ten years at Magdebourg in Prussia. He is standing on his tombstone in real chains of great weight — he appears pale and wild with despair." This exhibit has been honored with the company of the President of the United States and his family. (22 MAR 1792)

Thomas Sim Lee is elected governor. The Hon. Richard T. Lowndes is chosen senator in room of Hon. William Smallwood, deceased. (5 APR 1792)

Port Tobacco. John Alexander, hatter, from Philadelphia, advertises he has for sale ladies and mens hats, and white hats for the summer. (19 APR 1792)

George Plater and John Rousby Plater seek to settle the estate of George Plater. (19 APR 1792)

David Stuart and Notley Young are directors of the Patowmack Company. (26 APR 1792)

Port Tobacco. The partnership of Adam, Craik & Co. is dissolved by the death of Mr. Craik. Debts are to be settled. George Clements. (31 MAY 1792)

$12 reward offered for the return of Pee, a dark Mulatto, about 23 years of age, short and well set. He quitted my service about the 10th of April last, on pretense of petitioning for his freedom in the general court, and has been seen in Annapolis; had on a blue short coat, striped jacket, cotton overalls, shoes and stockings, but probably may change his dress, and endeavor to pass as a free man by the name of Butler, Shorter or Pembroke. Inquire of Henry Rozer, *Notley Hall*, Prince George's County. (21 JUN 1792)

Agreeable to the order of the orphans' court, will be sold at Port Tobacco on September 15th, from 50 to 100 hogsheads of tobacco; also at the late dwelling of William Smallwood, deceased, on Mattawoman, on November 20th, will be sold the whole personal estate, Negroes, horses, black cattle, sheep and hogs, furniture, including two elegant side tables for the reception of plate, a set of mahogany dining tables and chairs, a quantity of the most fashionable solid and French plate, elegant new coach with harness for four horses, corn, wheat, etc. William Craik, attorney in fact for Priscilla Hebbert Smallwood, Executrix. (26 JUL 1792)

For sale at the house of Thomas Crackles, Port Tobacco, on August 21st, 42 acres, part of that tract called *Mooreditch Resurveyed*, within 3 miles of Port Tobacco, to satisfy debts owed by Thomas Luckett. James Simmes, sheriff. (2 AUG 1792)

Along the Potomac River: Extracts from the *Maryland Gazette*, 1728-1799

WANTED. An industrious mechanic, capable of teaching psalmody in its different parts, who is willing to act as clerk and sexton to a Protestant Episcopal Church. Apply to the printing office. (13 SEP 1792)

July 27th. George Mason, of *Gunston Hall*, petitions the justices of Allegany County that he may mark a tract there called *Cove*. (13 SEP 1792)

Woodyard, August 28th. For sale in Upper Marlborough, on November 8th, twenty Negroes. Hannah West, Executrix of Stephen West, deceased. (20 SEP 1792)

Dr. Clagett is consecrated Bishop in New York. (4 OCT 1792)

Copies of the plan for the City of Washington are for sale. (4 OCT 1792)

The sheriff of Prince George's County has a Mulatto lad, about 10 years old, named Tom, who says he belongs to Daniel McCarty of Fairfax County. The owner is requested to collect him. (4 OCT 1792)

Strayed or stolen from *Haberdeventure*, a gelding. M.J. Stone. (11 OCT 1792)

John Tayloe will offer for sale in Fredericksburg on December 17th, 200 slaves. (11 OCT 1792)

For sale, a 510-acre tract of land, within 5 miles of Port Tobacco, called *Cool Springs*. Inquire of Alexander Hamilton, Piscataway. (18 OCT 1792)

Henry Rozer seeks the return of a runaway Mulatto named Tom, age 27, by trade a carpenter, "very fond of his hair wool and generally has it queued and tied with eel skin." He ran off with a Mulatto named Pee, who was brought back in August but ran away again. (18 OCT 1792)

William Courts died at *Milton Hill*, Charles County, on September 28th. He left a wife and three children [long obituary continues]. Betsey Courts, Executrix. (25 OCT 1792)

For sale on January 15th, at *Warburton*, the personal estate of George Digges, Esq., deceased. Included are slaves, stock, oxen, two mules from *Knight of Malta*, furniture, chariot with harness for four horses. Notley Young, Clement Hill and John Fitzgerald, Executors. (3 JAN 1793)

Died in childbed, at Port Tobacco, on December 13th, Mrs. Anne Davis, relict of [Ebenezer?] Davis, postmaster of that place. (10 JAN 1793)

Robert Brent is authorized to adjust the accounts of the estate of G. Digges, and asks that letters be directed to him at Mr. Young's in Washington. (10 JAN 1793)

Along the Potomac River: **Extracts from the *Maryland Gazette*, 1728-1799**

The lighthouse at Cape Henry, Virginia, is now completed; lamps were lit for the first time on the night of November 17th. (17 JAN 1793)

A list of letters in the post offices in Port Tobacco, *Allen's Fresh*, and Chaptico appear for the first time. [Allen's Fresh is near West Hatton]. (17 JAN 1793)

J.H. Stone posts a notice against trespassing on his plantation *Stepney*, on Beard's Creek. (31 JAN 1793)

Land is for sale in Prince William County, between 5 and 6,000 acres near and adjacent to Occoquan Run, and will be laid off in lots. Includes a mill seat and situation for a furnace. Apply to William Beale, Jr., at Tayloe's Neabsco furnace. John Tayloe, Presley Thornton. (21 FEB 1793)

Joseph Clark proposed to establish a circulating library in Annapolis. (28 FEB 1793)

Annapolis, February 18th. On Friday last, one of the Annapolis packets en route to Baltimore overset at the mouth of Magothy River. Nine people drowned including Benjamin Buckland, cabinet maker. (28 FEB 1793)

The horse *Paymaster* is at stud at *Stepney*, on South River; imported last summer from England by Col. Stone. John Craggs [pencilled in margin: Col. Stone]. (21 MAR 1793)

The horse *Hyder Alley* is standing at the seat of Osborn Harwood, near Samuel Rawlings. Richard Jones, groom. P. Emmerson. (28 MAR 1793)

Alexander Hamilton, of Piscataway, says collection of debts due the firm John Glassford & Co., at their late stores at Elk Ridge Landing and Annapolis are to be paid now to him. (4 APR 1793)

At *Brookfield*, in Prince George's County, departed this life, aged 61, Mrs. Sarah Contee, amiable consort of Thomas Contee, Esq., and daughter of the late Benjamin Fendall, Esq. [obituary continues]. (4 APR 1793)

The horse *Traveller* and [jack-ass] *Knight of Malta* are at stud at *Mount Vernon*. Anthony Whiting. (4 APR 1793)

Piscataway. The subscriber seeks employment of a bartender at his tavern at this place. Edward Edelen. (2 MAY 1793)

J.H. Stone will offer for sale on the 18th in Annapolis, household furniture, servants, and a few dry goods and hardware. Also, 200 hogsheads of good Maryland Patowmack tobacco. (9 MAY 1793)

$4 Reward. John McAtee, of Broad Creek, Prince George's County, seeks the return of a runaway Negro named Sall, "she calls herself Sall Short" .... (30 MAY 1793, see 20 JUN 1793)

A story having been propagated, injurious to me, that the French minister [Genet?] had met with insult at my house; justice to myself obliges me to declare, in this public manner, that so far from there being any foundation for this story, the minister did not put up at, nor was he in, my house during the short time he remained in this town on his route from the southward toward Philadelphia. John Suter, Georgetown. (30 MAY 1793)

The convention of the Episcopal Church of Maryland met at Easton on May 23rd ... Bishop Clagett presided ... Walter D. Addison, of Prince George's County, was made deacon. (6 JUN 1793)

$12 Reward. Edward Stonestreet seeks the return of a runaway Negro woman named Vick, age 17 years or thereabouts, and her child Lis, age about 12 months, from his house near Port Tobacco. (20 JUN 1793, see 18 JUL 1793)

The sheriff of Anne Arundel County, has Sall who belongs to John McAtee, of Prince George's County. (20 JUN 1793, see 30 MAY 1793)

A peculiar animal has been seen in the mountains of Carolina; biting people, between 12 to 15 feet high; of human form, but a head as big as the body; head contracts like that of a tortoise, etc. Called *Yahoo*, or *Chickly-Cudly* by the Indians. (27 JUN 1793)

An advertisement written by Italian nobleman almost 100 years old, "Sure and Certain Methods of Attaining a Long and Healthy Life," is for sale at the printers. W.L. Weems. (11 JUL 1793)

E. Valette & Co., is starting in Baltimore a circulating library of 2,500 volumes. (11 JUL 1793)

The sheriff of Anne Arundel County has Vick and child belonging to Mr. Stonestreet. (18 JUL 1793, see 20 JUN 1793)

Anthony Addison petitions the court to mark a tract called *Barnaby Manor*. (1 AUG 1793)

Betsey Courts offers for sale Negroes, stock, etc. of William Courts, deceased, at *Milton Hill*, Charles County. (1 AUG 1793)

The son of Joseph Clark, architect, is dead. (5 SEP 1793)

Along the Potomac River: **Extracts from the *Maryland Gazette*, 1728-1799**

The Vestry of St. John's Parish, commonly called King George, in Prince George's County, will petition to get the right in behalf of the parish to three acres of land whereon the lower chapel stands, commonly called Acque-Creek Chapel. Charles Tippeth, Registrar. (12 SEP 1793)

The cornerstone of the United States capitol was laid on September 18th [further details given]. (26 SEP 1793)

Frederick Stone, the only son of the late Thomas Stone, Esq., died in Princeton on the 4th, after a short illness [obituary continues]. (26 SEP 1793)

For sale on Friday, October 4th, at Mr. Richard Lanham's Tavern, between Piscataway and Upper Marlborough, 20 Negroes, furniture, stock, and a lease for one life on a 160-acre tract known by the name of *His Lordship's Kindness*; to satisfy debt from Charles Maddox to Nicholas Blacklock. (26 SEP 1793)

At *Blenheim*, Charles County, on the 4th, at 7:15 p.m., in his 18th year, Russell Lee, only surviving son of the late Philip Thomas Lee, Esq., has died from a fall from his horse [obituary continues]. (3 OCT 1793)

The estate of the late Thomas Crackels, of Charles County, is to be settled. Mary Crackels, Executrix. (3 OCT 1793)

By decree of the chancellor of Maryland, will be sold on December 19th, at King's Store, on Broad Creek, Prince George's County, 30-acre part of *Friendship*; 13-acre *Carricfurgus*, 49-acre part of *Low's Discovery*. Above lands are adjoining the lands of Henry Rozer, Esq., on the head of Broad Creek, and from their contiguity to the river Patowmack, and the flourishing town of Alexandria, must daily rise in value. (24 OCT 1793)

All those with claims against Edward Magruder, late of Prince George's County, deceased, whose debts will be sold to pay, are asked to present claims. Overton Carr. (24 OCT 1793)

On October 15th, departed this life at his seat near Port Tobacco, Mr. John Hanson, Sr., age 84; he left a very worthy woman languishing on her sickbed ... [married 61 years; obituary continues]. (7 NOV 1793)

Between 20 and 30 hogsheads of tobacco, of the estate of the late William Smallwood, Esq., will be sold at Port Tobacco on the 25th. Priscilla Smallwood. (7 NOV 1793)

Anyone who will undertake repairs to that part of the Stadt House, approved for use of the General Court, according to the designs and plans of Joseph Clark, architect, are asked to send in their bids. (19 DEC 1793)

Along the Potomac River: **Extracts from the *Maryland Gazette*, 1728-1799**

To be sold at Port Tobacco, on January 27th, part of two tracts: *Hawkins' Barrons* and *Sicamy* [Sycamore]; 80 acres, about 2 miles from Port Tobacco, and woodlands. For benefit of creditors of Francis Ware, Esq. (26 DEC 1793)

On Tuesday, the 21st, at Mr. Ross' tavern in Bladensburgh, will be sold the slaves of the estate of George Digges, Esq., deceased. (9 JAN 1794)

Peregrine Fitzhugh holds a lottery. A list of prize lands includes a dwelling plantation. (9 JAN 1794)

J. Halkerston has opened a tavern in Upper Marlborough, formerly occupied by Mr. Samuel Hamilton. (16 JAN 1794)

Sixpence reward is offered for the return of a runaway in August — Thomas Nevitt, an apprentice in the carpenters and joiners business, who has ever since constantly rejected my pressing solicitations to return. John Mahoney, carpenter. (23 JAN 1794)

A petition will be made to the Charles County court to mark the bounds of the tracts *Friendship*, *Run at a Venture*, and *Laurel Branch*. Thomas H. Marshall and Thomas Marshall. (23 JAN 1794)

Letters remaining in the post office at Upper Marlborough include one for Henry Rozer, Esq. (30 JAN 1794)

A proposal is detailed for the Portly Corps of militia. No one is to be under 220 pounds. (27 FEB 1794)

The Great Seal of Maryland is made. (27 FEB 1794)

A sale will be held at Butler Edelen's tavern, in Piscataway, on March 22nd, of a 50-acre part of a tract *East End*, of Edelen's *Hogpen Enlarged*. Sheriff. (6 MAR 1794)

The horse *High Flyer*, the property of John Craggs, is standing this season. (13 MAR 1794)

For Rent. A house and lot in Port Tobacco, formerly occupied by Dr. Warren. It has good gardens and a spring that can be made convenient to it. [I.E. Davis, pencilled in margin]. (27 MAR 1794)

John Francis Mercer resigns. A letter, dated April 13th, Marlborough, notes "extensive indisposition in my family delayed my attendance at Congress until a late period in the present session; increased illness recalled me suddenly, and will prevent my return..." He resigns his seat as Representative of the third Maryland district. (4 APR 1794)

John Addison, Jr. applies to the court to mark a tract called *Gisborough*. (4 APR 1794)

John Rousby Plater and Richard Smith apply to the court in Prince George's County to mark tracts called *Bachelor's Harbour* and *Swan Harbour*. (8 MAY 1794)

Verse on the death of the amiable and much lamented Miss Mary [Blackburn], of *Rippon Lodge*, Virginia. (22 MAY 1794)

For sale, on June 17th, a tract called *Blue Plains*, and a smaller one adjoining it called *Addison's Goodwill*, in Prince George's County, containing 500 acres. Late the property of George Fraser Hawkins, deceased, and now in the possession of Mr. William Bayley. Includes a dwelling, kitchen, meat house and dairy, tobacco house and barn. There is on another part of the land a tenement consisting of a dwelling, at present operated as a tavern, at which the ferry to Alexandria is kept. Sale at the tavern. William Kilty, trustee. (22 MAY 1794, and 13 NOV 1794)

Claims against the estate of the late Robert Brent, of Charles County, to be settled. Robert Brent, Executor. (22 MAY 1794)

John Craggs, of London-Town, offers for sale a mare and filly. (12 JUN 1794)

John Mandeville, of Alexandria, seeks the return of a runaway named Stephen, "sometimes called by his connections Stephen Bradley," a black man, likely plausible fellow, rather of a shining black ... sometimes preaches. (17 JUL 1794)

The sale of the tract *Blue Plains* to Nathaniel Washington is to be approved by the court. (17 JUL 1794)

Sixpence Reward. Ran away from Jacob Dodson, near Port Tobacco, on January 1st, an apprentice boy about 18 years old, named John Gray. (17 JUL 1794)

Edward Henry Calvert, near Upper Marlborough, seeks the return of a runaway Negro named Ned. (14 AUG 1794)

A camel is on exhibit in Annapolis. (16 OCT 1794; pictured 2 JUL 1795)

The inhabitants of Charles-Town, in Charles County, will petition the court to pass a law for a market in the said town. (23 OCT 1794)

Warren Dent died in Charles County on October 24th, in the 50th year of his age [obituary continues]. (30 OCT 1794)

Subscriptions are solicited for a novel by a citizen of Maryland, called "Maria, The Triumph of Perseverence." (6 NOV 1794)

On Monday last, John Hoskins Stone was elected governor of Maryland in the place of Thomas Sim Lee. (20 NOV 1794)

Along the Potomac River: Extracts from the *Maryland Gazette*, 1728-1799

The commencement at St. John's College. Oration by graduate John Carlyle Herbert, "On the Advantages of the Study of History." (20 NOV 1794)

The sale of the personal property of the late Samuel Hanson, Esq., of Charles County, will be held on December 26th. Henry H. Chapman, Esq., Executor. (20 NOV 1794)

John Addison is declared an insolvent debtor. (19 FEB 1795)

To be sold by N. Blacklock, for payment of debt from Benjamin Cawood: 16 Negroes, furniture, etc., at Bartholomew Carrico's tavern in Charles County, about 3 miles below Piscataway, on the road from there to Bryantown and Port Tobacco. (19 FEB 1795)

Mr. John Craggs is living at the South River ferry, near Annapolis. (19 FEB 1795)

The creditors of the estate of the late Gen. Smallwood, are to gather at Port Tobacco on March 19th, to petition for the sale of such of his lands to meet his debts. (5 MAR 1795)

The horse *High Flyer*, property of John Craggs, stands at South River Ferry, 4 miles from Annapolis. (24 MAR 1795)

The partnership of John Dabney & George Clements, in their store at Port Tobacco under the firm of George Clements & Co., is dissolved. (2 APR 1795)

The estate of the late Henry Digges, of Charles County, is to be settled. J. Digges and F. Digges. (21 MAY 1795)

An act for a bridge over Patowmack is approved. Books are open for subscriptions at Mrs. Suter's in Georgetown. Timothy Palmer, an artist eminently distinguished by the bridges he has lately built over the Merrimack River in Massachusetts, and the Piscataqua in New Hampshire is drawing plans for the bridge. (4 JUN 1795)

John H. Stone, of Annapolis, is selling part of a water lot in Port Tobacco. It includes a large wooden house with piazza [further description given] on it, and a large two-story dwelling, stable; also a tract about 3 or 4 miles of Port Tobacco of 400 acres. Apply to Humphrey Barnes, in Port Tobacco. (18 JUN 1795)

John Addison, Jr. will petition the court to mark the tract of *Gisborough Manor*. (2 JUL 1795)

The post office in Piscataway is mentioned. (16 JUL 1795)

For sale on September 19th, at the courthouse in Port Tobacco, will be 7,000 pounds of Gen. Smallwood's tobacco. (27 AUG 1795)

H.J. Stier has rented the tract *Strawberry Hill* near Annapolis. (10 SEP 1795)

To be sold at Mr. Koome's tavern in Piscataway, for debt due Joseph N. Baynes, of £2310, a 147-acre tract; *Wade's Adventure*, 218 acres; *Craft*, 37 acres, and *Ross Common*, 100 acres; contiguous to the town of Piscataway, on navigable water. (1 OCT 1795)

Francis Digges is elected to the Assembly for Charles County, and Edward Calvert for Prince George's County. (15 OCT 1795)

On January 2nd will be sold three lots in Port Tobacco, consisting of two acres adjoining the courthouse lot, in a square, fronting the streets all around. Four houses on it, two of which are taverns. Three other lots, 186 acres, five miles from Port Tobacco, 300 acres eight miles from Port Tobacco and Piscataway, and 170 acres in [Zachia] Swamp. Also slaves. Inquire of Charles Mankin for details. (29 OCT 1795)

John Hesselius, of *Primrose Hill* near Annapolis, has a stray mare. (29 OCT 1795)

John H. Stone is re-elected governor of Maryland. (12 NOV 1795)

Mr. Tayloe's horse *Grey Diomed*, will stand at *Mount Air*, near Piscataway. Inquire of Edward Edelin or Francis Tolson. (19 NOV 1795)

Col. John Addison's trustees will sell at Mrs. Suter's, in Georgetown, the property of John Addison; including a part of *Hawkins and Beatty's Addition to Georgetown*. Also on December 15th, at the house of John Addison, in Charles County, personal property: 12 slaves, 12 horses, 1 coachee and harness; hogs, ox, 2 carts, plough, 5 featherbeds, and furniture. William Baker, trustee. (19 NOV 1795)

John Brent petitions the court to mark his land called *Lynsay's Survey*. (24 DEC 1795)

An act is passed respecting the tract claimed by Thomas Digges, Esq., of Great Britain. (31 DEC 1795)

John Addison, Jr., will petition the court to mark the bounds of the tract *Gisborough Manor*. (11 FEB 1796)

The horse *High Flyer* is standing at stud at South River Ferry. John Craggs. (19 MAY 1796)

$16 Reward for the return of a dark bay horse stolen from Notley Young's *Forest Plantation*, branded "NY." Inquire of Thomas Soape, living at said plantation. (19 MAY 1796)

Advertisement for the proposed construction of a Flying Ark by Charles Sefton. (16 JUN 1796)

The creditors of John Alexander, late hatter, in Port Tobacco, are to bring in their claims to the subscriber living near Bean-town, in Charles County. William Hays, Sr., for Rachel Alexander, now Hays, Executrix. (23 JUN 1796)

Property of the late Thomas How Ridgate, in Charles-Town, Charles County, commonly called Port Tobacco, will be sold on August 16th: Lot 1 fronts south on the square, 70 feet where the courthouse stands, and 500 feet on St. George's Street, the principal entry to the town from the north. In the angle of said square and street stands a well-built framed house fronting south, 40'x28', two stories high with 2 brick chimneys at the end and dry airy brick cellar, the size of the house, with 2 fireplaces. The first story is a large store ... four rooms and passage upstairs ... house has piazzas and platforms on the north, south, and part of west end. On northeast of house is framed kitchen ... washhouse, etc. Behind is garden, 300 feet square. Lot 2 is 1-acre lot fronting St. Andrew's Street, for 140 feet. Has house. Lot 3 is 3-acres fronting St. Andrew's Street with unfinished house. (23 JUN 1796)

For sale on July 2nd, at Port Tobacco, the tract called *St. Matthews*, 204 acres, late the property of the Bishop of Chester, located 5 or 6 miles from Port Tobacco. (7 JUL 1796)

For sale, on July 4th, at Chaptico, St. Mary's County, part of *Chaptico Manor*. Inquire of William Marbury, agent for the state of Maryland. (7 JUL 1796)

Mrs. Eleanor Chapman died at *Green Hill* on July 20th, in her 29th year, the consort of Major Henry [Henley] Chapman ... youngest daughter of the late Samuel Hanson, Esq. [obituary continues]. (4 AUG 1796)

A petition to open a public road from Bean-Town to Charlestown, commonly called Port Tobacco. (29 SEP 1796)

Letters remaining in the post office at Piscataway include one for Mrs. Mary Hesselius, *Oxen Hill*; Capt. William Lyles, Broad Creek; and Miss Diggs, *Warburton*. Isidore Hardey, postmaster. (13 OCT 1796)

Francis Digges is elected to the House of Delegates. (20 OCT 1796)

Carlisle Fairfax Whiting, of Alexandria, graduated from St. John's College on October 21st, but was prevented by indisposition from taking a part in the public exercises of the day. (27 OCT 1796)

An act to make valid the sales of land made by Daniel of St. Thomas Jenifer while Agent for the State of Maryland. (5 JAN 1797)

Along the Potomac River: **Extracts from the *Maryland Gazette*, 1728-1799**

John Hesselius complains of trespassing at *Primrose Hill*, near Annapolis. Also, he offers for sale 686 acres, located 2 miles from Annapolis, on which is a commodious brick two-story house, 4 rooms on a floor, new brick kitchen adjoining, new stable, garden with fruit trees, etc. (5 JAN 1797)

Thomas G. Addison petitions to mark a tract in Prince George's County called *Prevention Enlarged*. (9 FEB 1797)

A portrait of George Washington has been commissioned by the Massachusetts legislature for the new state house. (9 FEB 1797)

Mr. Hesselius petitions the court to mark a tract in Anne Arundel County called *Young's Inn*. (9 FEB 1797)

A letter of George Washington seeks the whereabouts of forged letters appearing in 1777, said to have been in a portmanteau in the care of a Mulatto named Billy Lee, said to have been captured at Fort Lee. Seven letters [dates given], including one of 24 JUN 1776 to Martha Washington. (23 MAR 1797)

All persons indebted to the estate of John [Halkerston], late of Prince George's County, deceased, are asked to make payment. Elizabeth [Halkerston], Executrix. (6 APR 1797)

Shares in the Patowmack Company will be for sale on the third Monday in June ... at the house of Mr. John Gadsby, in Alexandria ... (4 MAY 1797)

J.H. Stone, of Annapolis, seeks to hire a single man who writes a good hand, understands accounts, and can teach reading, writing and arithmetic. (1 JUN 1797)

The horse *High Flyer* is covering mares at South River Ferry. John Craggs. (15 JUN 1797)

M.V. Stone offers for sale lands in Charles County: *The Dernier Resort*, 372 acres, 2½ miles from Mattawoman Creek; *Hawthorn*, 400 acres, lies on Port Tobacco Run, has several elegant sites for building, commanding a prospect of the village of Port Tobacco, the meanders of the creek, and range of hills ...; part of *Siccaney*, 104 acres ... one mile from Port Tobacco; *Equality*, my dwelling place, 640 acres of level land, about 2 miles from the mouth of Port Tobacco Creek. Lot and neat new house in Port Tobacco. I will also sell to humane masters several slaves. (15 JUN 1797)

October 1st. Mr. S. Love informs the gentlemen of the turf of Maryland that Mr. Tayloe's celebrated horse *Grey Diomed* will stand the ensuing season at his seat called *Salisbury*, in Loudoun County, near Alexandria, in Virginia. (5 OCT 1797)

Along the Potomac River: **Extracts from the *Maryland Gazette*, 1728-1799**

Lost, on the race ground near this city, on Tuesday last, a small French gold watch, single chased case, markers name and number unknown, a part of the enamel at the windup hole is broken off, marked on the end of the pendant, "MD," and has a pinchbeck seal and charm. Deliver to Mr. William Smallwood in Annapolis who offers 2 guineas reward. (5 OCT 1797)

Members of the House of Delegates: from Charles County, includes Henry H. Chapman; from Prince George's County, includes Thomas G. Addison and Charles Calvert. (12 OCT 1797)

Will be sold for a term of years at the subscriber's plantation, on November 28th, a parcel of valuable Negroes, horses, cows, plantation utensils, seine, batteau, sailing yawl, etc. John Hesselius. Will rent plantation. (16 NOV 1797)

$50 Reward, for Negro Jack, 5'9" ... has a remarkable scar on the top of his foot, but I forget whether left or right; he carried with him a greenish colored great coat of elastic cloth, with buff cuffs and cape, a white cashimer vest and breeches, a brown cloth vest and calico vest ... Negro likely belonged to the estate of Thomas Stone, in Charles County ... Inquire of Travers Daniel, Jr., Stafford County. (11 JAN 1798)

Bushrod Washington is appointed commissioner for the treaty with the Cherokees. (25 JAN 1798)

Remedy for hydrophobia is published. (5 APR 1798)

On February 10th, a Negro man was commited to the Kent County jail, who says he belongs to a Mr. Law, of the Federal City, and calls himself Esquire. Benjamin Hatcheson, sheriff. (10 MAY 1798)

Song of *Mount Vernon* published. As sung at the theatre by Mrs. Douglass, with universal applause. Words by Mr. McGrath. (24 MAY 1798)

> *Let Europe be proud of its seats so imperial,*
> *Its kingdoms, its cities, its palaces fair,*
> *And boast that all Nature her treasures doth there fill*
> *To cherish the senses of monarchs so rare.*
> *As thus each vain traveller his home makes the most of,*
> *In praising Mount Vernon I'm sure I'm not wrong,*
> *Mount Vernon containing what thrones cannot boast of*
> *Dear Liberty's guardian — the theme of my song.*
>
> *Be aristocrats vain of their high sounding titles,*
> *Their dukedoms, their lordships, their marquisites grand,*
> *All raised by devouring the honest mans vitals,*
> *By fraud and suppression thru slavery's land;*

Along the Potomac River: **Extracts from the *Maryland Gazette*, 1728-1799**

> *For me truly blessed with republican spirit,*
> *I'll sing of Mount Vernon, for there doth belong,*
> *One matchless in glory and each godlike merit,*
> *I mean the great Washington! — the theme of my song.*

The letters remaining in the post office at Port Tobacco include one for Henry Rozier, Esq., *Naucliff Hall*. (19 JUL 1798)

For sale, on October 18th, four or 500 acres in Frederick County, part of *Monocacy Manor* ... and on the 26th, that very excellent and beautifully situated farm in Charles County lying immediately upon the Patowmack River and bounded on one side by Chickamuxon Creek, containing 579 acres, lies about 15 miles from Alexandria and 6 from Dumfries ... improvements suitable for a tenant ... belonging to the estate of the late major-general [William] Smallwood. Inquire of John Campbell and Henry H. Chapman, Executors. (13 SEP 1798)

The subscriber [with several others] intends to petition the legislature at the next session for an act of insolvency. Thomas Marshall, Charles County. (20 SEP 1798)

Charles Mankin is moving to Baltimore in the fall, and will offer for sale on the 3rd Monday in November his lots in Port Tobacco, Negroes, and stock. (4 OCT 1798)

Thomas G. Addison, George Calvert are among those elected to the House of Delegates in Prince George's County, and Henry H. Chapman in Charles County. (11 OCT 1798)

Philip B. Key offers for sale a family of slaves: man, wife and 8 children, as it is too expensive to keep them together in town. (11 OCT 1798)

A letter for Mrs. Mary Hesselius, at *Oxen Hill*, and for Miss Digges, *Warburton*, remain at the post office in Piscataway. (11 OCT 1798)

George Dent is elected to Congress from the 1st district of Maryland, and William Craik the same from the third district. (18 OCT 1798)

Yesterday morning, the roof of the house in the occupancy of H.J. Stier, Esq., caught fire in several places, but by timely exertions the fire was prevented from doing any damage, except to the roof, which was considerably injured. (1 NOV 1798)

Henry H. Chapman is made speaker of the House of Delegates. (8 NOV 1798)

John Hesselius, of *Primrose Hill*, offers for sale several small tracts within 2 miles of Annapolis. (8 NOV 1798)

William Potts has graduated from St. John's College. (15 NOV 1798)

Peale Portrait, Miniature and Landscape Painter. In Mr. Johnson's house, on the hill, informs those who may please to encourage him in the practise of his profession, that none but approved likenesses shall leave his house. (22 NOV 1798)

> *Blest by the pencil, whose consoling pow'r,*
> *Soothing soft friendship in her pensive hour,*
> *Dispels the cloud, with melancholy fraught,*
> *That absence throws upon her tender thought*
> *Blest be the pencil! whose enchantment gives*
> *To wounded love the food on which he lives;*
> *Rich in this give, tho' cruel ocean bear*
> *The youth to exile from his faithful fair,*
> *He in fond dreams hangs o'er her glowing cheek,*
> *Still owes her present, and still hears her speak!*

In the sale of [William] Smallwood tracts on the Chickamuxon, 475 to 582 acres were sold at £5 per acre. (13 DEC 1798)

Thomas Atwood Digges, of *Warburton*, petitions to mark the bounds of *Warburton Manor* and *Frankland*. (24 JAN 1799)

John Hesselius warns against trespassing, or trusting or crediting anyone on account of him, without a line from him. (24 JAN 1799)

Penelope Jones petitions the court to mark tracts *Rich Hill* and *Thompson's Rest* (alias *Boarman's Content*) on Piscataway Creek. (7 FEB 1799)

William Adams, Executor, of Nanjemoy, wants those with claims against the estate of Rev. Walter Hanson Harrison to bring them in. (28 FEB 1799)

John Craggs, at South River ferry, has the horse *High Flyer* at stud. (21 MAR 1799)

Thomas A. Digges warns against trespassing. Also, he offers for rent *Swan Creek Landing*, *The Point* (or *Digges Landing*), the *Clifft*, and *Old Piscataway Landings*. (28 MAR 1799)

Charles Mankin is to move to Baltimore on May 1st, and will offer for sale on the 3rd Monday in April, lots in Port Tobacco, also three lots on the point in said town, with one small house. The first three lots all front the courthouse. Also, Negroes "which have no claim to freedom, [carriage] horses, and riding carriage [He says evil minded people said his last ad was a sham but he intends to sell]. (28 MAR 1799)

A poem on the death of Mr. McGrath, who died February 24, 1799, in Reading, Pennsylvania [of the theatre]. (4 APR 1799)

Along the Potomac River: **Extracts from the *Maryland Gazette*,** 1728-1799

A storm at the Calvert County courthouse blew down a house. Mr. Stone, chief justice of the district, was knocked down by a piece of timber and considerably hurt [details continue]. (2 MAY 1799)

For sale on June 11th at Port Tobacco, the house formerly occupied by the late Matthew Blair; large frame house, 46'x34', [dyone?] cellar and windows secure with iron stancheons; house divided into a large store room and three lodging rooms, well finished, two of them with fireplaces; on the south and west side is a range of piazzas supported by brick pillars, on the end of the main building are two wings, 24'x18', etc. (2 MAY 1799)

The Ricketts Equestrian Circus is playing in Annapolis. (23 MAY 1799)

Smallwood's executors offer for sale more land to pay debts, and on July 15th, eight or ten thousand acres on Mattawoman Creek. (30 MAY 1799)

The Maryland Medical Society is to be formed. (6 MAY 1799)

Virlinda, the wife of Henry Smallwood, of Charles County, has absconded from his bed and board. (25 JUL 1799)

John F. Mercer offers for sale seven or twelve hundred acres, part of Marlborough Neck, located 1½ miles on the Potomac, and 1 mile from the mouth of Aquia Creek on the south side. Includes an overseers house, plus 30 or 40 Virginia-born slaves raised on the land. West River, Maryland. (22 AUG 1799)

Lawrence Posey, of *Allen's Fresh*, Charles County, has a stray horse. (10 OCT 1799)

Francis Digges and Henry H. Chapman have been elected to the House of Delegates for Charles County; Messrs. Calvert and Addison, for Prince George's County. (17 OCT 1799)

Alexandria. An attempt that was made near Four Mile Run to rob the mail coach to Baltimore by three black fellows has foiled. (17 OCT 1799)

A day of mourning is proclaimed for the death of George Washington [eulogies given]. "In the long and lofty portico where oft the hero walked in all his glory, now lay the shrouded corpse."

[End]

INDEX

A

Abell
　S. 85
academies 55
　Lower Marlborough 67
　Philadelphia, Pa. 12
Accomptants 94
accounting rooms 51, 63
Ackakick, Md. 17
Acque-Creek Chapel 110
Acts of Assembly 5, 8, 20, 38, 39, 56, 61, 78, 86, 89, 91, 96, 100, 113-115
　bridge over Potomac River 105
Acts of Congress 102
Adair
　Cassandra 49
　Elizabeth 49, 50, 58, 61
　Robert 49
Adam
　Mr. 60
　Robert 22, 24, 30, 38, 46, 50, 52, 55, 65
Adams
　Humphrey 16
　Mr. 22
　William 45, 119
Adderton
　Joseph, Dr. 73
Addison
　Anne 12
　Anthony 109
　Eleanor 25, 26
　H. 14, 89
　Henry 26, 55
　Henry, Rev. 24, 65, 73, 89
　J. 100
　John 12, 14, 16, 26, 28, 33, 48, 56, 66, 74, 93, 113, 114
　John, Capt. 9, 12, 14
　John, Col. 25, 102, 114
　John, Jr. 104, 111, 113, 114
　Mr. 47, 120
　Mrs. 25
　Rachel (Dulany) 65
　Rebecca 67
　Rebecca (Dulany) 46
　Rev. 17, 45, 97
　Thomas 48, 52, 63, 64
　Thomas G. 116-118
　Thomas, Capt. 12
　Thomas, Hon. 25
　Thomas, Jr. 46, 47
　Walter D. 109
Addison's Ferry 25, 63
Aderton
　Jane 56
　Joseph 51
　Joseph, Dr. 56
Adjutants 69
advertisements 2, 5, 109, 115
Africa 21, 28
　windward coast of 27, 28
African ship 27
Agents 17, 25, 28, 47, 54, 115
Aikman
　William 58, 63
ailments 2
Aisquith
　William 60
Aix-la-Chapelle, Fra. 81
　peace declared 5
Albany, N.Y. 12
Aldermen
　Alexandria, Va. 29
Alexander
　Gerard 22
　Gerrard 6, 7
　John 106, 115
　Philip 30, 39, 45
　Rachel 115
　William 103
Alexandria Ferry 16, 62, 84, 97, 102
Alexandria, Va. 12-18, 20-35, 37, 39, 42, 44-47, 49-61, 63, 64, 66, 67, 69, 70, 72-80, 82-88, 95, 98, 101, 103, 104, 110, 112, 115, 116, 118, 120
　building church in 45
　Council, Aldermen and Mayor 29
　court day 34
　courthouse 90
　erecting at Hunting Creek Warehouse 5
　jail 38
　lottery 24, 25
　population 105
　prison to be built 38
　soldiers at 12
Algiers
　dey of 88
Allegany Co., Md. 107
Allen
　Bennett 47
　George 63
　John 63
Allison
　William 66
allspice 52
alms houses
　Charles Co., Md. 51
　Leonardtown, Md. 64
　Prince George's Co., Md. 51
　to be built 49
altarpieces 11
American Ambassadors 88
Amsterdam 79
Anacostia River 45, 52
anchors 19, 66, 76
Anderson
　Jonathan 92
　Joseph Horatio 60
　Mr. 75
Angola 26
animals 85, 109
Annapolis packets 108
Annapolis, Md. 1, 2, 4-6, 9-11, 15-19, 29, 31, 33, 35, 36, 39, 42-45, 49, 50, 53, 54, 56, 58, 60, 65-67, 71, 76-78, 80, 83, 84, 86, 88, 90, 92, 94, 96, 97, 103, 104, 106, 108, 112-114, 116-118, 120
　state house fire 100
　theatre 22, 55
　windmill at 24
Anne Arundel Co., Md. 14, 84, 103, 104, 109, 116
apothecary shops 97
apple orchards 53, 57, 60, 62, 64, 75
apprentices 49, 83, 88, 98, 111, 112
Aquia Church 53
Aquia Creek 54, 120
Aquia Run 82, 83
Aquia warehouse 46, 54, 82, 83
Aquia, Va. 14, 36, 49
Architects 60, 80, 83, 110

Ariss
  John 7, 18
arithmetic 54, 67, 116
arms 52
  cessation of 77
artillery 71
Artists 29, 113
Ashton
  John, Sr. 90
Assembly
  Maryland 9, 10, 14, 37, 64, 78, 79, 85, 87, 89, 93, 96, 98, 101, 102, 105, 114
  Virginia 24
assembly room
  building of 61
Attorneys 27, 60, 87, 88, 101, 106
  at law 1
  in fact 40, 75
auctions 44, 46, 48, 52, 54, 90
Aurora Borealis 2, 6, 9, 37
Authors 19, 54
Aventon
  Mardun Vaghn 31

B

Bachelors 38
  taxes on 18
Bailey's puppets 84
bake houses 21
bake ovens 21
Baker
  Thomas 17
  William 114
bakeries 48
baking 18
Bale
  John, cemetery of 46
balehouses 45
Ball
  Capt. 66
Ballendine
  John 17, 36, 48, 52, 53, 64, 65
balloons 80
  ascension 79
ballrooms 43, 79, 92
balls 1, 6, 22, 104
  building for 36
Baltimore
  Lady 1
  Lord 8
Baltimore Co., Md. 48

Baltimore, Md. 16, 18, 50, 53, 62, 68, 75, 76, 81, 108, 109, 118-120
bandy legs 37
Barbadoes 23, 33, 86
  freight to 30
Barbers 50
barges 75
Barker
  William 62
Barnes
  Abraham 12, 23, 64
  Abraham, Col. 26, 41, 58, 62
  Henry 97
  Humphrey 113
  Joseph 93
  Mr. 57
  Richard 57, 88
Barnet
  Col. 62
barns 45, 81, 104, 112
  shingled 44
Baron Trenck 106
barrels
  beer 103
  corn 91
  flour 66
  half, gunpowder 35
  Indian corn 47
  sugar 37
Barret
  Richard 26
Barrett
  Mr. 75
  Richard 27
Barrick
  John 99
Barry
  John 32
bars 22, 35
Bartenders 108
Bath, Va. 81
Batt
  Humphrey 2, 5, 9
batteaus 98, 117
Bayley
  William 112
Baylis
  John, Col. 44
  William, Capt. 17
Bayly
  William 75
Bayne
  John 62
  Thomas 99
  Thomas, Jr. 99

Baynes
  John 21, 27, 30, 41, 51, 55, 63, 65, 66
  Joseph N. 114
  Mr. 23, 57
bays 15, 71, 72
  structural 71
Beale
  William, Jr. 108
Beall
  Andrew 48
  Josias 64
Bean-town, Md. 115
Beane
  John H., Col. 91
Beane's Tavern 91
Beans
  Colmore 15
  Henrietta 95
  J.H. 84
  John 101
  John H., Col. 95
  William 15
Beard's Creek 100, 108
beards 23
bearskin coats 41
bearskin frockcoats 21
Beason
  brand of 86
bed-clothes 50
beds 34, 50, 63, 69, 120
beef 71
beer 103
beggar's opera 10
Belaa
  John, Jr. 17
Belhaven, Va. 7-9, 11-13, 50
  lottery 8, 9
Bell-Town, Md. 3
Belmont, Va. 19
Belt
  H. 77
  Joseph 9
  Thomas 47
Benedict, Md. 24, 66, 73
Benger
  Elliott, Esq. 8
Berkeley Co., Va. 1, 63, 81, 84
Bermuda 54
Berry
  William 48, 89
Betton
  J. 94
Bigfoot 109
bill of rights 94
billiard tables

Along the Potomac River: Extracts from the *Maryland Gazette*, 1728-1799

for sale 30
London 22, 35
billiards 6
bills of exchange 28
birthdays 9
Bishop of Chester 115
Bishops 107
black cattle 99, 106
black furred hats 71
black satin waistcoats 25
black silk breeches 25
black velvet 87
Blackburn
   Capt. 12
   Col. 10
   Hugh 44
   Mr. 10
Blacklock
   N. 113
   Nicholas 98, 99, 101, 110
Blacksmith shops 60, 62
Blacksmiths 4, 8, 28, 51, 59, 76
Bladensburg, Md. 3, 6, 12, 13, 15, 21, 40, 51, 53, 56, 64, 76, 79, 87, 98, 99, 111
   laying out 29
   lottery 29
Blair
   Matthew 97, 120
blankets 69
blasphemy 3
Blate
   John 78
Block Makers 49
Bloomsbury Square 66
Blue Ridge Mountains 58
boarders 58
boarding 36
boarding houses 81
boats 28, 43, 44, 59, 65, 67
   lost 89
Bohemia, Md. 34
boilers 73
bonds 53
bookcases
   mahogany 98
books 24, 30, 54, 69
   borrowed 8
   Case of the Episcopal Church... 76
   for sale 13, 32, 103
   law, for sale 63
   Laws of Virginia 47
   lost 6
   Maria, The Triumph of Perseverence 112

Origin of Civil Government 90
   subscriptions 84, 90, 112
Booksellers 58
Boon
   Henry 87
Booth
   William 65
boots 10
Boston rum 52
Boston, Mass. 17, 22, 49, 82
   fire 25
Botetourt Co., Va. 105
Boucher
   Mr. 55
   Rev. 51, 55, 66, 69, 70, 74
boundaries
   of District [of Columbia] 103
Bowden
   Mr. 23
Bowdon
   George 19, 21
Bowen's Waxworks 106
Bowes
   Richard 30, 34
Bowie
   Allen 66
   Fielder 102
   John 61
   Robert 102
   Walter 102
   William 87
Bowles
   James 1
   Rebecca, Mrs. 1
boxes 50
   misdirected 20
Boyd's-Hole, Va. 28
Boylan
   Mary 101
   Thomas 101
Braddock
   Gen. 15, 16
Bradley
   Stephen 112
brass 51
breakfast
   not eating 102
Breaton
   Thomas 62
breeches 24, 25, 29, 117
Breeches Maker 53
Brent
   Chancellor 86
   Clare 54
   Dorothy 102

George 48
Henry 16, 54
John 114
Mary 86
Mr. 67
Robert 27, 46, 48, 86, 88, 101, 102, 107, 112
Robert, Jr. 78, 89
Robert, Sr. 101
William 35, 40, 41, 48, 71, 74
Brentown, Va.
   lands of 45
Brereton
   Thomas 53
Brethren 92
Brewer
   Joseph 85
breweries 39
Brewers 59
Brice
   Ariana 6
   John 33
   John, Esq. 6
Brick Church 74
Bricklayers 13, 58
Brickmakers 19
bridges 29, 63
   over Potomac River 105, 113
   plans for 113
   Severn River 42
   to be built 98
Brigadier General 75
Brigantines
   Ann & Elizabeth 60
   Brittania 53
   Fairfax 8, 11, 53
   Fortitude 80
   Hawke 24
   Molly 23
   Ranger 80
      attacked 75
   Success 12
Brigs
   Betty 54
   Marquis de la Fayette 77
   Peggy Stewart 65
   Swift, to be sold 55
bristles
   hogs' 92
Britannic Majesty 77
British America 52
British Army 73
British ships 72

Briton's Bay 28
Broad Creek 2, 5, 7-9, 12, 19, 25, 31, 36, 39, 50, 53, 74, 87, 105, 109, 110, 115
Broad Creek warehouse 75, 102
broadcloth coats 40
broadcloths 85
Brockenbrough
  Col. 31
Brodus
  Samuel, Capt. 53
Bronaugh
  William, Jr. 21
  William, Sr. 21
Brook
  Mr. 62
Brooke
  Baker 78
  Rev. 55
  T. 96
  Thomas, Jr. 1
Brookes
  William 34
brooms 11
Brown
  Gustavus R. 62, 95, 100
  Gustavus R., Dr. 84, 98
  Gustavus Richard, Dr. 81
  Gustavus, Dr. 30, 64, 101
  Richard, Rev. 100
  William 35
brown sugar 86
Bruce
  John 72
brush making 92
Bryantown, Md. 113
Buckingham
  John 41
Buckland
  Benjamin 108
  William 58, 59, 61, 66
buildings 7, 8, 10, 14, 36, 39, 50, 56
  destroyed by fire 89
  draughts of 8
  Executive department 104
  ferry 97
  miniature 8
  stone 48
  tenant 57, 76
  wooden 3
Bullet
  Cuthbert 95
bulls 72, 73, 101
Bunbury

Thomas, Jr. 69
Burgesses 99
Burgoyne
  Roger 38
burials 19, 43, 51, 75, 87, 101, 105
Burrell
  Alexander 40, 55
Bushop
  Elizabeth 6
Bushrod
  John, Maj. 7
businesses
  Adam, Craik & Co. 106
  Alexander Brown & Co. 29
  Alexander Cunningham & Co. 60
  Barnes & Ridgate 57
  Carlyle & Dalton 12, 15, 18, 21, 23-25, 31, 32, 34, 35, 39, 55
    dissolved 69
  Champe & Hunter 26, 27
  Christie & Stone 68
  Craik & Hanson, dissolved 69
  Crosbies & Trafford 27, 33
  Davenport, Strather & Lane 59
  dissolved 113
  E. Valette & Co. 109
  Edward Trafford & Sons 21
  Edward Trafford, Esq. & Sons 19
  George Clements & Co. 113
  Green & Rind 34
  Hooe & Harrison 101
  Hugh Blackburn & Co. 44
  J.H. Stone & Co. 92
  James Todd & Co. 40
  Jenifer & Hooe 69
  Jennifer & Hooe 68
  John Champe & Co. 21
  John Glassford & Co. 20, 37, 73, 108
    store books 35
  John Jamieson & Sons 56
  John Petty & Co. 91, 102
  Nicholas & Valentine Peers 98
  partnership dissolved 17, 69, 106
  Patowmack Canal Co. 83
  Patowmack Co. 31, 90, 95, 96, 106, 116
  Reid & Stewart 9

Robert Adam & Co. 52
Stewart & Armour 9
Thompson & Magruder 63
Wallace & Muir 77
Butcher
  Jonathan, Rev. 66
Butchers 30
Butler
  Mr. 106
buttons 40, 85, 87
by-Oist? 60
Byrd
  Col. 21
Byrn
  Patrick 35

C

Cabinet Makers 31, 59, 108
cables 19
calendar
  adopted 9
Calvert
  Ariana 80
  Benedict 3-5, 9-11, 36, 37, 55, 69, 80, 83, 93, 99
  Benedict, Hon. 61
  Charles 61, 117
  Edward 114
  Edward Henry 112
  Elizabeth 93
  George 118
  Gov. 42
  John 48
  Mr. 36, 43, 120
Calvert Co., Md. 7, 10, 11, 57, 71, 88, 93, 120
calves 100
camels 112
Cameron, Va. 7, 9
Campbell
  Colin 104
  Isaac, Rev. 84, 90
  John 118
  Thomas 35
  Thomas, Capt. 33
  William 90
camps 13, 15, 34
canals 65
cancer
  cure for 9
candles 6
candlesticks 11, 77
Cane
  Margaret 42

124

canes 96
Cannon
   Grace 39
Cape Henry, Va. 62, 108
capes 117
   crimson velvet 85
capitol
   cornerstone laid 110
   sites for 104
   Williamsburg, Va. 3
Captain John's Run 49
Carey
   Peter 16
Carlisle 31
Carlyle
   John 7, 21, 22, 26, 29, 30, 38, 53, 56, 60, 65, 66
   John, Col. 25, 67
   Mr. 18, 22
   Sarah (Fairfax) 25
Carne
   Mr. 60
   Richard 71
Carolina mountains 109
Carpenters 14, 29, 59, 61, 100, 111
   forge 34
Carr
   John 4
   Overton 66, 69, 74, 110
   William 30
carriage guns 18, 26, 28, 75
carriages
   repair of 29
Carrico
   Bartholomew 113
Carrico's Tavern 113
Carroll
   Billy 29
   Charles 47, 52, 104
   Daniel 7, 16, 48, 52, 91, 103
   Daniel, Jr. 101
   Mary (Darnall) 47
Carrollsburg, Md.
   formed 52
Carrollton, Md. 104
carts 114
Carvers 29, 59
Casburn
   John 35
cashimer vests 117
casks 45, 86
Casturn
   John 66
Catholics 56
cattle 5, 12, 63, 73, 76, 80, 82,
   88
   black 106
   for sale 14
Caulkers 9
Causin
   G.B. 76, 94, 96
   Gerard Blackiston 102
Caverley
   Mr. 76
Cawood
   Benjamin 113
Cecil Co., Md. 44, 47
Cedar Point 39, 43
cedar posts 61
Cedar Run 55
cellar stairs 11
cellars 7, 9, 10, 30, 33, 35, 39, 44, 45, 50, 51, 63, 68, 70, 79, 83, 84, 88, 115, 120
cemeteries
   Aderton Family 51
   Bale Family 46
census 102, 105
cents 87
cessation of arms 77
chains 106
chair houses 72
chairs 63, 69, 72, 77, 106
chamber organs 32, 80
Chambers
   James 25
Champe
   Col. 30
   John 21
   John, Col. 22
Chancellor of Maryland 110
Chapel Point, Md. 54
   to be laid out 78
chapels 1, 4
   lower, King George Parish 110
Chapman
   Eleanor (Hanson) 115
   Henry H. 96, 103, 113, 117, 118, 120
   Henry H., Maj. 115
   John, Dr. 98, 101, 103
   Lucy 33
   Mary 50
   Nathan 33
   Nathaniel 7
Chaptico, Md. 108, 115
chariots 86, 94, 103, 107
charity-working school 14
Charles Co., Md. 4, 6, 8, 11, 12, 15, 17, 18, 20, 23, 25,
   27, 28, 30-32, 34, 36, 37, 40, 42, 43, 47, 50-53, 57, 59, 62, 65, 67, 70, 72, 74, 76-78, 81, 83, 88-90, 94-96, 99, 102, 103, 105, 107, 110, 112-118, 120
   alms house 51
   brethren of 92
   court 88, 111
   court day 83
   courthouse 62, 68, 87, 113, 115, 119
   free school 51, 60, 61
   free school lands 64
   inhabitants 78, 79, 94
   Justices 105
   record office, building of 105
   school 34
Charles II 102
Charles Town, Md. 20, 97, 112, 115
   inhabitants 98
Charles, Earl of Tankerville 23
Charles, Lord Baltimore 8
Charleston, S.C. 61
Charlestown, Md. 47
Charlotte Hall
   school now building 85
Charter
   Mrs. 30
charters 34, 54, 63
   wanted 27
Chase
   Jeremiah 15
   Samuel 55
cherry trees 81
Chester Co. 79
Chester River 95
Chestertown, Md. 17, 49
Chew
   Joseph 12
   Richard 105
Chickamuxon Creek 118, 119
Chickamuxon, Md. 52
Chickly-Cudly 109
Chief Justice 12, 53, 120
chimneys 8, 11, 17, 21, 36, 40, 42, 48, 58, 60, 68, 69, 72, 81, 91, 105, 115
Chincoteague, Md. 3
Chinese stone 2
chintzes 25
Choppawansick Creek 41
Christianity 101
Christie
   John, Capt. 82

125

Christmas 11, 103
Church of England 56
churches 7, 46
  ad posted in 43
  Alexandria, Va., to be built 66
  Aquia, Va. 14, 53
  building at Falls Church 45
  building in Alexandria, Va. 45
  building of 56
  completing inside 64
  enlarged 43
  enlarging 38, 39, 42
  Episcopal 76
  Episcopal, Maryland 109
  Eversfield's chapel 34
  of Truro Parish, upper 40
  Old Falls, decayed 36
  organ for 32
  Piccawaxon 72
  Piscataway 72
  Pohick 10
  Port Tobacco 18
  Presbyterian, to be built 53
  Prince George's Co., Md. 74
  Protestant 70
  Protestant Episcopal 107
  Roman Catholic 79
  Roman Catholic chapel 70
  South River 96
  St. John's 43
  to be built 28, 44
  to be built at the falls 40
  Trinity Parish, to be built 53
  Truro Parish 44, 61
  Truro Parish, building of 36
Churchwardens 11, 40, 45, 56, 61
churchyards 61
cider 75, 86, 104
circuses 120
City of Washington 105
  plan for sale 107
Clagett
  Bishop 109
  Dr. 107
Clajon
  Mr. 17
Clark
  Charles 102
  Joseph 108, 110
  William 90
Clarke
  Abraham 71
  Reuben, Capt. 82

clean knives 10
Clements
  George 106, 113
Clergymen 96
Clerks 78, 89, 107
Clifford
  John 62
Clifford's Ferry 70, 77, 80
Clifton
  William 2, 14, 27, 58
Clifton's Ferry 30
clock repairing 39
Clockmakers 34, 39
closets 10
cloth 55
clothes 40, 50, 55, 89
clothing
  for sale 18
clouds 119
clubs 86
coach houses 45
coachees 114
coaches 13, 80, 106
coal 40
coal wood 64
coat of arms 24
  Lee Family 1
Coates
  Thomas 97
coats 29, 40, 62, 87, 106, 117
  stolen 85
Cockermouth, Eng. 82
coffee 52
Coffee Houses
  Alexandria, Va. 29
  Annapolis, Md. 56, 72
coffee pots 77
cohorns 28
coinage 87
  establish U.S. mint 88
Colchester, Va. 22, 30, 31, 33, 44-46, 58, 65, 66, 78, 83
Collector of Revenue 98
Collector of Taxes 95
Collectors 57
colleges 84, 100, 104, 113, 115, 118
Collet
  James 53
Colliers 59
Collington Branch 74
Columbia
  territory of 105
Columbian Magazine 91
Columbine
  Thomas 62

Colvill
  Frances 46
  John 25, 28, 43
  John, Capt. 2
  Mr. 41
  Thomas 28, 43, 46
Colville
  Thomas 28
  Thomas, Col. 44
comets 20, 22, 38
Commanders 34
Commissary General 20, 58
Commissioners 12, 28, 29
  appointed 103, 117
Commissioners of the Peace 6
commissions
  appointed 91
compting rooms 40, 78
concerts 36
confiscated property 73, 74, 76, 89, 92
Conn
  William 99
Connell
  John 66
Constables
  Charles Co., Md. 43
constitution 91, 95
  amendments to 94
  published 91
Contee
  Benjamin 77
  Mary (Craufurd) 90
  Richard 90
  Sarah (Fendall) 108
  Thomas 24, 51, 56, 57, 105, 108
Continental Congress 68
convict servants 5, 18, 20, 21, 23, 40, 46, 47, 55, 59
convict ships 45
convicts 3-5, 20
Conway
  Robert, Capt. 67, 69
Cooke
  George 16
  John 93
Cool Springs 55, 63, 64, 85
  La Fayette village 85
Coolidge
  Judson, Capt. 24
Copher
  William 88
Copithorn
  John 18, 37
copper mines 17

126

copper pieces 84
copper tea kettles 11
Coreshil
   Thomas 47
corn 52, 53, 91, 99, 106
corn houses 5, 45, 79, 81
Corneil
   Peter 100
cornerstones
   U.S. capitol 110
corpses 120
cotton 6, 13, 71
council 85
   Alexandria, Va. 29
   His Lordship's 3, 15, 18, 20, 45
   Maryland 41, 45, 50, 85, 99
Council of State
   Maryland 50
Count Dillon 76
Count Rochambeau 76
counterfeit bills 49
counterfeit double doubloons 6
counterfeit milled dollars 5
counterpanes 25
counting rooms 7, 83, 84, 88
country born slaves 22
country cloth 71
country villa
   to be built 83
Court
   William 74
Court of Exchequer 1
courthouse lot
   Port Tobacco, Md. 114
courthouses
   Alexandria, Va. 35, 90
   Charles Co., Md. 62, 68, 78, 79, 87, 105, 113, 115, 119
   Fairfax Co., Va. 46
   Prince George's Co., Md. 3, 4, 8
   St. Mary's Co., Md. 26, 32
   Stafford Co., Va. 35, 46
   Westmoreland Co., Va. 49
Courts
   Betsey 107
   Charles Co., Md. 79
   Elizabeth 67
   John 6
   Richard H. 105
   William 72, 107
courts (public) 3, 24, 53, 63
   Calvert Co., Md. 93
   Charles Co., Md. 79, 83, 87, 88, 94

establish new county 94
Prince George's Co., Md. 65, 94
Prince William Co., Va. 63
Provincial 12
St. Mary's Co., Md. 94
cows 25, 31, 117
   gives live birth 100
Cox
   Polly 70
Crabb
   Henry Wright 3
Crackels
   Mary 110
   Thomas 110
Crackles
   Thomas 101, 106
Cragge
   John 105
Craggs
   John 97, 108, 111-114, 116, 119
Craig
   David 22
   John 22, 60
Craigg
   John 24
Craik
   James 25, 28, 51, 58, 62, 73
   James, Dr. 69
   James, Sr. 83, 88, 98
   Mr. 106
   William 90, 99, 102, 106, 118
Crane
   George 89
Cranston
   Andrew 28
Craufurd
   David 90
   Mary 90
Crawford
   Mrs. 7
Crawford's Old Fields 7
creditors 49, 53, 56, 62, 111, 113, 115
creeks 104
   Aquia 54, 120
   Beard's 100, 108
   Broad 2, 5, 7, 8, 12, 19, 25, 31, 36, 39, 43, 50, 53, 74, 75, 87, 102, 105, 109, 110, 115
   Chickamuxon 118
   Choppawansick 41
   Dogue 1, 16

Great Hunting 1, 7
Hunting 2, 5
Lions 71
Little Hunting 14, 16
Machodock 90
Mattawoman 56, 116, 120
Nanjemoy 23, 74, 81
Oxon 16
Piscataway 41, 78, 84, 119
Pohick 44
Port Tobacco 54, 70, 75, 78, 94, 102, 105, 116
Quantico 62, 95
Rock 1-3, 6, 8, 9, 99
Swan 119
Cricket matches 13, 14
crimes 32, 73
   adultery 57
   beastiality 19
   bigamy 89
   burglary 5
   counterfeiting 6
   cutting a sealed half bushel 4
   felony 37
   murder 6, 7, 43, 81
   robbery 51, 52, 73, 120
   shoplifting 14
   stabbing 104
crimson velvet capes 85
Crookshanks
   Capt. 14
crop notes 52
crops 53, 94
Crosbies
   Mr. 27
Crouch
   Henry 29
   Joseph 11
cuffs 117
Cunningham
   Alexander 60
Curling
   Daniel 26
currency 25, 27, 28, 30, 49, 56, 84
Currier 10
Custis
   J.P. 72
custom houses 57

D

Dabney
   John 113
dairies 44, 112

Dalton
  John 7, 15, 22, 45, 46, 54, 65, 69
  Mr. 50
dancing 19, 42
Dancing masters
  wanted 40
dancing schools 18
Daniel
  Travers, Jr. 117
Darkins
  Richard 37
Darnall
  Anne, widow 8
  Henry 27
  Mary 47
  Robert 66, 83, 93
Darrell
  Mr. 4
  Sampson 8, 47
Dartmouth 18
Davenport
  Mr. 59
Davis
  Anne 107
  Cuthbert, Capt. 27
  Ebenezer 107
  I.E. 111
  Thomas 69
  William 31
Dayly
  John 32
de la Sumat
  John 45
deacons 109
deaths 7, 10, 15, 75, 81, 82
  Adams, Humphrey 16
  Addison, Eleanor 25
  Addison, Rachel (Dulany) 65
  Addison, Thomas 52, 64
  Baylis, John, Col. 44
  Beans, Henrietta 95
  Benger, Elliott, Esq. 8
  Blackburn, Mary 112
  Blackburn, Mr. 10
  Blate, John 78
  Braddock, Gen. 16
  Brent, Dorothy 102
  Brooke, Rachel 96
  Brown, Gustavus, Dr. 30
  Buckland, Benjamin 108
  by lightning 36
  Calvert, Ariana 80
  Calvert, Charles 61
  Cannon, Grace 39
  Carlyle, Sarah (Fairfax) 25
  Carroll, Daniel 7
  Chapman, Eleanor (Hanson) 115
  Chapman, John, Dr. 101
  Charles, Lord Baltimore 8
  Colville, Thomas, Col. 44
  Contee, Sarah (Fendall) 108
  Crouch, Henry 29
  Crouch, Joseph 11
  Davis, Anne 107
  de la Sumat, John 45
  Dent, George, Col. 12
  Dent, Warren 112
  Digges, Charles 49
  Digges, Mrs. William 18
  Dulany, Daniel 12
  Dulany, Walter, Hon. 58
  Fairfax, William, Col. 18
  Fendall, Anne 83
  Fowke, Gerard, Capt. 77
  Frazier, Thomas 19
  Gordon, Christian, Mrs. 52
  Green, Jonah 46
  Green, Nathaniel 87
  Hambleton, Arthur, Rev. 72
  Hanson, Elizabeth 57
  Hanson, John, Hon. 79
  Hanson, John, Sr. 110
  Hanson, Robert, Col. 4
  Harrison, Dorothy 10
  Harrison, Robert H., Hon. 100
  Hawkins, Josias 99
  Henderson, Jacob, Rev. 8
  Hopkenson, Thomas, Rev. 94
  Jenifer, Elizabeth (Hanson) 19
  Jenifer, Walter Hanson, Dr. 85
  Johnston, George 44
  Jones, Benjamin 16
  Jordan, John 54
  Key, Philip, Hon. 41
  King George II 25
  Lee, Grace 99
  Lee, Richard, Hon. 89
  Lee, Russell 110
  Leidler, John 59
  Mackubin, John 10
  Magruder, John 6
  Marlow, Mr. 42
  Mason, Anne 34
  Mason, Mary 54
  McGrath, Mr. 119
  McKenzie, Donald 7
  Mercer, John 47
  Milton Hill 107
  Mulliken, Thomas 37
  Murdock, Anne (Addison) 12
  Negro man 23
  Philip Barton 17
  Plater, George, Hon. 15, 105
  Plater, Mrs. 6
  Ridgate, Thomas How 100
  Rousby, Mr. 7
  Schneider, John 54
  Scott, George 54
  Smith, Mary 64
  Somervell, James, Dr. 7
  St. Thomas Jenifer, Daniel of 102
  Stoddert, John Truman 42
  Stone, David 56
  Stone, Frederick 110
  Stone, Margaret 91
  Stone, Mary 105
  Stone, Thomas, Hon. 53
  Stone, Walter 105
  Stonestreet, Thomas 54
  Swift, Theophilus, Rev. 31
  Tasker, Benjamin 25
  Tipton, Jonathan 17
  Washington, George 120
  Washington, Lucy (Chapman) 33
  Williams, Richard, Capt. 9
debtors 91, 97, 100, 113
debts 4, 28, 33, 48, 52, 55, 56, 68, 81, 85, 93, 97-99, 101, 106, 108, 110, 113, 114, 116, 120
  British 87, 98
DeButts
  John 55
  Lawrence, Rev. 55
Deen
  Capt. 68
deer 86
Deering
  James 25
deerskins 37
Delaforce
  Joseph 59
delegates 82, 83, 92, 96
Dent
  Elizabeth 98
  Gen. 70
  George 62, 96, 102, 118
  George, Capt. 37
  George, Col. 12
  John 70

Mr. 42
Mrs. 95
Sarah 70
Thomas 57, 71
Thomas, Capt. 98
Warren 68, 112
Dentists 72, 76
deserters 12, 13, 34, 68
deserts 80
desperadoes 75
Difficult Run 28
Digges
  C. 19, 30
  Charles 26, 30, 34, 37, 43, 46, 49
  Edward 32, 81
  F. 113
  Francis 114, 115, 120
  G. 107
  George 78, 79, 85, 92, 94, 96, 99, 101, 105, 107, 111
  Henry 32, 113
  Ignatius 7, 14, 16, 33, 86
  J. 113
  Mary 86
  Miss 118
  Thomas 114
  Thomas A. 119
  Thomas Atwood 119
  William 7, 14, 16, 24, 25, 28, 30, 32, 33, 40, 41, 45, 47, 55, 78
  William, Mrs. 18
Diggs
  Miss 115
Dillon
  Count 76
dimes 87
dining 21, 29, 42, 70, 106
dining rooms 22, 35
Dinwiddie
  Gov. 15
disabled slaves 100
discharge papers 13
distilleries 73
divorces
  Boylan, Mary 101
Dixon
  Capt. 65
docking 36
docks 18, 42, 77
Dodson
  Jacob 112
  William 78
  Wm. 86
dogs 100

Dogue Creek 1, 16
Dogue Run farm 27
dollars 66, 77, 84, 87, 90
  counterfeit 5
Doncastle
  John 41
  Mr. 27
Doran
  Patrick 2
Dorchester Co., Md. 4
double dimes 87
double doubloons 6
doubloons 6
Douglas
  James 30
Douglass
  Mrs. 117
Dowson
  Benjamin 19
Doyne
  Robert 74
dragoons 4
drawings
  sale of goods 30
dress wigs 10
drinking 6, 16, 42, 70
  toasts 22
drownings 10, 100, 108
drums 29
dry goods 108
Dublin, Ire. 36
Ducking Stool Point 2
dueling 78
duels 44
Duke of Lancaster
  last will of 38
Dulany
  Benjamin 68, 74, 76, 77
  Daniel 12-14, 20, 27
  Daniel, Hon. 65
  Daniel, Jr. 5
  Elizabeth 92
  Grafton 63
  Lloyd 92
  Rachel 65
  Rebecca 46
  Walter 13, 45, 92
  Walter, Hon. 46, 58
Dumfries, Scotland 51
Dumfries, Va. 20-22, 25, 30, 31, 33, 37, 44, 46, 49, 50, 52, 53, 55, 58, 62, 63, 65, 71, 82, 83, 95, 98, 103, 104, 118
Duncanson
  Willis 3

Duncastle
  John 20
dungeons 106
Dunkirk 79
Durham Parish 67
Dutch servants 42
Duvall
  G. 90
  Gabriel 85, 87
  Marsh M. 84, 85
dwelling houses 7, 9, 10, 16, 23, 25, 35, 39, 46, 48, 58, 60, 66, 69, 75, 79, 80, 82, 84, 94, 99, 104-106, 112, 113, 116
  fires 42
  for rent 33, 60, 64
  for sale 44, 45, 64, 70, 74, 81, 88, 102
  framed 104
  log 44
dwelling plantations 56, 67, 70, 74, 75, 97, 100, 111
Dyer
  Walter 85

E

eagles (monetary unit) 87
Earl of Chatham 49
Earl of Tankerville 23, 25, 28
  lands of 28
Earthenware Makers 42
earthquakes 16, 17, 19, 55
East-Indies goods 28
Eastern Branch 5, 12, 29, 32, 45, 55, 75, 76, 104
  ferry 30
  shoals, removing 29
Eastern Branch Ferry 21
Eastern Shore 24, 82
Easton, Md. 109
Edelen
  Butler 111
  Edward 67, 74, 108
Edelen's Tavern 111
Edelin
  Benedict 91
  Edward 114
  Edward, Jr. 61
  James 48
Eden
  Gov. 57, 59, 62
Edenburg, Md.
  being layed out 54

Edenburgh
  John 13
eel skins 107
Egerton
  Peter 54
Eilbeck
  Anne 6
  William 6
elastic cloth 117
elections 2, 9, 12, 14, 17, 19,
  29, 42, 68, 82, 83, 85, 88,
  92, 96, 97, 99, 102, 105,
  106, 112, 114, 115, 118,
  120
Elk Ridge Landing 55, 108
Ellzey
  Thomazin 61
  William 65
elm trees 79
Elvira, Md.
  town to be called 47
Emmerson
  P. 108
  Peter 105
employment 10, 11, 14, 17, 19,
  26, 28, 38, 59, 83, 94, 108,
  116
Engineers 64
England 9, 15, 30, 36, 49, 50,
  66, 74, 105, 108
English convicts 1
English gardener 67
English servants 6, 41
English whalebone 19
Engravers 65
entertainment 2, 32, 38, 57, 71
enumeration of the inhabitants
  102
Episcopal Church 76
  of Maryland 109
epitaphs 42
Erith, Kent, Eng. 8
Errington
  Capt. 43
Essex Co., Va. 46, 78
estates 11, 73, 86, 93, 95, 96,
  98, 101, 103, 106, 107,
  110, 112, 113, 116, 119
  for sale 85
  life 97
Europe 14, 52, 97, 117
European goods 28, 37
Evans
  Joshua 56
Eversfield's chapel 34
exportation 37

exports 62
eye brows 23
  shaved 86
eye water 78, 86

F

Fabre
  Bartholomew, Capt. 33
factors 20
Fairfax
  Bryan 65
  Col., Hon. 14
  G.W., Col. 7
  George William 18, 21, 22,
    24, 40
  George William, Hon. 63
  John 90, 91
  Mrs. 24
  Sarah 25
  William 25
  William, Col. 18
Fairfax Co., Va. 1-4, 6-8, 10,
  13, 21, 31, 49, 58, 63, 66,
  80, 107
  court day 14, 52, 69
  courthouse 46
fairs 1, 3
falls 29, 32, 36, 40, 45, 48, 52,
  53, 56, 63-65
Falls Church, Va.
  building church at 45
Falmouth, Va. 30, 100
false teeth 76
Farmers 39, 101
farming 59
farms 75
  for rent 104
  for sale 86
Farrell
  Kennedy 3
Farriers 36
Fauquier Co., Va. 45, 55
feast days 9
feather beds 99, 114
Federal city 104, 117
felons 41
felt hats 24
fences 88
fencing 19, 26
Fendall
  Anne 83
  B., Dr. 94
  Benjamin 18, 40, 108
  Benjamin, Dr. 72, 83

  Dr. 76
  John 23
  Philip Richard 82, 103
  Phillip 57
  Phillip R. 104
  Rev. 68
  Sarah 108
ferries 28, 31, 33, 39, 41, 47,
  51, 52, 54, 58, 62, 66, 70,
  112
  Addison's 48, 63
  Alexandria 16, 84, 97, 102
  Clifford's 70, 80
  Clifford's, for rent 77
  Clifton, William 2
  Clifton's 30
  Eastern Branch 21, 30
  for rent 96
  Hooe's 40, 67, 74
  Jones' 2
  Leidler's 59
  Posey's 16, 52
  Rock Hall 97
  South River 76, 113, 114,
    116, 119
  Thompson's 2
ferry boats 31, 33
  lost 20
ferry buildings 97
ferry houses 70
fiddles 74
fields 1, 3, 7, 13, 20
Finlay
  Mr. 68
fire engines 15
  experimental 93
  for sale 72
fire places 22, 33, 35, 39, 40,
  44, 45, 50, 51, 63, 79, 81,
  115, 120
fires
  Aquia church 14
  arson 6
  Boston, Mass. 22, 25
  brig Peggy Stewart 65
  Col. Fitzhugh's storehouse
    65
  Dumfries, Va. 25
  Gov. Calvert's house 42
  house of Benedict Calvert 10
  house of H.J. Stier 118
  house of Hon. Phillip Lee 1
  house of Lucy Hatton 6
  house of Thomas Fleming 42
  house of William Fitzhugh 72
  John Glassford & Co. store

books 35
Port Tobacco, Md. 91
Printing-Office 72
prison in Upper Marlborough, Md. 6
Richmond, Va. 89
Stadt House 91
state house, Annapolis, Md. 100
threat of 43
tobacco house 95
tobacco houses 96
tobacco warehouses 72
wheat and rye 95
Williamsburg, Va. 3
firewood 36
fish 59, 71, 84
  destruction of 51
fish houses 44
Fisher
  John 92
  Joseph 65
  Patrick 65
fisheries
  Mattawoman Creek 56
Fishermen 79
fishing 2, 10, 78
fishing landings 66, 76
Fishkill, N.Y. 96
Fitzgerald
  John 83, 95, 107
  John, Col. 78
Fitzhugh
  Col. 65
  Peregrine 83, 89, 111
  William 5, 33, 53, 55, 58, 72, 74, 82, 83
  William, Col. 7, 50, 72
  William, Esq. 9
  William, Hon. 58
Fitzpatrick
  John 32
fives yards 75
flags 81
Flanders 4
flats 52, 67
  for sale 34
Fleming
  Thomas 8, 42
flooring 23
floors 70
flour 52, 77
  branded "Beason" 86
  in barrels 66
  Philadelphia superfine 86
flour houses 39

Flower
  Sarah 58
flying ark
  to be built 115
flying gout 54
Forbes
  John 101
forfeited estates 73
Forge Carpenters 34
forged letters 116
forges 22, 44, 93
Forster
  Ralph 62
Fort Cumberland, Md. 29
  town layed off 35
fort guns 1
Fort Lee 116
Fort Peircall 17
forts 12
Fossit
  Thomas 47
found
  anchor 66
  battoe 98
  cask marked "N-F" 45
  felt hats 24
  horses 37
  prayer book 4
  red steer 89
  stray bull 72
foundations
  State House laid 54
Four Mile Run 28, 46, 58, 120
Fowke
  Gerard 23, 51
  Gerard, Capt. 77, 78
  Richard 69
fowl 84
fowling 78
  landings 76
fox hunts 47
foxes 47
foxing 36
France 45, 77, 78
Franklin
  Benjamin 12
Fraser
  George 23
  Verlinda 66
Frazier
  George 14
  Thomas 18
Frederick Co., Md. 8, 10, 37, 43, 73, 118
Frederick, Md. 16
Fredericksburg, Va. 18, 26, 27,

30, 31, 34, 58, 63, 83, 93, 100, 107
fair 44
Jockey Club 63
population 105
Fredericktown, Md. 23, 31, 43
freeholders 56
French fisherman 79
French nation 12, 16
  war declared 17
French plate 106
frescoes 60
Fricker
  John 40, 41
frigates
  Choptank 66
frockcoats 41
fruit trees 116
  injured 88
Fry
  Joshua 12
Furguson
  Robert 81
furnaces 44, 108
furniture 1, 10, 11, 13, 40, 48, 63, 67, 71, 72, 76, 80, 85, 98, 99, 101, 103, 106, 107, 110, 113, 114
  mahogany 77
  stay 19
Furry
  Rachael 68
fustian frockcoats 41

G

Gadsby
  John 116
Gaither
  Ann 18
  Samuel 18
galleries
  church 36, 40, 45
gallows 23
Galwith
  Jonas 99
Gambia River 28, 32
Gambia slaves 33
gaming 6
Gammell
  William 20, 35
Gantt
  Thomas, Jr. 29
gaol yards 102
Gaolers 47, 104

gaols 19, 69, 102
  Chester Co. 79
  Dumfries, Va. 104
  Prince George's Co., Md. 42
Gardeners
  English 67
gardening 59
gardens 21, 22, 51, 79, 111, 115, 116
  paled in 7, 33, 35, 45, 50, 57
  walled in 44
  walled up 39
  watering 72
Gardner
  Capt. 80
  William 45
garrets 72
Garvey
  Lucas 59
Gasford
  Samuel 55
gates
  palisaded 61
Gawey
  Lucas 37
General Court 110
  Maryland 100, 101, 106
  Virginia 24
Genet
  French minister 109
gentleman's table 10
Gentlemen's Magazine 9
George Tavern 25, 35, 41
  for rent 22
Georgetown, Md. 9, 13, 27, 32, 40, 47, 49, 60, 64, 76, 90-92, 109, 113, 114
Ghiselin
  Reverdy 97
Gibson
  John 16, 54
Gildard
  James 28
Gilpin
  George 83, 95
  William 68
gilt buttons 40
ginger 52
Glasgow, Scotland 29, 31, 38, 44, 60
glass windows 72
Glassford
  John 20, 35, 37, 73, 108
Glebe lands 10
  Truro Parish 45
Gloucester Co., Va. 92

Gody
  John 27
Gold Coast
  Negroes from 33
  slaves 21
gold plate 18
gold rings 1
gold watches 18, 117
gondolas 67
Goodwin sands 79
Gordon
  Christian, Mrs. 52
  George 2, 13
  Robert 2, 19
Gothic phrenzy 78
Gough
  Mr. 62
gout remedy 92
Governor's Council
  Maryland 41
Governors 1, 48, 57, 59, 68, 76, 85, 87, 99
  Maryland 14, 15, 22, 43, 62, 88, 92, 95, 96, 105, 106, 112, 114
  Virginia 12, 15, 105
Graham
  Dr. 52
  Patrick 66
  Richard 20, 50
  William 40
grain 76
grain sithes 76
grammar schools 51, 56
grampus 3
grass 75
grass sithes 76
Gravelly Hill 75
graveyards 51
Gray
  George 56
  John 112
Grayson
  Benjamin 22, 44
  Mr. 94
  William 52, 96
Great Britain 7, 20, 23, 35, 37, 41, 54, 59, 64, 70, 114
Great Falls 29, 93
  canal around 65
Great Falls, Va. 55
Great Hunting Creek 1, 7
Green
  C., Rev. 11
  Catherine 46
  Charles, Rev. 13

  Frederick 71
  George 85
  Jonah 46
  Jonus 5
  Mr. 34
green hams 58
Greenbury Point 42
Greene
  Nathaniel 87
Greenway
  Joseph, Capt. 79
Gretter
  Michael 47
Griffith
  Samuel 67
grist mills 44, 46, 48-50, 70, 78, 93
grooms 35, 36, 40, 60, 66, 100, 108
Grymes
  Benjamin 22
guineas 14, 50, 60, 61, 77, 90, 92, 117
Guiney trade 9
gum [wood] 59
gun work 69
gunpowder 35
Gunpowder River 50
guns 67
  firing in streets 103
  firing of 11, 29
Gunston Hall 1, 100
Gunston, Va. 58
gunwales 59
Gwinn
  John 94

H

Hagan
  Nathaniel 103
hair wool 107
Hale
  Barnhard, Sir 1
half crown notes 27
half dollars 87
Half King 12
Halkerston
  Anne 71
  Elizabeth 116
  J. 111
  John 71, 79, 101, 116
  John, prisoner 91
  Mrs. 35, 48, 56, 69

Hall
  Francis 89
  John 102
  Martha 89
  Notley 67
  Thomas 59
Hambleton
  Arthur, Rev. 72
  William, Capt. 50
Hamilton
  Alexander 58, 65, 70, 102, 107, 108
  Burditt 47, 72
  Dr. 57, 62
  Samuel 111
Hammersley
  Henry 86
Hammitt
  John 74
hams
  green 58
Hancock
  John 85
Handeser
  James 49
handkerchiefs 20
Hanson
  Dorothy 10
  Eleanor 115
  Elizabeth 19, 57
  John 11, 42
  John, Hon. 79
  John, Jr. 27, 35, 37, 98
  John, Sr. 110
  John, the Younger 6
  Robert 47, 51
  Robert, Col. 4, 10
  S. 68, 74
  Samuel 11, 28, 32, 50, 51, 74-77, 79, 113, 115
  Samuel, Jr. 41
  T. 77, 90
  Theodore 52
  Thomas 79, 80
  Thomas H. 77
  Walter 19, 38, 51, 57, 62, 69, 76
  Walter, Rev. 119
  William 8, 34, 70
Hanson's Branch 57
harbours 47, 71, 72, 95, 105
Hardey
  George 27
  George Dent 91
  Henry, Sr. 99
  Isidore 115

hardware 108
Hardy
  George 71
  George, Jr. 27
  Henry 99
  Thomas 71
Harford, Md. 75
Harmer
  Robert 56
Harness Makers 29
harnesses 80, 86, 99, 101, 106, 107, 114
Harper
  Ann 13
  Christopher 13
harpsicords 94
Harrison
  Benjamin, Col. 1
  Col. 67
  Dorothy 10
  John Hanson 37
  Richard, Col. 10
  Robert H., Hon. 101
  Robert Hanson, Hon. 100
  Walter H. 101
Hartshorne
  William 95
Harwood
  Osborn 108
  Thomas 1
  Thomas, Jr. 13
Hatcheson
  Benjamin 117
hats 24, 55, 71, 87, 106
Hatters 106, 115
Hatton
  Lucy, Mrs. 6
Hawkins
  George F. 60
  George Fraser 112
  George Frazier 85
  John 75
  John Stone 34
  Josias 99
  Mary 57
  Mrs., infidelity 34
  Susanna J. 85
  Susannah T. 96
hay 86
Hayes
  Alexander, Capt. 62
Hays
  Rachel 115
  William, Sr. 115
Hayward
  Thomas 18

hedges 68, 79
Heidy
  Philip 92
Henderson
  Alexander 30, 33, 46, 65
  Archibald 33, 37
  Jacob, Rev. 8
Hendricks
  James 64
Henry
  Mr. 94
Herbert
  John Carlyle 113
  William 63, 84, 87
Herring Bay 105
Heryford
  George 21
  John 21
Hesselius
  John 67, 114, 116-119
  Mary 115, 118
  Mr. 116
Hewit
  Thomas 18
hiccory switches 3
Hicks
  William 60
Hill
  Clement 107
His Lordship's
  Honourable Council of State 45
His Lordship's Agent 47
His Lordship's Council 3, 15, 20, 54
His Majesty 1
His Majesty's
  arms 21
  Dominions 8
  Justices of the Peace 21
  seven-year passengers 39
His Majesty's 35th Regiment of Foot 52
His Majesty's arms 21
His Majesty's Council 18
Hodskin
  Allen 70
Hogarth
  Mr. 19
Hoget
  John 47
Hoggins
  Peter 5
hogs 5, 7, 99, 106, 114
hogs' bristles 92
hogsheads 54, 62, 72, 75, 95,

102, 106, 110
damaged tobacco 21
holidays
   Christmas 103
   Thanksgiving established 77
Holkins
   Thomas 58
Holme
   John 31, 34
Hooe
   Capt. 2
   Gerard 67
Hooe's Ferry 40, 67, 74
Hopkenson
   Thomas, Rev. 94
Hore
   William 8
Horne
   John 65
   Pooling 65
horse pens
   graveyard as 51
horse races 1, 3, 13, 20, 23,
   36, 47, 50, 58, 65, 77
   Alexandria, Va. 22, 26, 31
   Annapolis, Md. 5, 7, 26, 45,
     50, 55, 76
   Baltimore, Md. 62
   Bladensburg, Md. 12, 87, 98
   Calvert Co., Md. 71
   judges in 27
   Leedstown, Va. 5
   Piscataway, Md. 41, 44, 47,
     50, 81, 96
   Port Tobacco, Md. 6, 72
   Prince George's Co., Md. 62
   Queen Anne, Md. 85
   Upper Marlborough, Md. 7,
     46, 53, 77
horse yards 79
horses 2, 5, 7, 10, 25, 31, 32,
   36, 38, 39, 50, 72, 73, 80,
   82, 88, 100, 105, 117
   accidents 37
   Achilles 55
   Aeriel 30, 35
   Ajax 97
   Arabian 73
   Bay Bolton 56, 60, 65, 67
   bay geldings 103
   branded "NY" 114
   carriage 119
   Chatham 74, 77, 90
   Comet 74
   Cub 74
   Curious Dentalus 74

   Cyprus 74
   Dauphin 77
   Dutchman 47
   English chesnut filly 34
   fall from 110
   filly 58, 62
   for sale 32, 34, 41, 96, 99,
     101, 106, 112, 114
   found 37
   Frederick Jones 67
   Ganky 62
   gelding 56
   Gimcrack 46
   grey colt 31
   Grey Diomed 114, 116
   Harmony 57
   High Flyer 111, 113, 114,
     116, 119
   Hyder Alley 97, 108
   Hyder Ally 100, 105
   in custody 5
   Jockeys 97
   Jolly Roger 48
   Jolly-C 36
   Leonides 72
   Little Driver 50
   lost 27, 54
   Magnolio 90
   mares 17
   Miss Colvill 26, 40
   Othello 66, 68, 74, 76
   Ovid 72
   Paymaster 108
   Primrose 62
   Ranger 55, 61
   Regulos 53
   Regulus 57, 66
   Rockingham 103
   Roebuck 74, 90
   shoeing 56
   Silverlegs 50, 53
   Slim 62, 77
   Stella 74
   stolen 4, 9, 13, 27, 28, 32,
     61, 63, 64, 84, 107, 114
   stray 20, 21, 23, 30
   stray bay 16
   stray mare 12
   strayed 32, 36, 45, 56, 66,
     84, 90, 107, 114, 120
   Tamerland 74
   Tanner 62
   Trainers 97
   Traveller 36, 40, 46, 74, 108
   Vendome 7
   Venetian 97

   Volunteer 50
   Why Not 57, 62, 77
   Young Traveller 26, 30
Horseshoers 76
hounds
   lost 28
House
   Penelope 14
House Painters 23, 39
house servants 44, 101
house wenches 49
household furniture 50, 56, 63,
   66, 75, 108
houses 11, 50, 60, 72, 85, 116
   for rent 30, 58, 63, 66, 111
   for sale 13, 15, 21, 28, 33,
     35, 38, 44, 46, 57, 59, 71,
     73, 84, 91, 95, 120
   framed 115
   wooden 113
Howe
   Mr. 59, 71
Hoxton
   Walter 76
Hughes
   David 4
   Nathan 33
   Samuel 88
hulls 18
Humphrey
   Col. 73
Hunt
   James 56
Hunter
   George 54
   George, Rev. 78
   Jane 48
   John 22, 30, 48
   Mr. 22, 32, 68
   Rev. 79
   William 12
Hunting Creek 2
Hunting Creek Warehouse
   erecting a town at 5
hunting saddles 4
Hutchinson
   William 56
Hutton
   Margaret 69, 70
   Mrs. 70
Hyde
   Samuel 5
hydrophobia
   cure for 96
   remedy 117

I

ice 42, 72, 80
importation 62
indented servants 8
indentured servants 34, 58
Indian conference 12
Indian corn 47, 76, 94
Indians 16, 17, 109
  Cherokee 117
  scalping 17
infidelity 34
inhabitants
  Charles Co., Md. 78, 79, 94
  Charles Town, Md. 98, 112
  Prince George's Co., Md. 94, 102
  St. Mary's Co., Md. 94
  U.S., enumeration of 102
injured unfortunate 54
injurious stories 109
Innes
  Col. 13
Innkeepers 40
insolvent debtors 91, 97, 113, 118
inspection houses 5
insurance offices 53
Intendant of the Revenue 78, 80, 84
Ireland 4, 14
Irish convict servants 46
Irish linens 58
Irish servants 16, 20
Irishmen 66
iron 69
iron boilers 73
iron furnaces 36
iron spits 36
iron stancheons 120
islands 71

J

jackasses
  Knight of Malta 90, 100, 103, 107, 108
  Royal Gift 90, 100, 103
  Tickle Pitcher 17
jackets 62, 71, 106
Jackson
  James 6
  John 6
  Low 6
  Maj. 104
  Jacques
  Denton 66
jail fever
  deaths from 45
Jailers 66
jails
  Alexandria, Va. 38
  Fairax Co. 13
  Fairfax Co., Va. 6
  Kent Co., Md. 117
Jamaica spirits
  in hogsheads 52
James River 86
Jamestown, Va. 3
Jamieson
  John 56
Jarrold
  Thomas 40
Jenifer
  Daniel 19, 26, 31, 45, 48, 62, 67, 69, 75, 103
  Daniel, Jr. 88, 103
  Daniel, Sr. 103
  Elizabeth (Hanson) 19
  Walter Hanson, Dr. 85
Jenkins
  Edward 97
  Jason 87
  Win 99
jennies 90
Jennings
  John 2
Jernegan
  Henry 32
  Mr. 24
Jeudy
  John 39
Jewellers 39
Jobbers 52
Jockey Club 65
  Fredericksburg, Va. 63
Jockeys 97
John of Gaunt 38
Johnson
  Capt. 5
  Mary Cleaverly 88
  Mr. 119
  Rinaldo 98, 99
  T. 95
  Thomas 82, 83, 88, 96, 103
  Thomas, Jr. 68
Johnston
  Capt. 27
  George 22, 30, 37, 44, 46, 51
  George, estate 51
  Robert 20
  Samuel 30, 58
  Sarah 46, 50, 51
Joiners 23, 61, 66, 111
Jones
  Benjamin 16
  Charles 2, 98
  Penelope 119
  Richard 108
  Thomas 63
Jordan
  John 54
Justices 19, 21, 56, 100, 120
  Alexandria, Va. 68
  Allegany Co., Md. 107
  Charles Co., Md. 4, 20, 43, 105
  Prince George's Co., Md. 4

K

Kennedy
  Daniel 64
Kent
  Emmanuel 58
Kent Co., Md. 49, 50, 58
  jail 117
Kent Island, Md. 2, 72, 89
Kentucky 88
  new state formed 84
Keppel
  Comm. 15
Key
  Edmund 19, 22
  Francis 11
  Philip 37, 57, 102
  Philip B. 118
  Philip Barton 17
  Philip, Hon. 41
  Phillip 1
kid mittens 20
Kilty
  William 112
King
  Francis 38
King & Queen Parish 61
King Charles
  beheaded 23
King George Co., Va. 69, 90
King George the Second 25
King George's Parish 1, 4, 38, 39, 110
King's Store 110
Kingsbury
  Demilion 51

Kingston Parish 92
Kingston, Jamaica 17, 43
Kinsman
  Janet 29, 30
  John 24, 29
Kirk
  James 52
  Mr. 51
Kirkpatrick
  John 30, 31, 33, 34
  Mr. 34, 37
  Thomas 33, 34
Kirton
  John 97
kitchen furniture 63
kitchen utensils 76
kitchens 7, 15, 22, 33, 35, 38-40, 44, 45, 58, 68, 70, 72, 75, 79, 94, 104, 105, 112, 116
  framed 81, 115
knives 10, 78, 87
knives and forks 77
Koome
  Mr. 114
Koome's Tavern 114

L

Laborers 44
lace 41
Laidler
  Capt. 57
  J. 57
Lammond
  John 6
lamp of life went out 10
lampblack 98
Lancaster, Pa. 92
land [see "tracts"]
  deeds 89, 102
  for rent 28, 39, 40, 47, 94, 119
  for sale 37, 39-41, 43, 46-48, 50, 52, 55, 56, 58, 60-62, 69, 71, 72, 74, 75, 82-84, 87, 90-93, 98, 105-108, 112, 113, 116, 118-120
  free school 55
  prizes 111
  sales by Daniel St. Thomas Jenifer 115
  under litigation 81
landings 5, 9, 15, 16, 25, 31, 33, 40, 41, 47, 52, 55, 59, 66, 76, 89, 108, 119
Piscataway, Md. 26
Rock Creek 2
landscapes 11, 119
Lane
  Benjamin 71
  Joseph 57
  Richard 71
Lange
  James, an Englishman 15
languages
  English 54
  French 10, 11, 13, 14, 17
  German 14
  Greek 14, 54
  Italian 14
  Latin 14, 54
Lanham
  Richard 110
Lanham's Tavern 110
Lansdale
  Charles 53, 60, 91
lanthorns 10
last will and testaments 38, 54, 71, 73, 100
Law
  Mr. 117
Lawrie
  James 31, 42
  James, appointed Recorder 29
Laws of Virginia 47
Lawson
  Mr. 68
  Thomas 31, 34, 48, 66
Lawyers 47
Layman
  William 83
leases
  for life 110
  for sale 74
Leatch
  Andrew 63
leather
  scalloped 4
leather breeches 29
Lebanon, Pa. 96
lectures 92
Lee
  Billy 116
  Capt. 25
  Grace 99
  Hannah 34, 37
  Henry, Hon. 105
  Philip Ludwell 19
  Philip Thomas 110
Phillip, Hon. 1
Richard 37
Richard, Hon. 34, 89, 99
Russell 110
Thomas 83
Thomas S. 95
Thomas Sim 106, 112
Thomas, Col. 1
Leeds, Eng. 82
Leedstown, Va. 5
Leidler
  Elizabeth 59
  John 59
Leidler's Ferry 59
Leitch
  Andrew 63, 65
  Joseph 65
Leonard
  Charles 52
Leonardtown, Md. 16, 23, 27, 28, 32, 58, 60, 64
letters 107, 111, 118
  forged 116
  in post office 86, 92, 94, 108, 111, 115, 118
  protest 88
  Washington, George 116
levies 102
  building gaol and gaol yard 102
  for building bridge 98
  repairs to courthouse 105
Lewis
  Thomas 1
liars 48
liberty pole and flag 81
libraries 32
  at Bohemia, Md. 34
  circulating 33, 58, 108, 109
  for sale 8, 69, 70
lies 68
Lieweiler's Warehouse 74
lighthouses 62, 108
  to be built 86
lightning 1, 11, 36, 84, 87
limes 2
  in barrels 37
limestone land 84
limning 11
Lindsey
  William 78
lines 15
Lions Creek 71
liquors 4, 21
  Spanish 15
Little Hunting Creek 14, 16

Littlemore
 Richard 60
Liverpool, Eng. 17, 19, 21, 27, 28, 33, 53
livery lace 41
Lloyd
 Edward, Col. 74
Locke
 George 98
locks
 lower falls 65
locust posts 57
lodges
 Port Tobacco, Md. 92
lodging 36
lodging rooms 50
Lomax
 Mr. 54, 82
Lomax's Tavern 83
London mahogany furniture 77
London plate 77
London, Eng. 9, 10, 14, 22-24, 27, 31, 43, 46, 51, 63, 80, 81, 89
London-Town 105, 112
long boats 10
looking glasses 11
looms 86
Lord
 David 46
Lord Baltimore 8
Lord Botetourt 53
Lord Stair's Regiment 4
Lorton, Eng. 82
lost
 black leather pocket book 87
 boats 89
 clouded cane 96
 dog named Ponto 100
 ferry boat 20
 furniture in fire 1
 gold 96
 gold watch 117
 horse 27, 54
 hound 28
 lottery tickets 23
 medal 9
 Parish book 6
 silver snuffbox 2
 Tuesday Club proceedings 71
lots
 for rent, Alexandria, Va. 30, 39
 for rent, Port Tobacco, Md. 111

for sale 33, 51
for sale, Alexandria, Va. 5, 23, 35, 44, 50, 59
for sale, Belhaven 8, 9
for sale, Cameron 7, 9
for sale, Colchester, Va. 44
for sale, Edenburg, Md. 54
for sale, Georgetown 9
for sale, Newport 95
for sale, Pig Point, Md. 84
for sale, Piscataway, Md. 70, 91, 95, 99
for sale, Port Tobacco, Md. 38, 48, 68, 97, 99, 113-115, 119
formed, Carrollsburg, Md. 52
lotteries 23, 111
 Alexandria, Va. 22, 24, 25
 Annapolis, Md. 36
 Belhaven 9
 Belhaven, Va. 7, 8
 Bladensburg, Md. 29
 Bohemia, Md. 34
 clearing Patuxent River 51
 Edenburg, Md. 54
 LaFayette village 85
 Port Tobacco, Md. 35
 prizes listed 34
 Upper Marlborough, Md. 21
 Winchester, Va. 25
Loudon Co., Va. 23
Loudoun Co., Va. 54, 56, 63, 76, 116
Love
 Charles 19
 Philip, Lieut. 31
 S. 116
 Samuel, Jr. 76
Lowe
 Henry 7
 James 50
 Mr. 96
Lower Cedar Point 2
Lower Marlborough Academy 67
Lower Marlborough, Md. 28, 82
Lowndes
 Christopher 3, 15
 Francis, Capt. 24
 Richard T., Hon. 106
Lowrie [also see "Lawrie"]
 John 50
Luckett
 John Boone 63
 Thomas 106
 Thomas Hussey 99

lumber houses 40
Lunatick Club 56
lutestrings 25
Lyle
 Mr. 62
Lyles
 Hilleary 20
 W. 73
 William 57, 62, 73
 William, Capt. 115
 William, Jr. 64, 66, 78

M

machines
 perpetual motion 51
 pile-driving 89
Machodock Creek 90
Machodock River 52
MacKenzie
 Daniel 24
Mackubin
 John 10
Maddins
 Scarlet 48
Maddox
 Charles 110
 Walter 20
Maddox's Old Field 20
Madiera
 in pipes 26
Magdebourg, Prussia 106
Magistrates 12, 53
 Charles Co., Md. 30
Magne
 Mr. 21
Magnett
 Ezekial 32
Magothy River 108
Magruder
 Edward 76, 110
 Hezekiah 70
 John 6
 John Read 74
 Mary 70
 Mr. 70
mahogany bookcases 98
mahogany dining tables 106
mahogany furniture 77
mahogany plank 31
mahogany silver mounted case 77
Mahoney
 John 111
mail 73, 75

Along the Potomac River: **Extracts from the *Maryland Gazette*, 1728-1799**

mail coaches
  robbery of 120
Mamazink 71
Managers 8, 9, 22, 24-26,
  29-31, 36, 48, 58, 59, 95,
  103
Mandeville
  John 112
Mankin
  Charles 79, 95, 98, 99, 114,
  118, 119
Mann
  George 85
Mann's Tavern 102
Manning
  John 41
mansion houses 48, 79
mantel pieces 36
manumission 100
maps 30
marble columns 73
Marbury
  William 115
market houses 7
  Annapolis, Md. 11
  Winchester, Va. 25, 28
market prices 99
markets 112
marking instruments 63
Marlborough Neck, Va. 120
Marlborough, Md. 4
Marlborough, Va. 44, 47, 111
Marlow
  Mr. 42
  Samuel Middleton 28
Marquis de la Fayette 81
marriages 10, 70, 81, 85
  Adair, Elizabeth 49
  Addison, Thomas, Jr. 46
  annuled 92
  Bowles, Rebecca, Mrs. 1
  Brice, Ariana 6
  Carroll, Charles 47
  Darnall, Mary 47
  Dulany, Daniel, Jr. 5
  Dulany, Rebecca 46
  Eilbeck, Anne 6
  Fitzhugh, William, Esq. 9
  Key, Francis 11
  Lee, Hannah 34
  Lowndes, Christopher 3
  Mason, George, Esq. 6
  Mercer, John F. 83
  Plater, George 1, 34
  Posey, John 49
  Ross, Anne Arnold 11

  Ross, David, Dr. 6
  Rousby, Mrs. 9
  Sprigg, Miss 83
  Tasker, Elizabeth 3
  Tasker, Rebecca 5
  West, Stephen 12
  Williams, Hannah 12
Marshall
  James 20, 22, 26, 30, 37, 50,
  57
  John 27
  T. Hanson, Capt. 52
  Thomas 22, 31, 97, 111, 118
  Thomas H. 111
  Thomas Hanson 22, 53, 56,
  59, 62
  Thomas, Dr. 100
marshes 81
Martin
  Luther 91
Martinico 69
Martinique Gazette 88
Maryland 12, 13, 16, 25, 32,
  35, 47, 49, 54, 60, 65, 74,
  80, 82-84, 86, 95, 118
  counties in southern 55
  Great Seal 111
  House of Delegates 102,
  115, 117, 118, 120
  Virginia 82
Maryland boys 12
Maryland Constitutional
  Convention 93
Maryland currency 28
Maryland Gazette 4, 32, 34, 44,
  46
Maryland General Court 100,
  101
Maryland Medical Society
  to be formed 120
Maryland Patowmack tobacco
  108
Maryland Point 67
Maryland Society of the
  Cincinnati 102
Mason
  Anne 34
  George 7, 22, 46, 61, 65, 80,
  87, 93, 95, 107
  George, Col. 34, 58
  George, Esq. 6
  George, Jr. 80, 87, 89
  George, Mrs. 1
  Mary 54
  Mr. 94
  Thompson 27

Thomson 26, 28, 32, 41, 54,
  65
Massachusetts 113
  state house 116
Massachusetts legislature
  commissions portrait 116
Massey's heirs 76
masters 18, 23
Mastin
  Francis 52
masts 19
mates 24, 82
  of Capt. Montgomery 15
mathematics 59
Mattawoman Creek 56, 84,
  106, 116, 120
Mattawoman, Md. 42
Matthews
  Ignatius 78
  Ignatius, Rev. 76
  William 75
Maurlbourgh 98
Maxwell
  Nancy 70
Mayors
  Alexandria, Va. 29
  Annapolis, Md. 2
McAtee
  John 109
McBride
  Hugh 43
McCabe
  Henry 33
McCain
  Marmaduke 89
McCarty
  Daniel 11, 13, 50, 53, 65, 74,
  107
  Mr. 55
McCrae
  Allen 21, 22, 30
McGrath
  Mr. 117, 119
McHenry
  J. 91
McKenzie
  Donald 7
McLaughlin
  Mary 4
McPherson
  William 65
meadows 45, 59, 64
measles 78
meat houses 15, 33, 35, 39, 44,
  45, 68, 72, 81, 112
Mechanics 107

Medcalf
  John 47
medical instruments 42
medicine 98
  for sale 103
Meek
  Francis 67
meeting houses 53
Mercer
  George 25, 35
  George, Col. 29, 63
  James 58, 95
  John 20, 44, 47
  John F. 83, 92, 96, 98, 120
  John Francis 91, 111
  John, Col. 95
  William 52
Merchants 3, 6, 12, 18, 20, 22, 26-30, 33, 34, 37, 39, 43, 45, 46, 49, 54, 59, 60, 63, 65, 80, 84, 90, 94, 100, 105
Merrimack River 113
merrymakings 6
Messenger
  Joseph, Rev. 73
metal buttons 87
metals 29
Middleton
  Ignatius 46
  Mr. 77
  Samuel 50
Middleton's tavern 77
Milborn
  John 33
military
  1st Maryland Regiment 68
  appointment 69
  army 76
Military Officers 18
militia 17, 67, 70
  Portly Corps 111
milk houses 70, 81
milk pots 46
mill houses 44
mill seats 108
Millby
  Robert 4
mills 32, 44, 46, 48-50, 70, 78, 82, 93, 108
  Port Tobacco 99
  water 5
mills (monetary unit) 87
millstones 77
  hand 31
Mine Bank 48

mines
  saltpetre 49
miniatures 119
mining 17
Ministers 10
Mintier
  Ninian 40
Mitchel
  Collin 4
mohair buttons 85
molasses 33, 69, 86
  in hogsheads 37
monetary units 84, 87
money 12
Montgomerie
  Thomas 53, 63
Montgomery
  Capt. 15
Montgomery Co., Md. 98, 101
monuments 73
  memory of Washington 86
Moore
  Cassandra (Adair) 49
  John 49
  William 21
Morlay, France 18
Morphy
  John 20
Morris
  Hugh 69
Morrison
  Robert 38
mortar and pestle 11
Morton
  Mr. 40
Moss
  John 56
mountains
  Carolina 109
mourning 120
Muir
  John 22, 23, 80
Mulattoes 2, 21, 29, 32, 37, 55, 78, 80, 83, 89, 106, 107, 116
mulberry 59
mules 27, 107
Mulliken
  Thomas 37
Mundell
  Robert 28, 35, 73
Munrow
  Dan 66
Murdock
  Anne 12
  Mr. 1, 14

  Samuel, Capt. 26
  William 12, 42
Murdock's Old Fields 1, 14
Murphy
  John 23
Muschett
  Mungo 97
music 19, 94
  to be published 52
musical instruments 29
  bassoon 19
  drum 80, 87
  fiddle 19, 74
  flute 19
  harpsicord 94
  violin 19
Musicians 6, 54
muskets 4
muslin 63

N

nails 55
  making 69
Nanjemoy Creek 23, 74, 81
Nanjemoy, Md. 10, 21, 25, 28, 53, 72, 78, 105, 119
natural curiosities
  house for 87
Naval Officers 1, 15
naval offices
  Alexandria, Va. 93
  Charles Co., Md. 18, 40
navigation 51
  growing difficult 95
  Potomac River 29, 64, 82, 86, 105
Nayler
  George, Jr. 77
Neabsco Furnace 66, 108
Neabsco Iron Works 31, 43, 48
Neale
  Edward 24, 89
  Leonard, Rev. 87
necessary houses 35, 75, 76
necessary outhouses 40
needles 11
Negro quarters 5
Negroes 38, 41, 50, 58, 65, 71, 76, 79, 81, 86, 87, 92, 100, 104, 109, 117
  died 23
  for hire 28
  for sale 28, 31, 33, 37, 56, 69, 73, 74, 83, 85, 88, 96,

139

99, 100, 102, 103, 105-107, 110, 113, 118, 119
   for sale, term 117
   mortgaged 100
   prisoner 6
   runaways 16, 21, 27, 43, 48, 80, 85, 87, 102-104, 109, 112
   Spanish pirates 3
Nevitt
   Thomas 111
New England 53
New Hampshire 113
New York 9, 34, 97, 107
Newport 101
Newport, Md. 19, 27
Newport, Va. 95, 98
newspapers 5, 8, 34, 46, 88, 96
   advertising stray horses 23
   Maryland Gazette
      expiring 44
      office 32
      suspended 71
   Virginia Journal & Alexandria Advertiser 82
Newton
   Isaac, Sir 20
Nicholson
   Col. 62
nicking 36
Noble
   Joseph 60
   Mary Anne 41
Norfolk, Eng. 89
Norfolk, Va. 62
North Carolina regiment 13
North Sea 79
Nottingham 57, 62

O

Occoquan Furnace 17
Occoquan Iron Works 33, 43
Occoquan River 19, 44, 45
Occoquan Run 108
Occoquan Works 93
Odell
   Edward 64
Office of Preservation 73
officers 14
offices 44, 48
Ogle
   Benjamin 100
   Gov. 48

Ohio 61
Ohio Company 35, 46
Ohio River 12, 13, 58, 86
old age 23, 30, 45, 64, 102, 109
old chapel land 60
old fields 1, 3, 7, 13, 14, 20
Onion Iron Works 75
operas 10
orations 113
orchards 16, 44, 104
   apple 53, 57, 60, 62, 64, 75
   cherry 81
   peach 45, 60, 72
ordinaries 49, 52, 63
Ordinary Keepers 4, 9
ordnance field pieces 73
Organists 20, 38, 52, 61
organs 32, 80
Ormsby
   John 18
orphans' court 106
Orr
   John 33
osnabrigs 13
Oston
   Thomas 99
outbuildings 70
outhouses 16, 31, 40, 94, 104
over mantles 29
overalls 106
overfloat watermills 64
Overseers 7, 10, 45, 90, 97, 120
overseers houses 120
oxen 101, 107, 114
Oxen Hill, Md. 25
Oxen list 99
Oxon Creek 16
oysters 59, 71
   swamp 71

P

Paca
   William 55, 68
packets 108
Pagan
   John 2, 7, 9, 11, 18, 29
Painters 11, 49, 60, 64, 119
   signs 35
palisaded gates 61
Palmer
   Timothy 113
pamphlets

Introductory Discourse to An Argument... 98
Pamunkey Neck, Md. 31
pantrys 39
paper 63
paper currency 25, 27, 49
Paris, France 79
parishes
   Durham 67
   King & Queen 61
   King George's 1, 4, 38, 39, 110
   Kingston 92
   Port Tobacco 8, 20, 31, 38, 52, 72
   Queen Anne's 64
   St. Anne's 4, 6
   St. Barnaby's 8
   St. John's 38, 42, 110
   Trinity 53
   Truro 10, 36, 40, 44, 45, 61
parliament
   President of 81
Parnham
   John 102
passengers 80
   7-year 39
   from convict ship 45
pasturage 40
pastures 33, 90
Patapsco, Md. 3
Patowmack Canal Company 83
Patowmack Co. 96, 106, 116
patriots 22
patterns 69
Patterson
   John 23, 25, 28
   Joseph 29
   Susannah 48
Patuxent River 15, 21, 24, 26, 72, 84, 101
   clearing chanel of 51
Payne
   Daniel 30
   William 11
Payton
   Mr. 49
Peabody
   Capt. 80
peach orchards 45, 60, 72
Peake
   John 16
Peale
   Charles 49, 64
   Charles Wilson 29, 35, 39
   Mr. 87, 119

Along the Potomac River: **Extracts from the *Maryland Gazette*,** 1728-1799

Peale's Museum 95
peasants 73
Peers
   Nicholas 88, 91, 94, 98
   Valentine 88, 91, 94, 98
pelicans 95
Pemberton
   Samuel, Capt. 28
Pembroke
   Mr. 106
pencils 119
Perrin
   M. 77
peruke makers 21
Peruvian Bark 64
Peter
   Robert 29
petitions 78, 79, 87, 89, 92-94, 97, 98, 101, 102, 107, 109, 111-116, 118, 119
Petre
   Catherine, Rt. Hon. 27
petticoats 71
Pettit
   John 18
Petty
   John 102
Pewterers 56
Peyton
   Henry, Col. 50
phætons 94, 101
phials
   for eye water 78
Philadelphia, Pa. 12, 17, 18, 31, 57, 62, 65, 71, 75, 78, 80, 106, 109
   convention in 91
   state house 91
Philee 63
Phillips
   Teresia Constantia 43
Philosophers 79
Philpot
   Brian, Jr. 8
Philpott
   Benjamin 42
physic 83, 85, 88
Physicians 9, 30, 42, 45, 52, 56, 57, 62, 64, 69, 73, 83, 85, 88, 98
physick 98
piazzas 113, 115, 120
Piccawaxon Church 72
Pickett
   Heathcoat 16
pieces of eight 7, 8

Pierce
   Isaac, Jr. 49
   Isabel 1
Pig Point, Md. 27, 51, 55, 84
Pile
   William 64
pile driving machine
   to be built 89
Piles' Warehouse 52
pillars 120
pillory 2, 4
pilot boats 69, 82
Pilots 69, 82
   rules for 92
Pimmit Run 52
pine rails 61
Piper
   Henry 52
pirates 3
Piscataqua River 113
Piscataway Church 72
Piscataway Creek 41, 78, 84, 119
Piscataway, Md. 1, 5, 6, 10, 17, 19-24, 26-28, 30, 35-38, 40, 41, 43, 44, 47-51, 54, 55, 57, 58, 60-68, 70, 71, 73-76, 78, 81, 84-86, 90, 91, 95-97, 99, 101, 102, 107, 108, 110, 111, 113, 114, 115, 118
   post office 113, 118
pistol shot 59
pistoles 13, 66
pistols 78
   for sale 41
pitch 41
plaister 81
plaistering 21
plans
   City of Washington 107
plantation utensils 74, 76, 117
plantation work 76
plantations 9, 12, 16, 21, 23, 25, 32, 36, 38, 40, 45, 56, 57, 60, 63, 66, 67, 72-74, 84, 86, 87, 97, 99, 101, 102, 108, 114, 117
   for lease 73
   for rent 58, 117
   for sale 76, 81, 84
Planters 36, 75
planters' work 69
Plasay
   Mrs. 22
   Widow 37, 38

Plasterers 61
plate 106
   French 106
   London 77
   of parish 45
   stolen 1, 18
Plater
   Col. 54
   George 1, 3, 27, 28, 34, 37, 38, 64, 86, 93, 103, 106
   George, Col. 6
   George, Hon. 15, 105
   George, Jr. 102
   Hannah (Lee) 37
   John Rousby 106, 112
   Mrs. 6
plats 58
plays
   The Rivals 88
ploughs 114
pocket books
   lost 87
poems 13
poetry 92, 119
Pohick Church 10
Pohick Creek 44, 61
Pohick Run 58
Pohick warehouse 58
Point Lookout 41
poisoning 15
poisons 93
pokeweed juice 9
poltergeist story 96
Pomonkey Neck 56
Pooley
   A. 11
poor 49
Poplar Island 66
population census 105
pork 99
Port Tobacco Creek 54, 70, 75, 78, 94, 102, 105
Port Tobacco Mill 99
Port Tobacco Parish 8, 20, 31, 38, 52, 72, 73
Port Tobacco Run 116
Port Tobacco warehouse 70
Port Tobacco, Md. 4, 6, 10, 18-20, 23, 24, 26-32, 34, 35, 38, 40-42, 46, 48, 49, 54, 56, 57, 60, 62, 64, 66, 68-72, 74-79, 82-94, 97, 98, 100-102, 104, 106, 107, 109-113, 115, 116, 118
   inhabitants 91

141

post office 118
Portly Corps 111
portmanteaus 116
portraits 49, 119
   Washington, George 116
Portugal 77
Posey
   Belain 89, 91
   Elizabeth (Adair) 49, 58, 61
   John 31, 32, 34, 49, 58
   John, Capt. 49, 50, 52, 61
   Lawrence 120
   Thomas 36
Posey's Ferry 16
post offices 92
   Allen's Fresh, Md. 108
   Annapolis, Md. 86
   Chaptico, Md. 108
   letters in 94
   Piscataway, Md. 113, 115, 118
   Port Tobacco, Md. 108, 118
   Upper Marlborough, Md. 111
Post Riders 18, 53, 75
   robbed 73
   wanted 39
Postmaster General 8, 12
Postmasters 107, 115
Pot House 17
Potomac River 1, 2, 5, 8, 12, 14, 16, 18, 20, 21, 23, 24, 26-28, 30, 31, 36, 39, 40, 43-46, 49, 50, 52, 53, 55-59, 62-66, 69, 70, 73-76, 78, 80, 82, 84, 86, 92, 95, 98, 100, 102, 105, 110, 113, 120
   falls of 48
   Monocacy Manor 118
   navigation of 29, 82
   upper falls of 32
Potomac, Va. 28
potteries
   Rumney, Edward 2
pottery 17
Potts
   John 90
   Richard 92
   William 118
Powell
   William 50
power of attorney 67
Prather
   Thomas, Col. 29
Pratt
   Henrietta 57

Henry 57
Mulattoes 57
prayer book 4
Presbyterian church
   to be built 53
President of Congress 79
Presidents 97, 103, 104, 106
   Maryland Constitutional Convention 93
   Maryland Senate 68
   Patowmack Co. 95
   Virginia 25
Prince George's Co., Md. 1, 2, 4, 5, 7-10, 13, 14, 16, 19, 20, 25, 26, 28, 30, 31, 34, 36, 37, 39, 40, 42, 43, 47, 49-51, 53, 54, 56, 57, 61, 62, 64-67, 69, 70, 73, 74, 76, 78, 79, 84, 85, 87, 89, 91, 93, 95, 97, 99-102, 105-110, 112, 114, 116-118, 120
   alms house 51
   courthouse 8
   courthouse in disrepair 3
   courthouse repairs 4
   free school 48, 61, 74
   free school land 63
   gaol 42
   House of Delegates 92
   inhabitants 94, 102
   public prison 9
   school 3, 11
Prince William Co., Va. 4, 37, 53, 54, 59, 62, 74, 81, 83, 93, 95, 108
   court held 63
Prince William militia 17
Princeton, N.J. 110
Printers 5, 6, 19, 32-34, 46, 47, 71, 109
printing offices 30, 72, 76, 107
printing presses 33
prisoners 75, 91
   escaped 42
prisons 6, 14, 86, 87
   Alexandria, Va., to be built 38
   escapes 18
   Prince George's Co., Md. 9
privy houses 39
processions 29
proclamations 77, 87, 95
promissory notes 13
Proprietor's Agent 54
Protestant Episcopal Church 107
Protestants 14
Provence 81
Provincial Court 12
public houses 11, 26, 28, 33, 35, 42, 58, 68, 75
public sales 21, 22, 77, 88, 100
   Alexandria lots 5
public vendues 19, 31, 33
Pump Makers 49
Punch's head 50
punishment
   caned, burned 44
punishments
   bored through tongue 3
puppet Punch's head 50
puppets
   Bailey's 84
Pye
   Charles 86
   Walter 86, 93, 100

Q

Quantico Creek 62, 95
Quantico, Va. 10, 52
quarries 62
Quartermaster General 14
quarters 32, 81
Quebec
   Reduction of 21
Queen
   Henry 40
Queen Anne, Md. 1, 16, 19, 27, 61, 84, 85
Queen Anne's Co., Md. 17, 27, 58
Queen Anne's Parish 64
Queen's Town, Md. 4
Queen-Tree 101

R

rabbits 2
race grounds 117
   Alexandria, Va. 26
   Annapolis, Md. 26
Ralls
   John 46, 53
Ramsay
   Anthony 8
   Col. 78
   Mrs. 22
   William 7, 8, 11, 17, 18, 22,

25, 29-31, 35-38, 41, 63, 65, 66
William, founder of Alexandria, Va. 29
William, Hon. 68
Rangers 5
Rappahannock River 27, 62
rattlesnakes 4
Rawlings
  Aaron 13
  Capt. 15
  Samuel 108
Reade
  Robert, Rev. 49
reading 67, 116
Reading, Pa. 119
Receiver General 47
record offices
  Charles Co., Md. 105
Recorder
  Alexandria, Va. 29
recruiting song
  printed 13
red steer 89
Reeder
  B. 95
  Benjamin 91
  Thomas 72
Reeves
  Thomas Charles 88
  Thomas Courtney 88
refugee barges 75
regiments 12, 13
Registers 39
Registrars 110
Reid
  Andrew 9
remedies
  cancer 9
  gout 92
  hydrophobia 96, 117
removals 29, 37, 43, 119
repairs
  carriages 29
  courthouse 4, 105
  public wharf 22
  Stadt House 80, 110
  watches 39
Representatives 6, 9, 12, 17, 25, 28, 42, 44, 57, 111
revenue offices 93
rewards 1, 23, 31, 32, 40, 41, 43, 64, 65, 81, 91, 96, 104, 106, 109, 111, 112, 114, 117

Rhodes
  John 47
Richie
  Mr. 33
Richmond Co., Va. 31
Richmond, Va. 92-94
Ricketts' Equestrian Circus 120
Ridgate
  Elizabeth 101
  Mr. 57
  Thomas How 93, 100, 101, 115
riding carriages 119
riding chairs 99
Rigden
  Edward 51
rigging 15, 20
Rind
  Mr. 34
  William 33, 47
rivers [see name] 2, 72
roads 5, 7, 19, 20, 31, 37, 57, 58, 62, 71, 75, 79, 86, 87, 113, 115
  near the wood yard 2
  post 31, 45
robe-coats 19
Roberson
  Mr. 59
Robinson
  Charles 31
Rochambeau 73
  Count 76
Rock Creek 1, 3, 6, 8, 9, 99
Rock Creek Landing 2
Rock Hall Ferry 97
roebucks 67
Rogers
  J. 57
  William 59
Roman Catholic Church 79
Roman orator 49
ropewalks 15
Rose
  Thomas 98
Ross
  Anne Arnold 11
  David 9, 23, 33, 39
  David, Dr. 6
  Hector 22, 30, 52
  John 11
  Mr. 111
Ross' Tavern 111
Rousby
  John 7, 9
  Mr. 7

Mrs., widow 9
rowboats 67
rowgalleys
  Protector 67
Royal American Magazine 59
Rozer [or Rozier]
  Eleanor 89
  Henry 16, 24, 26, 30, 36, 46, 48, 52, 67, 74, 89, 93, 106, 107, 110, 111, 118
  Miss 94
  Mr. 36, 40
  Mrs. 1
  Thomas 86
rozin 41
rugs 58
rum 33, 40, 52, 101
  in hogsheads 37
Rumney
  Edward 2, 6
  William, Dr. 52
Rumsey
  James 81
  Joseph 93
runaways 1-6, 8, 9, 12, 13, 15, 16, 18-21, 23-27, 29, 32-34, 37, 40-43, 46-48, 50, 51, 55, 58, 59, 61-67, 69, 71, 74, 78, 80, 83-87, 89, 92, 102-104, 106, 107, 109, 111, 112
runways 23
Rusbatch
  Samuel 60
Rutland
  Thomas 94
rye 95

S

S.C.
  Mrs. 3
saddlers 29, 35, 39, 49
saddles 4, 37
Sadler
  Richard 61
sailing yawls 117
Sailors 42
sails 19, 20
Salem, N.J. 101
salt 28
saltpetre mine 49
Sandy Point 57, 67
Savannah, Ga. 87

143

Along the Potomac River: Extracts from the *Maryland Gazette*, 1728-1799

Savary
  P. 84, 102
saw mills 44, 93
saws 31
Sawyers 31
scars 78, 80, 117
Schneider
  John 54
School Teachers 36
schoolhouses 20
Schoolmasters 1, 3, 11, 24, 34, 48, 51, 64
schools 17
  building of 24
  Charles Co., Md. 34, 51
  Charlotte Hall 85
  dancing 18
  free 48, 55, 60, 61, 63, 64, 74
  free, St. Mary's Co., Md. 20
  grammar 51, 56
  grammar, erecting of 22
  Prince George's Co., Md. 3, 11
  St. Mary's Co., Md. 1
  Talbot Co. charity-working 14
schooner rigged boat 24
schooners 18
  Anne Maria 68
  for sale 2, 33, 34
  George 52
  Hope 82
  Industry 34, 37
  Lucy 69
  Saltana and George 69
  Virgin 40
  Why Not 77
Scotch coal 40
Scotchmen 24, 29, 66
Scotland 36
Scott
  George 54
  Gustavus 82
  Gustavus R. 99
  James 37
  John 83
  Rev. 54
  Richard 98
  Zachariah 57
scroll heads
  on schooner 2
Seahorn
  Christopher 84

seals
  pinchbeck 117
Sears
  William 53
seas
  cessation of arms 77
Sebastian
  Benjamin 39
Secretarys 90
  Maryland 15, 25, 27
Seelig
  Michael 25
Sefton
  Charles 115
seine 117
seine hauling 10, 13
Selkeld
  Henry 53
seminaries 83
Semmes
  Ignatius 23, 26, 32, 38, 40
  Mary 40
Semple
  John 30, 93
Senators 96, 106
Senegal River 32
servants 1-6, 8, 9, 11, 13, 15, 16, 18, 20, 21, 23, 24, 26, 31, 33, 34, 41-44, 46-48, 50, 51, 54, 55, 58, 59, 62, 63, 86, 108
settlers to Ohio 61
Severn River 11, 42, 104
Sewell
  William 21
sewing cases 18
Sextons 107
shalloons 40
Sharpe
  Gov. 14, 15
shaving wigs 10
shavings 14
Shaw
  John 72
sheds 21
sheep 72, 73, 101, 106
sheetings 58
sheets 4, 24
Shenando Falls 36
Shenandoah River 63
sheriffs 12, 13, 17, 38, 41, 62, 78, 81, 85, 102, 106, 107, 109, 111, 117
  fees due as 93
shingles 3, 39
ship bread 18

Ship Tavern 47
ship work 69, 76
Shipbuilders 42
Shipping Hole, Md. 33
ships 2, 10, 15, 19, 27, 50, 59, 67, 95
  African 27
  Alexander 26
  Alexandria 18
  Alice 26
  Baltimore 24
  British 72
  Catherine 31
  Christian 32
  clearing of 93
  convict 45
  Fair Lily 38
  Fishburn 14
  Hicks 34, 39
  insurance for 53
  Irish cutter 82
  Jane 43
  Jenifer 25
  John & Presley 31
  loading 62
  Mary & Anne 66
  Molly 69
  Neptune 39
  Notley 81
  Ocean 65
  Osgood 14
  parts 19
  Peggy 27
  Phoenix 23
  Prince Edward 12
  Royal Charlotte 33
  Sampson 79
  sprung a leak 82
  Swan 46
  Thames Frigate 5
  to Europe 97
  Trial 43
  True Blue 21
  Two Friends 80
  Upton 28
  Wilson 24
ships of war
  British 71
Shirden
  John 41
shirts 29, 40
shoals 29
shoes 10, 106
shop furniture 103
shops 15, 29, 35

Shorter
  Mr. 106
shorthand gentlemen 93
side tables 106
sign painting 35
silk 63
silk bonnets 71
silver 51
silver buckles 1
silver handled knives and forks 77
silver mounted case 77
silver snuffboxes 2
silver spoons 37
silver teapots 46
silver watches 25
Silversmiths 39
Simmes
  James 106
Simmons
  Jonathan 97
  Thomas, Capt. 75
Simms
  Joseph 68
sithes 76
sixpence 27, 111, 112
skating 42
Skinner
  Mary 50
  Walter 50
Skinners 53
skittle alley 75
slander 95
slaves 5, 10, 21, 27, 28, 43, 48, 50, 58, 75, 82
  country born 22
  disabled 100
  for hire 59
  for sale 14, 26, 28, 32, 33, 37, 42, 50, 52, 67, 71, 73, 76, 78, 80, 98, 101, 107, 111, 114, 116, 118
  manumission 100
  runaways 80, 87
  to hire 65
  Virginia-born 120
slip partitions 79
slips 19
sloops 8, 11, 18
  large sea 35
  Nancy, Virginia-built 41
  Ranger 57
Slye
  Mrs. 75
small pox 21, 42

Smallwood
  Gen. 113
  Henry 120
  Priscilla 110
  Priscilla Hebbert 106
  Virlinda 120
  William 25, 37, 42, 57, 62, 82, 88, 92, 95, 102, 106, 110, 117, 119, 120
  William, Hon. 72, 85, 106
  William, Maj.-Gen. 118
Smith
  Basil 56
  John 34
  John Addison 99
  Nathaniel 15
  Richard 112
Smith's houses 62
Smith's Point 20
Smith's shops 8, 64
Smith's tools 69
Smiths 69
Smithys 40
smoaks 67
smoke houses 22, 35, 58
snakebite 2
Snicker's ordinary 63
Snows
  Alexandria 21
  Brent 26
  Favourite Polly 33
  Norfolk 63
  Virginian 27, 33
snuffboxes 2
Soape
  Thomas 114
Society of the Cincinnati
  Maryland 102
soil 75, 76, 79
soldiers 4, 13, 32
  at Alexandria, Va. 12
soldiers' uniforms 78
Somervell
  James, Dr. 7
Sommerville
  Capt. 39
songs
  Mount Vernon 117
Soper
  Leonard 45
  Nathan 95
South
  John 31
South River 14, 76, 100, 104
South River Church 96

South River Ferry 113, 114, 116, 119
Spanish America 52
Spanish liquor 15
Spanish pirates 3
Speakers 118
spectators 29
Speers
  Thomas 66
spinets 77
spoons 37
  engraved 51
Sprigg
  J.R. 92
  Miss 83
springs 13, 57, 58, 111
Sprotson
  Croasdale 61
St. Andrew
  feast of 29
St. Anne's Parish 4, 6
St. Barnaby's Parish 8
St. Clair
  John, Sir 14
St. George's Island 75
St. John's Church 43
St. John's College 113, 115, 118
  opens 100
St. John's Parish 38, 42, 110
St. Kitts 37
St. Martins 80
St. Mary's Co., Md. 1, 11, 15, 17, 19, 22, 27, 28, 34, 38, 40, 41, 53, 55, 57, 59-63, 71, 74, 85, 86, 98, 102, 115
  courthouse 26, 32
  free school 20, 61
  inhabitants 94
  public school 1
St. Mary's River 17, 24, 72
St. Mary's, Md. 19, 25, 75, 81
St. Thomas Jenifer
  Daniel 17, 25, 32, 36, 41, 47, 51, 54, 59, 68, 78, 80, 84, 87, 90, 91, 93, 96, 100, 102-104, 115
stables 15, 22, 25, 33, 35, 38-40, 44, 46, 61, 63, 72, 81, 104, 113, 116
  framed 79
Stadt House 80
  fire at 91
  repairs needed 110

Stafford Co., Va. 1, 14, 34, 40, 41, 46, 47, 53, 55, 74, 83, 95, 117
   courthouse 35, 46
stage coaches 19
stages 90
Stamp Distributor 44
stamp tax 44
stancheons 120
Stanley
   Edward, Capt. 32
State Houses
   foundation laid 54
Stationers 63
statues
   Lord Botetourt 53
Stay Making 15
Staymakers 19, 20, 35, 39, 60
stays 20
Steel
   Matthew 13
steel (metal) 24, 69
steers 97
Stephen
   Adam 13
Steptoe
   James, Col. 57
sterling 28
Stevens
   Mr. 100
Stewart
   Antony 65
   Dr. 103
   James 52
Stier
   H.J. 114, 118
stills 73
stock 74, 75, 107, 110, 118
stockings 24, 106
stocks 18, 54, 90
   James River 86
Stoddert
   Benjamin 2
   Benjamin C. 88
   John T. 37, 42
   John Truman 42
stolen
   gold watch 18
   grey horse 27
   horse 64
   horse from stable 61
   Negro girl slaves 58
   pinchbeck watch 93
   puppet Punch's head 50
   roan mare 63
stolen goods 11

Stone
   Col. 103, 108
   David 56
   Frederick 110
   H. 104
   J. 95
   J.H. 92, 97, 108, 116
   J.H., Col. 68
   John H. 84, 102, 113, 114
   John H., Col. 83
   John Hoskins 112
   John Hoskins, Hon. 105
   M.J. 100, 107
   M.V. 116
   Margaret 91
   Mary 105
   Mr. 120
   T. 82, 83
   Th. 57
   Thomas 53, 62, 68, 88, 95, 100, 110, 117
   Thomas, Hon. 91, 92
   Walter 90, 105
Stone masons 47
stones 62
   extract poison 92
Stonestreet
   Edward 109
   Henry 86
   Mr. 109
   Thomas 54
store books 35
store rooms 120
   for rent 83, 84
storehouses 5, 7, 38, 40, 45, 46, 63, 65, 70
   for rent 7, 75, 88
Storekeepers 27
stores 5, 18, 21, 24, 26, 27, 35, 37-40, 48, 55-57, 65, 68, 75, 99, 102, 103, 108, 110, 115
   Pagan, John 2
Stoy
   W. 96
Stratford, Va. 19
streams 78
Street
   Capt. 80
   St. George's 115
streets 69, 103
   Cameron 53
   Charles Town, Md. 98
   Church, Annapolis, Md. 35
   Port Tobacco, Md. 114
   Royal 53

St. Andrew's 115
town of Newport, Va. 95
strings 94
Stuart
   David 106
subscriptions
   for bridge building 113
sugar 33, 40, 52, 86
   in barrels 37
suits 10, 88, 102
   breach of promise 3
   libel 6
sulkeys 101
Sullivan
   John 37
Surgeons 51, 75
surgery 69, 83, 88, 98
surveys
   Upper Marlborough 91
Suter
   John 109
   Mrs. 113, 114
Suter's Tavern 90
Sutlers 15
Sutton
   John 39
swamp oysters 71
Swan
   Mr. 35
sweepstakes 58
Sweet Springs, Va. 105
Swift
   Mary, widow 64
   Rev. 32
   Theophilus, Rev. 31
swords 73

T

Tabb
   Mrs. 92
tabbies 19
tabby stays 20
tables 10, 63, 69, 77
   mahogany dining 106
   side 106
Tailors 65, 68, 69
Talbot
   Mrs. 30
Talbot Co., Md. 2, 14, 57, 92
Taliaferro
   Lawrence 103
tammies 40
tar 41

Along the Potomac River: **Extracts from the *Maryland Gazette*, 1728-1799**

Tasker
  Benjamin 1, 3, 25
  Benjamin, Hon. 5, 12
  Col. 26, 40
  Elizabeth 3
  Rebecca 5
Tavern Keepers 39, 53, 101
taverns 15, 18, 27, 38, 46, 48,
  49, 62, 63, 66, 69, 108,
  111, 112, 114
  Beane's 91
  Carrico's 113
  Edelen's 111
  for rent 31, 35, 37, 41, 79
  for sale 69
  George 22, 25, 35
  Koome's 114
  Lanham's 110
  Lomax's 83
  Mann's 102
  Middleton's 77
  Ross' 111
  Ship 47
  Suter's 90
  The Sign of the Ship 29
  Ware's 103
Tax Collectors 99
taxables 20
taxes 18, 62, 64
  delinquent 99
  stamp 44
Tayloe
  Col. 33
  John 17, 31, 33, 43, 63, 107,
    108
  John, Hon. 48
  Mr. 114, 116
Tayloe's Neabsco furnace 108
Taylor
  James 51
  Margaret 25
Taylors 35, 39
tea kettles 11, 45
Teachers 54, 60, 67
teapots 46
teas 65, 77
Tebbs
  Daniel 81
  Widow 85
teeth 76
tenant buildings 57, 76
tenants 41, 58, 118
tenders 67
tenements 99, 112
tents 42

Terrasson
  M. 77
testimonials 2
Thanksgiving
  holiday established 77
theatres 117, 119
  American Company 88
  Annapolis, Md. 55
  building in Annapolis, Md. 22
  opening 22
  plays 88
  stage actors 24
  Virginia Company 10
theodolite 9, 77
thickets 75
Thomas
  John Allan 87
  John, Lieut. 67
Thomason
  Mr. 84
Thompson
  C. 97
  Dekar 30
  Henry 2
  Joseph 37
  William 34
Thomson
  William, Sir 1
Thornton
  Col. 33
  Presley 17, 34, 108
  Thomas, Rev. 52
Throgmorton
  Robert 81
tickets 7-9, 22-25, 30, 34, 54
Tilghman
  Col. 73, 95
timber 80, 120
Tipper
  James 30
Tippeth
  Charles 110
Tipple
  William, Capt. 14
Tipton
  Jonathan 17
tithables 52
titles 58
toasts 22, 69, 70
tobacco 4, 20, 23, 24, 27, 28,
  33, 38, 39, 53, 54, 75-77,
  79, 84, 94, 95, 97, 106,
  110, 113
  damaged 21
  destroyed 72
  lost from Broad Creek

    Warehouse 102
  Maryland Patowmack 108
  tobacco barns 16
  tobacco droguers 2
  tobacco flats 11, 69
  tobacco houses 2, 5, 32, 44,
    64, 76, 81, 94, 96, 112
    burned 95
  tobacco inspection 62
  tobacco inspections 84, 95
  Tobacco Inspectors 102
  tobacco warehouses 72
Todd
  James 40
Todd's Bridge, Va. 49
Tolson
  Francis 97, 114
  John 31
tombstones 66, 106
tongues
  bored through 3
torries 69, 70, 73
tortoise shell case 93
tortoises 109
Tothill
  Anna 15
  Richard 15
tracts 9, 83
  A Penny Worth 1
  Abingdon 72
  Addison's Folly 105
  Addison's Goodwill 112
  Addition to Littleworth 55
  Admirathoria Manor 93
  Allen's Fresh 103, 108, 120
  Bachelor's Harbour 112
  Barbadoes 99
  Barker's Hazard 62
  Barker's Lot 62
  Barnaby Manor 109
  Batchelor's Hope 97
  Battersee 50
  Bell-Air 100
  Bellair 48
  Belmont 19, 44, 46, 66, 68
  Belvoir 63, 65
  Benfield 77, 96
  Berry's Enclosure 89
  Betty's Delight 88
  Beulah 53
  Blenheim 89, 99, 110
  Blue Plains 112
  Boarman's Content 119
  Brenton 46, 48
  Brooke Court Manor 98
  Brookfield 108

Along the Potomac River: Extracts from the *Maryland Gazette*, 1728-1799

Burbridge 28
Cain's Purchase 75
Cameron 7, 9, 86
Carricfurgus 110
Causin-Manor 96
Cedar Hill 83, 94
Chaptico Manor 115
Charlotte Hall 63, 64
Chevy Chase 47
Clarkson's Purchase 105
Clean Drinking 6, 98
Clifft 119
Clifton's Neck 16
Clish 43, 44
Come by Chance 99
Constitution Hill 61, 67, 68
Convenience 76
Cool Springs 107
Cove 107
Craft 114
Crane's Low Grounds 89
Darketh 105
Darnall's Lodge 93
Deer Range and Meadows 60
Digges Landing 119
Duncaster 76
Durham Freehold 97
East End 111
Enfield Chase 100
Equality 116
Eton 61
Exeter 101
for sale 14, 16, 23, 30, 78
Forest Plantation 114
Four and One Half Gallons of Rum 16
Frankland 94, 105, 119
Friendship 110, 111
Geeseborough Manor 99
Girls Delight 62
Gisborough 12, 75, 104, 111
Gisborough Manor 113, 114
God's Gift 60
Governor's Field 60
Green Hill 77, 115
Grub's Venture 89
Gunston 58
Gunston Hall 107
Haber Deventure 48
Haberdeventure 104, 107
Hanson's Plains Enlarged 48
Hanson's Progress 105
Harmony Hall 57
Harwood 97
Hawkins and Beatty's

Addition to Georgetown 114
Hawkins Lot 60
Hawkins' Barrens 99
Hawkins' Barrons 111
Hawthorn 116
Hazard and Never Fear 60
Hermitage 3
His Lordship's Favour 45
His Lordship's Kindness 5, 93, 110
Hogpen Enlarged 111
Holly Spring 89
Hopkins Folly 4
Hoskinson's Folly 3
Joseph and Mary 98
Kent Fort Manor 71
Kittockton 25, 28
Knave's Disappointment 1
Land-over 28
Landover 97
Larkin's Forest 100
Laurel Branch 111
Lee Hall 57
Littleworth 55, 101
Long Ordinary 35
Lordship's Manor 99
Low's Discovery 110
Luckett's Benefit 99
Lynsay's Survey 114
Maiden Bradley 99
Major's Choice 85, 91
Mankin's Folly 99
Mankin's Venture 99
Marlborough 44
Marmion 72
Mattapony 59
Mellwood Park 86
Merry Thought 60
Middleton 81
Mile's End 93
Mill Run 93
Mistake 88
Moisditch 99
Monocacy Manor 118
Mooreditch Resurveyed 106
Mount Air 114
Mount Airy 69, 80, 93
Mount Arrarat 97, 100
Mount Asaph 90
Mount Azile 84
Mount Calvert 26
Mount Pleasant 9
Mount Vernon 78, 80, 81, 90, 91, 103, 108, 118
Nanjemoy 47

Naucliff Hall 118
Newport 88, 92
Nick'd Him 60
Nonesuch 45
Northampton 64
Notley Hall 46, 67, 86, 94, 106
Old Piscataway Landings 119
Oxen Hill 52, 79, 80, 89, 102, 115, 118
Oxmon-Town 99
Pasbetansay 69
Poplar Hill 66
Poplar Neck & Addison 3
Poynton Manor 74
Prevention Enlarged 116
Primrose Hill 114, 116, 118
Puddington 104
Puddington Harbor 104
Rich Hill 119
Ridgely's Addition 100
Riley's Discovery 61
Rippon Lodge, Va. 112
Rock Hall 97
Ross Common 114
Rousby Hall 33, 72
Rovers-Delight 49
Rozer's Refuge 93
Rozier's Refuge 105
Run at a Venture 111
Rural Hall 74
Salisbury 116
Saturday's Work 8
Sicamy 111
Siccaney 116
Simmons Delight 4
Something 60
Sotterley 86, 93
Sotterly 103, 105
Speedwell 8
Squire's Purchase 60
St. Bernard's 102
St. Elizabeth 76
St. Johns 41
St. Mary's Freehold 60
St. Matthews 115
St. Peter's 60
Stepney 104, 108
Stratford 19
Strawberry Hill 90, 114
Strife 99
Swan Creek Landing 119
Swan Harbour 99, 112
Sycamore 111
Taylortown 98

148

Along the Potomac River: **Extracts from the *Maryland Gazette*,** 1728-1799

The Addition 93, 105
The Dernier Resort 116
The Hermitage 4
The Lodge 93
The Point 119
The Vineyard 96
Theobald's Hill 104
Thomason's Chance 101
Thompson's Rest 119
Tomsonton 105
Torthorwald 56, 60
Townhill 104
Wade's Adventure 114
Warburton 78, 79, 94, 107, 115, 118, 119
Warburton Manor 94, 105, 119
Westwood 54
White Hall 92
Widow's Mite 1
Wilkerson's Throne 101
Woodberry's Harbour 72
Woodcock's Range 100
Wynn's E. & W. Littleworth 55
Young's Inn 116
trade
  affected by small pox 21
tradesmen 68
Trafford
  Edward 19, 21
  Mr. 27
traitors 69
transports 71
travelers 80
Treasurers 46, 95
Treasury of Maryland 98
treaties
  with the Cherokees 117
trees
  cherry 81
  elm 68, 79
  fruit 88, 116
trenches 16
trespassers 88, 99
trespassing 100, 108, 116, 119
trials 69
tribal scars 27
Trinity Parish 53
Triplett
  Francis 20
  Thomas 53
  William 43
troops 67
trumpets 29
trunks 50

Truro Parish 10, 36, 40, 44, 45, 61
trustees of the poor 49
Tuesday Club 9, 71
Turner
  Charles 52
  John B. 93
  Zephaniah 57
turning instruments 94
turpentine 41
Tutors 14, 54
Tyler
  Elizabeth 70

U

U.S. Congress 73, 75, 77, 82-85, 102, 111, 118
U.S. Navy 105
Undertakers 14, 80
uniforms
  soldiers' 78
universities
  commencement 78
Upper Marlborough, Md. 6, 7, 10, 15, 18, 19, 32, 37, 46, 49, 53, 62, 64, 74, 77, 83, 90, 91, 104, 107, 110-112
  Assembly of 59

V

Valette
  E. 109
Vallette
  Elie 64
Van Braam
  Mr. 11
Vennell
  William 19
venom 2
vessels 42, 44, 62, 72, 77, 89, 92, 104
  insurance for 53
  large sea 59
vessels wanted 30
vestries 18
  King George Parish 110
  King George's 110
  King George's Parish 1, 39
  meeting of 40
  Port Tobacco Parish 8
  St. John's Parish 42, 110
  Truro Parish 10, 36, 61

vestry houses 61
  buildling of new 64
Vestrymen 55
vests 117
views of houses 11
violins 19
Virginia 1, 2, 6, 8, 9, 16, 17, 22, 23, 25-27, 29, 31, 35, 37, 45, 51, 67, 68, 78, 80, 81, 84-86, 96
  population 105
Virginia Convention 95
Virginia currency 28, 30, 36, 37, 56
Virginia Regiment 18, 31, 34
Virginians 67
volunteers 17

W

W__d
  Joseph 10
W__n
  Mary 10
Waddle
  Jonathan 61
Wade
  John 24
  Zachariah 62, 102
  Zachariah, Capt. 60
Wagener
  Peter 4, 31
wagons 69
wainscot 11
waistcoat patterns 69
waistcoats 25, 40, 87
Waite
  William 13, 18
Wakefield
  John 61
Wales 102
  Andrew 59
Walker
  David 60
  Henrietta 84
  Michael 36
walking on water 2
Wallace
  Herbert 16
  Hugh 3
Walmsley
  Charles S., Hon. 27
wanted
  captain for sloop 35
  Carpenter 92

charter 97
Dancing Master 40
journeymen cabinet makers 31
mahogany plank 31
manager 58, 59
Mechanic 107
Organist 52
Post Rider 39
Schoolmaster 48, 51, 64
skinner & breeches maker 53
Teacher 60, 67
woman to manage house 53
Ware
   Francis 38, 42, 111
   Mr. 98
Ware's Tavern 103
warehouses 8, 9, 21, 50, 52-54, 72
   Aquia 82, 83
   Broad Creek 75, 102
warm springs
   public 81
Warman
   William Berry 89, 91
Warren
   Dr. 111
wars 80, 98
washhouses 115
washing 36
Washington
   Augustine 7
   Bailey, Col. 82, 83
   Bushrod 117
   City of 105, 107
   City of, plan 107
   Col. 13, 23
   G. 95
   Gen. 68-70, 73, 78, 80, 81
   George 13, 17, 26, 27, 40, 45, 46, 58, 60, 61, 63, 65, 66, 83, 86, 116, 118
   George, arrives in N.Y. 97
   George, dies 120
   George, elected President 97
   George, journal of 12
   George, President 104
   Lawrence 4
   Lawrence, Maj. 7
   Lucy (Chapman) 33
   Maj. 12
   Martha 116
   Mrs. 68, 71
   Nathaniel 112
   Samuel 33, 52
Washington Co., Md. 88

Washington College 83
watch cleaning 39
watches 18, 25, 62
   for sale 41
   French gold 117
   pinchbeck 93
water 39, 44, 45, 75, 78, 84, 92
   navigable 93, 114
Watermen 44, 69
watermills 64
Waters
   Robert 41
Watkins
   Thomas 102
Watson
   Ann 13
   John 32
   Joseph 29, 30, 61
   Josiah 76
waxworks 106
wearing apparel 1
weather
   earthquakes 16, 17, 19, 55
   hail 36
   hail storm 84, 87
   lightning 11, 36, 84
   rain and snow 3
   severe gusts 36
   storms 25, 120
   tornado 10
   very hot 57
   violent 79
   wind 82
Weavers 4, 39, 47
Webster
   Thomas 89
   William 66
Weedon
   George 63
Weems
   Mason, Rev. 103
   W.L. 109
   William Locke 10
weirs 79
Wells
   Daniel 30
wells (water) 35, 44, 62
Welshmen 4
West
   Hannah 107
   Hugh 3, 12
   John 2, 38, 46
   John, Jr. 36
   Stephen 12, 27, 54, 107
West Hatton, Md. 108
West River, Md. 120

West's ordinary 63
West-Indies 27
western branch 37
Westmoreland Co., Va. 5, 7, 18, 21, 32, 49, 52, 74
whalebone 19
whales 3
whaling sloops 82
wharves 60
   Bladensburg, Md. 29
   repairing in Alexandria, Va. 22
   Upper Marlborough, Md. 21
wheat 52, 53, 86, 95, 99, 106
Wheeler
   Charity 91
   Elizabeth 85, 91
Wheelwrights 51
whipping 2-4, 43, 44, 47
Whitcomb
   Benjamin 20
White
   Capt. 81
   Mr. 94
Whitehaven, Eng. 32, 60, 65
whitewashing 21
Whiting
   Anthony 103, 108
   Carlisle Fairfax 115
Wicomico River 40, 98
Wicomico Warehouse 21
wife for sale 82
wigs 10, 24
wild deer 86
Wilkinson
   Anne 70
   William M. 90
Willett
   Mary 56
   William 56
Williams
   Evan 62
   Hannah 12
   Jane 3
   Otho H., Col. 75
   Richard, Capt. 9
   Thomas 98
Williamsburg, Va. 2, 3, 12, 13, 45, 53, 58, 69, 71
   capitol to be rebuilt 5
Willis
   Francis, Jr. 63
Willoughby
   Robert 4
Wilmington
   John 13

Wilson
  Lingan 26
Winchester, Va. 13, 21, 28
  lottery 25
Windmill Point, Md. 24
windmills 24, 44
windows 39, 120
windward coast 28
wine 77
wings 120
Winship
  Maria 92
  Winn 92
Winter
  John 23
  Mr. 43
Wisendon
  Robert 8
wives 89
wolves
  destroying of 96
Wood
  William 54
Wood Yard 9, 12, 13, 52, 54, 74, 107
wood yards 2
woodlands 111
wool 71
Wootton
  Singleton 74
  William Turner 28
workhouses 64
writing 67, 116
Writtle
  Richard 21
Wye River 33
Wynn
  Hezekiah 84
  John 55

Y

Yahoo 109
yearlings 25
yellow buttons 85
yellow gilt buttons 40
Yeocomico, Md. 67, 93
Yorkshire, Eng. 82, 102
Young
  Benjamin 89
  Mr. 107
  Mrs. 67
  Notley 29, 32, 46, 52, 55, 77, 87, 92, 95, 101, 106, 107, 114
  Robert 73

Z

Zachia Swamp 45, 98, 114

No Surname

[ ]
Antony 102
Archibald 83
Benjamin 104
Billie 48
Billy 18
Bob 37, 74, 87, 92
Charles 87
Clajon, a Parisian 14
Clem 80
Cupid 27
Daphne 103
Davy 21
Dick 12, 21, 80, 87, 89
Esquire 117
Frank 104
George 79
Harry 43, 85
Henny 103
Jack 16, 27, 117
Jerry 78
Joe 103
John 66
Kitt 81
Lis 109
Marcus 104
Monica 71
Ned 112
Neptune 27
Pee 106, 107
Peras 27
Sall 109
Scipio 48
Stephen 112
Tom 107
Towermill 86
Vick 109
Watt 87
William 32

www.ingramcontent.com/pod-product-compliance
Lightning Source LLC
Chambersburg PA
CBHW070910160426
43193CB00011B/1415